# Reaching for
# HOPE

# Reaching for

# HOPE

## An LDS Perspective on
## Recovering from Depression

MEGHAN DECKER AND
BETSY CHATLIN, LCSW

BOOKCRAFT®

*For my best friend and husband, David,*

*and for my delightful daughters*

*Rachel, Mary Beth, Ruth, Elise, and Rosalind.*

*I wanted to provide an easy Eden*

*for my family, but I am grateful*

*for the wisdon we gained together instead.*

*—M. D.*


*For Gene, Laurie, Kristina, and Jani.*
*—B. C.*

**Library of Congress Cataloging-in-Publication Data**

Decker, Meghan.
  Reaching for hope: an LDS perspective on recovering from depression / Meghan Decker and Betsy Chatlin.
    p.  cm.
  Includes bibliographical references.
  ISBN 1-57345-849-X (pbk.)
    1. Depression, Mental—Religious aspects—Church of Jesus Christ of Latter-day Saints. 2. Depressed persons—Religious life. 3. Decker, Meghan. I. Chatlin, Betsy. II. Title.
BX8643.D44 D43 2000
248.8'625—dc21

00-044495

Printed in the United States of America        15778-6740

10   9   8   7   6   5   4   3   2   1

All names in this book have been changed,

with the exception of the primary authors and their families.

In addition, in some cases further identifying

details have been altered.

# Table of Contents

# Acknowledgments

*From Meghan*

The Lord has blessed Betsy and me in our ability to work together to produce this book. It would have been impossible without his direction.

We also had the encouragement and help of many friends and family members. My parents, Ed and Colleen Peters, provided a home environment that encouraged initiative, faith, study, writing, and lots of discussion and questioning. Those characteristics helped me to fight depression's grip. My brother, Kevin, and his wife Pam have given me loving encouragement throughout my life, and especially during the writing of this book. My husband David, and my children Rachael, Mary Beth, Ruth, Elise, and Rosalind have been willing to put up with the days that I have produced more pages than meals. Thank you, David, for all the fresh bread, waffles, and quesadillas.

My family has also been willing to expose some of our not-quite-healed wounds in the hope that our experiences will help others through their own dark times. I thank David and Rachael for the writing they have done, and David and Mary Beth for their willingness to wade through the completed manuscript and make editorial suggestions, all of which were useful.

I also acknowledge the other readers who helped us when Betsy and I were too close to the manuscript to see it clearly. Jerelyn Decker (David's mother, a highly intelligent woman with wonderful editorial skills and the unusual ability to wait to be asked for her opinion), Margot Baker, Denise Palmer, and Kristen Baker all helped us with the final manuscript.

We appreciate the passion and strength of the contributions we have received from women who were willing to delve deeply into painful emotions to respond to our requests for their stories. Though we cannot thank them by name, we applaud their selflessness and courage. None of them considered herself a writer, yet the power of their experiences speaks strongly to the reader.

David Decker contributed the bishop's viewpoint, and Kurt Southam wrote from the perspective of a stake president. I thank them for their contributions, and also for the wise, tender leadership they have provided in their callings.

Finally, it seems unfair that Jennifer Adams's name doesn't appear as a co-author. She is our editor at Deseret Book and has put a great deal of labor into refining the manuscript we presented. In addition, I've enjoyed working with Emily Watts, also of Deseret Book, as she tried to decide what to do with this manuscript that appeared out of the blue. Her encouragement and her commitment to publishing a book on clinical depression have been instrumental to our success in bringing this book to you.

*From Betsy*

When I consider all the choices I have made in my life, I am grateful to remember that almost all of my really good ones involved having someone I loved or respected view the "best" in me.

I wish to thank all those who, as major influences in my life have inspired me, propelled me, and sometimes even confronted me to choose the more excellent way. My personal cheerleaders include my mother, my uncle Phil, my aunt Elbie, my cousin Nancy, my cousin Bow, and my daughters, Laurie, Kristina, Jani; Elder Mike Enfield, Elder Mark C. Porter, Elder Ron Bitter (the three missionaries who taught me the restored gospel of Christ); my first ward family, including Bishop Ted Lansing, Doris Lansing, Linda, Lydia, and Carolyn; my BYU coalition, including Mary Lou, Marsha G., Darlene, Carol G., Dr. J. Joel Moss, Dr. Lamar C. Berrett, Jim S., Linda Kay, George, Sharon T., Bishop Berrett, Karen M., Sue B., MaryBeth W., Bishop Sterling Albrecht; my amazingly wonderful neighbors for twelve years, including Dixie, Bill, Bishop Bud Mix, Mary, Joan, Hilda, Werner, Jon, Bishop J. Lewis Taylor, Betty S., Alton, Win, Dawnetta, Rulon (the world's greatest home teacher) and Don Corbett.

Beginning my new career in social work, a whole new world of contributors to my life emerged: Marge E., Luta, Gene, Jan, Jill, Karie,

Brad, Dick Mac., Joy, Opal, Ginny H., Beth C., Annie A., Carol M., Ann B., Connie B.P., Kassie, Jan B., Jan and Bill R., Lana, Derrill, Dell, President Randy Wilkinson, Carol G., Sara, Rebekah J., Margie, Nancy A. Also to my new friends of Kalamazoo, MI: Pam, Marlene, Arlene, Lisa, Shawna, Gail, Kim, Julie, Cathy, Judi, Lynn, President Dana Nickens, and Bishops Erickson, Cowles, Thomas, and Kellogg. And to my newest friend in Kalamazoo: Meghan Decker, without whom—obviously—this book would never and could never have been written.

Final thoughts and big thanks to the eight women who courageously and graciously shared their stories with you, our readers, and to the three psychiatrists who read selected excerpts for clinical and psychiatric accuracy: Dr. Joy Ely (retired, former Medical Director of Southwest Utah Mental Health), Dr. Ted Wingate (current Medical Director of Kalamazoo County Community Mental Health), and Dr. Gabrielle Lieberg (staff Psychiatrist at KCCMH). And finally, to Greg, the Chili's manager who put up with the four hour lunches as we initiated our book in the Chili's booth.

# *Weeping May Endure for a Night*

Denise is in the Young Women's presidency in her ward. The girls love and admire her. She graduated from BYU, where she met her husband, a successful and kind man who loves her and their four children. He is an involved father and regularly takes his wife out on a date to give her a break from her responsibilities. Denise has lots of friends; she is considered an intelligent, funny, giving woman. Why does she wish she were dead?

Denise is a victim of clinical depression, a brain disorder in which her own distorted thoughts affect her perception of the world around her and bury her in a deep pit of hopelessness and despair. She finds herself unable to feel the comfort of the Spirit; when she prays she feels that a lead ceiling covers her head. She is sure the Lord considers her unworthy of his comfort or direction.

We, Meghan and Betsy, have suffered under that same ceiling, felt the same hopelessness and despair that you may be experiencing now. We are intimately acquainted with the agony of depression, a dark mist that seems to rob life of all joy and purpose. And out of that darkness, we come as messengers to tell you that there is hope. You can recover, and you will again love life and feel joy.

The primary purpose of this book is to inspire hope in women who are somewhere in their own passage through depression.[1]

Depression is a physical affliction. You did not choose to feel this way.

Clinical depression manifests itself in negative thoughts, hopelessness, and an inability to feel joyful emotions, such as the emotions associated with the direction of the Holy Ghost. The Lord has not left you. He will be watching over you and bestowing direction even when you are unaware or incapable of noticing.

Well-meaning friends and family members may encourage you to pray, read your scriptures, do an act of service, or count your blessings. No doubt you have tried these things again and again and again. What used to work doesn't work anymore. How can you explain to others what is going on in your mind? How can they understand?

You may think you are alone, but you are not. One of every three women will experience depression at some point in her life. This is not just sadness; it is a physical disorder that manifests itself in emotional as well as physical symptoms. The World Health Organization declares clinical depression is the number one women's health problem today.[2] If you were to talk to the other women at church who are depressed (and we promise you, there are some) you would be amazed at the similarity of your feelings and experiences. You would also be surprised at *who* these fellow-sufferers are, working so hard to hide their despair and carry on valiantly behind a pasted-on smile.

Looking out the window as we write this book, we see trees that have weathered a difficult winter beginning to put forth the first young leaves of spring. You will be like these trees. Though you may now, in the darkness and chill of your depression, feel that hope is gone, you will again feel warmth and light. As you leave your winter of depression behind you and begin to reach for hope, you will one day return to joy, richness, and light.

We share our insights and experiences with you to testify that there is a way back to the light, joy, and happiness that will become part of your life again. Meghan is a writer who has experienced clinical depression in her own life. Betsy is a therapist who understands depression intimately, both professionally and personally. We have combined our talents to offer you solace, understanding, and hope.

As you read this book, you will notice that some chapters are stories, while others are educational and clinical. We have tried to use both narrative and informative chapters to give you a more complete picture of clinical depression.

In addition to our words, we have provided a number of real-life, autobiographical stories of Latter-day Saint women who have struggled with depression. Though their names are altered, their experiences are used with their express permission in the hope that their stories will be of help to lift the burdens of others. You may recognize your own story in their words. All of these brave sisters testify of the healing that has brought happiness back into their lives.

As the Apostle Paul wrote, we now say to you: "Therefore ye are no more strangers . . . but fellowcitizens with the saints" (Ephesians 2:19).

If you have found yourself a stranger in the desolate land of depression, you may recognize in this book your fellowcitizens who have traveled through desolation toward hope, and who have found that "we have endured many things and hope to be able to endure all things" (Article of Faith 13).

We, Meghan and Betsy, hope for your hope.

---

1. This book is written primarily to LDS women suffering from depression. The authors speak from their own experience and include the experiences and voices of many other LDS women. Yet depression is not a gender-specific disease. Many men also suffer from depression. Although the pronouns used in this book are feminine and the examples come from women, there is much here to benefit men suffering from depression as well.
2. Joannie M. Schrof and Stacy Schultz, "Melancholy Nation," *U.S. News and World Report*, 8 March 1999, 57.

# Toward Hope: A Personal Perspective

*This chapter is from Meghan's personal experience.*

"Mom, please, the missionaries are going to be here for dinner soon. You've got to come downstairs!" My twelve-year-old daughter stands looking down at me curled on the floor in a corner of my bedroom. My daughter is becoming frantic, not only because of the dinner; I am not acting the way I should, not the way any mother should. With a great effort I respond, "You'll just have to tell them we can't do it tonight. Or maybe Dad will get home in time. I don't know. I can't do this." The familiar feelings of hopelessness and helplessness close in on me. "I just can't do this." I curl up tighter, trying to find a way to *escape the everyday pressures around me, searching for a place of quiet inside myself that would let me stop thinking or responding. "I can't do this."*

*I am relieved when my tearful daughter leaves me.*

*My husband, David, does come home, and he makes waffles for the family and the missionaries, as well as making excuses for me. I am not feeling well, he explains. He comes and talks to me, asks me what he can do, and shares my feelings of confusion and helplessness.*

*I don't know who I am anymore, but I know who I'm not: myself. I miss Me. I can remember feeling discouraged only late at night and knowing it was the result of fatigue, that I would have my enthusiasm back in the morning. Now hopelessness is my constant companion. I wistfully look back on the person I have been. I like her, admire her "can-do" attitude. In college I pushed through the master's degree program in half the time of many of my classmates, despite pregnancy and a new baby, while continuing to teach undergraduate classes, take classes myself, and write my thesis. Challenges were fun, and David and I worked as a team to take on whatever came our way. Now I feel alone and incapable. What happened to me? What have I become?*

*The evolution into this sad, scared woman has been an insidious one. Even now, I wonder if this isn't the result of some odd, persistent mood. Maybe if I fast and pray again, read scriptures more earnestly, do an extra act of service for someone outside the family every day, I could shake off this gloom. But I've tried all these things over and over, and still my darkness doesn't lift. In my distorted reasoning I can come to only one conclusion: it must be a terrible flaw deep inside of me. If I no longer feel the Spirit—no comfort, no burning, no joy—then it must be God withdrawing himself from me. He doesn't withdraw from us for no reason. I'm not worthy. It must be me.*

Was the change evident to anyone else? I did my best to ensure it was not. I smiled when I was supposed to, fulfilled my callings, tried to be kind to others. I hugged my private despair to myself like a secret treasure. But

❧

I became quiet, and my fear of burdening others by exposing them to the darkness I was feeling condemned me to solitary torment.

One of the first changes I noticed in myself was a new hesitation when approaching challenges. I had always been willing to take nearly anything on, confident that with enough effort things would work out. I used to wake up each morning eager to start on the project I had planned—painting a bathroom, installing new software on the computer at the Family History Center, sewing Halloween costumes, or figuring out how to change the oil in the tiller. Attending a Relief Society home-making meeting was exciting because of the friends I would see there, or the new skill I would learn, and I anticipated the pleasure of the evening's meeting all day.

But mornings began to come too soon, and not merely because of the time spent with the baby during the night. Now I mistrusted myself. I didn't feel ready for the days with their challenges, even the simple ones like making sack lunches or having dinner ready at night. While before I was invigorated by the admiration and love I felt for my friends, now I was overwhelmed by the thought of measuring up to them. Worse, I began to suspect their motives, to wonder if they were really as I had seen them. The world around me began to darken and close in.

As time went on, I felt more and more isolated. Simply speaking to friends in passing became an effort. I started withdrawing from the exertions of friendship. I would brood over light comments and examine them for their underlying meaning. When I saw two friends together, I assumed they didn't want me around, and their welcomes were only required courtesy.

Most of all, emotional closeness was just exhausting. I made feeble excuses to a close companion with whom I had exercised for years, and I lost her friendship as she sensed my withdrawal and misinterpreted it. But the effort was too great for me to correct the misunderstanding.

When my visiting teachers came, I was inattentive and distracted. Mostly I was afraid that they would ask me how I was doing. I felt instinctively that I should confide in no one. I was ashamed of my problem and worried about gossip. I also didn't see how anyone could help me. Sensing my distraction, they left feeling hurt and unwelcome. I was relieved that they had not asked about me—so I wouldn't have to lie again—and at the same time hurt by their lack of interest.

Why did I feel so strongly that no one should discover my inner darkness? Perhaps it was partly because my husband was their bishop, and I didn't want to let him or them down. I'm sure my pride prevented me from admitting that I was no longer the self-reliant woman I had always been. I was used to being the strong one; I didn't know how to accept emotional support from someone else. I didn't want my children to think that anything was wrong. Most of all, I just hoped this would pass quickly—that I would pull myself out of it.

It was around this time that the bishops in our stake, including my husband David, were asked to read *One Heart, One Flesh,* by Carlfred Broderick. David suggested that I read it as well. The changes in me were having an effect on my family and marriage. All of us were confused, hurt, angry, and scared. As I read this small book, one chapter captured my attention. He briefly talked about clinical depression, its manifestations and possible treatments. *This is like what's happening to me,* I thought, but at the same time my mind recoiled from the thought that I could be "depressed." I thought of women I know who talk about being depressed. *I'm not like that!* But if I was not, then what exactly was I like? I didn't know myself anymore. I didn't like myself anymore.

I had a similar experience my senior year of high school. I seemed to be having deep mood swings. At that time, after extensive medical testing the doctors had decided I had temporal lobe epilepsy, and I was treated with anti-seizure medication. This was in spite of the neurologist saying my EEG showed nothing of the sort. He thought the problem was rooted in an emotional disturbance. But the psychologists thought I was well-adjusted. We were at an impasse, and my doctor decided on medication that, if it cured nothing, at least numbed me to the point that I no longer complained.

After a year or two, I stopped taking the medication on my own. The doctor was not monitoring me at all, and I had a renewable prescription.

I simply made the decision myself. I seemed to do okay, so I decided not to think about what had happened and just move on. Later I found the medication I had been taking would cause severe birth defects, and I was glad I stopped taking it on my own before marrying and having children.

I can't place too much blame on the doctors for their inability to accurately diagnose my condition. Today we know that clinical depression is rooted in chemical imbalances in the brain, which are certainly influenced by outside factors and biological changes as well as emotional turmoil. In a sense, the doctors were right. The problem was both physiological and psychological.

After reading Dr. Broderick's book, I kept wondering if my experiences, both past and present, could be the result of depression. Even though I recoiled at the idea, it kept with me until at last I decided something had to be done. I could not go on as I was, even if the thought of going to a doctor for depression was disgraceful. I went at last out of desperation.

Worn by months of melancholy, and encouraged by Dr. Broderick's assurance that medical help can make a difference, I called my family physician. David met me for lunch after my appointment. The doctor had explained to me that sometimes periods of depression are brought on by external events; another type of depression is the result of a change in the chemistry of the brain, for no apparent reason. This can resolve itself after several months or years. Medication can speed up the process, getting things back in sync. I left with a bottle of antidepressants in my purse. I cried at the restaurant when I told David about the medication; so far, having to rely on drugs just made me feel like more of a failure.

I was taking Zoloft, and I was lucky. Some people play trial and error with many medications before finding one that helps them. I responded quickly and found my mind clearer, my hopes for future happiness renewed, and the lead ceiling which covered me during my prayers dissolved. I felt as if I were resurrected, and in a sense I was. I was brought out of what seemed to me a living death into a world alive again with color, with hope, and with possibilities of joy.

During this first period of recovery, I was able to look back and see how distorted my thinking had become. I had previously had a difficult time determining whether I was locked in despair or merely accepting life's realities after years of pretending to myself. Now I could see that the glass I had been looking through was dim, indeed. I began to be able to tentatively participate in my world again. I had never physically withdrawn; but emotionally I was so battered by the storms within that I had withdrawn from closeness with friends, both because I had so little to give and because I feared the results if I lost my self-reliance by unburdening myself. I was worried about my friends seeing me as a whining leech. I didn't want them to resent me. I felt that if I had nothing to give, then I ought not to demand and take. Even as I began to feel better, I still held myself back, just in case I was still too weak to be an asset to a friendship. It has been a hard lesson to learn that this kind of false self-reliance is actually self-destruction.

This is my experience. But as I have talked to friends and family members about their own experiences with clinical depression, it seems that this self-imposed isolation transcends individual personality traits or circumstances. Withdrawal is common, as is the impression that these feelings are unique to *me*, that no one else has ever experienced, or deserved, this inward despair. Compounding this solitude is the common misconception that depression is easily solved by putting a smile on one's face or singing a happy song. I tried in every way I could to change my attitude. This wasn't simply discouragement; I was in a deep, dark abyss, with only the memory of the light above. I had no *reason* to be depressed. I was blessed with all that I ever desired, and more. I didn't choose depression: it chose me.

Most agonizing of all to the faithful Latter-day Saint is the spiritual wasteland that is home to depression. I sought in desperation for the familiar, though increasingly distant, comfort of the Spirit. This was especially trying and difficult to understand, because the last few years of our lives had been the most spiritually fulfilling. We had been called to work in the Washington D.C. Temple as ordinance workers for our stake; in addition, my husband's responsibilities on the stake high council had included the stake temple trip which was the culmination of a year's planning on the part of every active member of the stake. Those years seemed to be a time when the heavens were open to us, and the direction of the Spirit was a daily occurrence.

Yet as the world began to darken around me, I prayed and read my scriptures, fasted and took meals to new mothers, and applied myself with renewed energy to my calling, without ever feeling the comfort or burning of the Holy Ghost. This was the hardest part of my depression to understand, both doctrinally and emotionally. I had always believed anything else might be wrested from us, but not our relationship with our Heavenly Father. Yet as I prayed, I felt that lead ceiling above my head. It was as if I picked up a phone to hear and feel a presence at the other end, but instead got only a dead line.

As I look back now, I can see that the Lord was directing me in many of the decisions I made. I know I received inspiration in my callings, from planning stake Young Women camps to writing scripts for our visiting teaching seminars. I felt the Lord's guidance and instruction intellectually. In retrospect, I can see his hand guiding me to the places I needed to find help. I know that the Lord was watching over me, even at those times when I was unaware of his presence. But I could not feel the emotions associated with the Spirit. No burning, no comfort, no overwhelming joy. It was as if I were seeing the world in black and white, not color. Something fundamental was missing.

Almost every clinically depressed person I have talked to in the Church has been tormented by these same experiences. Part of our test in this earth-life is a physical test, and even our minds—with agency intact—are subject to physical ailments that affect our perceptions. This shouldn't be surprising; when my children are tired or hungry I understand that they may feel irritable until they rest or eat. Depression is similar to this, except it is unrelenting in its effects. The physical ailment which affected my perception and distorted my thinking was depression. Just as many cancer patients are not healed by priesthood blessings, so my physical and emotional condition was not healed by scripture study and good works. Despite all my efforts, I was never able to feel the warm comfort of the Holy Ghost bringing peace to my soul. I don't understand this spiritual loss completely, but I know from my experience that it is real, and I know that at the time it is happening, we usually attribute this apparent abandonment to unworthiness. I never doubted the Lord, or his atoning sacrifice. I did doubt that I was worthy of his blessings. My inability to feel the swelling of the Spirit in my heart confirmed to me all my worst thoughts about myself. This inability to feel the Spirit is part of the illness; the challenge is to be able to recognize and accept the ways in which the Spirit continues to operate in our lives.

*At the end of a temple recommend interview with the stake president I prepare to leave, still uncertain inside myself about my worthiness. No, not uncertain. Why would the Lord want someone like me inside his house? President Southam shakes my hand, looks me in the eye, and says firmly, "You are good, Sister Decker!" He says it as if it is his testimony. I can almost find it in me to believe him. I hang on to his conviction for a long, long time.*

The physician warned me that the initial dosage of Zoloft often has to be doubled. In my case, I unconsciously felt that if I had humbled myself enough to take this stuff in the first place, it was enough. Surely my reliance on something chemical would not need to be increased. But in a few weeks I found myself sitting on the floor of my basement family room, looking at the dress-up clothes and toys spread around the room. I sat still, not knowing where to start, paralyzed into inaction by the feeling that this was just too much—and I knew I was slipping back. At the doctor's advice, my dosage of the drug increased. With mixed feelings of resentment and gratitude, I began my days and ended them with a little blue pill, which seemed to be my lifeline to a stable, happy life. I felt weakened by my dependence. But I clung to my doctor's promise that often all that was needed was for the medicine to establish a chemical pattern in my brain and, once established, my own body would take over: firing all the correct electrical impulses, emitting and reabsorbing the correct chemicals. I believed that all I needed was a little help to get going, and this purely physiological problem would resolve itself. It was much better to think of myself as having a temporary physical problem than as having a problem that was related to my spirit.

After six months, I asked my husband for a blessing, and I began to decrease my dosage. I eventually stopped taking any medication at all. This was an answer to my prayers. I felt triumphant in my independence. But I never felt completely well. I was still tentative. I was still careful, waking up in the morning wondering if I would be asked to do more that day than I could handle. The smile on my face was genuine, now, but it lacked confidence and depth.

Over the next two years, I struggled to understand the correct balance. I desperately wanted to be independent of the medication, but at times I recognized that, both for me and for my family, I needed its help.

*"Mary Beth, we need to go through your flash cards again. You have to go out for the bus soon: Come on!" She doesn't want to, and I don't want to, but we've got to work on this. I hold up a card: "Okay, what's this?" I wait impatiently. She guesses halfheartedly. "Come on, Mary Beth! Let's get with it!" I know I'm not doing this well. So does she. She gets irritated and snaps at me. I explode and throw the cards in her face. At the look of shock on her face I slide down to the floor, bury my head in my hands, and cry. This is the last my children see of me as they head out the door for the day. It's obvious to me again that, like it or not, I need Zoloft. I am angry: how could the Lord do this to my family? Where is my control over my own life? I've always felt that even if no one else came through, I could depend on myself. Yeah, right. As long as I don't run out of little blue pills.*

This time was like a slow roller-coaster: several months with medication, then several without. But I was never truly *me*, never completely confident in my ability to pull it all off. Perhaps this was simply the beginning of wisdom, I thought, a recognition of my own inherent weakness and vulnerability. My testimony of the Atonement deepened. I recognized my dependence on the Savior and appreciated his empathy as I realized the limits of my own compassion, even for myself. I also began to realize the individuality of each of our trials, and the complete inability of anyone to truly understand another's tribulation. All of this I recognized as valuable growth; yet at the same time, I knew I was standing on crumbling ground.

*It's nearly dawn, and I have been staring out the window into darkness for hours. Last night I realized how miserably I am failing as a mother. I have five daughters; the responsibility for giving them a good start in this earthly life rests in my hands, and it is clear to me I am failing. Who knows what serious mistakes they will make as a result of my struggles and failures? The future seems very simple to me now; if something were to happen to me, David would remarry a good woman who would rectify my mistakes. They can all be happy again. Why should they suffer any more? After reading "it is better that one man should perish than that a nation should dwindle and perish in unbelief" during family scripture study (1 Nephi 4:13), I know my conclusion is the right one. I even feel the Lord is confirming my decision. I would not be with my family forever anyway; I simply don't have the strength to endure the trials of this life. I've been tested and found wanting, but that is no reason for them to be injured. This is the best thing for all of us.*

It's a measure of how severely distorted my thinking had become that I believed death was good and right. I saw myself as the source of all strife, all trouble, all trial to the people I loved. This experience occurred during a time that I was without medication. As I pondered my conclusions through the days that followed, I felt I was being very rational. My main concern was not to cause any more pain to my family.

For several days I was preoccupied, thinking about my decision and wondering how to manage the next step. David, sensing my withdrawal, thought it was the result of distress between him and me. As I was leaving to take the kids to a movie one Saturday afternoon, he asked if I was going to talk about what was bothering me, or just let it continue to fester between us. I was in a quandary. I had my mind on internal matters, and I had been unconsciously quiet and distant around him, but I certainly hadn't meant to make him think I was upset. What was I to do? Let him continue to believe I was unhappy with him and our marriage or have a theatrical scene explaining that I wouldn't be around much longer? Even the word *suicide* seemed to me highly melodramatic. I simply wanted to solve my family's problems, not draw attention to myself.

Eventually, after a long silence, and only because I didn't want him to continue thinking that I was angry, I explained the cause of my pre-occupation. We were sitting on opposite sides of the floor in our bathroom, and I explained very rationally the circumstances that led to my conclusion. I was unemotional and felt sorry for upsetting him. He listened carefully, acknowledging the tone I had set by responding in an equally objective tone. Only when I said I had to go, because the movie would be starting soon, did he hold me to him, crying as he pled, "Don't leave me! Please don't leave us!" Somehow, inside my emotionally and rationally addled mind, I recognized that I wasn't an interchangeable unit, to be replaced when worn out. His love for me, Meghan, not just "wife," made itself clear to me.

I decided to hang on to my life, not because I valued it, but because he did. In spite of all I had put him and our children through, I recognized that he still saw worth in me. I resolved to trust his vision. But for the next few months, I had very curious experiences related to suicidal thoughts. Though I had rejected self-destruction as an alternative, it seemed I could not rid it from my mind. Suicide would thrust itself into my thoughts at odd times and places. I was continually pushing it out of my mind. I had never thought much about death before, and certainly not suicide; now I would be walking down the aisle in the grocery store and suddenly think: "No more grocery shopping after this life." I might be sorting socks and wonder, "If something happened to me and David remarried, I wonder if she'd know what to do with the unmated socks?" Some of these thoughts were funny, at times, but overall they were disturbing.

After a few months of these random and intrusive thoughts, however, my youngest daughter had an experience that demonstrated her need for me and the understanding that only I could give her. She wanted her mother, and no one else could take my place. Following this recognition of my importance to her, I was no longer troubled by these unwelcome destructive thoughts. I began taking medication again, and this time thanked Heavenly Father for its existence. I was frightened by the path on which my distorted thinking had placed me, and so I reconciled myself to my continued dependence on the antidepressant. I recognized that my ability to evaluate my own stability was flawed, almost fatally.

I can see two lifelines that pulled me through this difficult time. One was my awareness of someone else's unconditional affection and respect. I was actually surprised by the depth of my husband's love for me. Because I had lost so much respect and affection for myself, I assumed I was equally unlovable to everyone else. I also had managed to distance myself from friends, and they had not seen through my elaborate masquerade to the desperate needs underneath. I don't know that I even would have believed them if they had worked to convince me of their love and concern. But to see my usually controlled husband in tears was enough of a shock to convince me of his sincerity. I felt truly valued by someone else, and that was essential.

The other lifeline was my daughter's need: I was convinced that only I could help her. This unique need was vital, because if someone else had been able to step in, my usefulness would have been diminished. To be truly needed, and irreplaceable, is a strong evidence of worth. I required this external proof of worth, because I had none inside.

Months later I realized I was again feeling hopeless and alone. It was necessary to increase the dosage of my medication again, until eventually I was taking quadruple the original dose. I was at the maximum dosage level for the drug and was beginning to experience side effects that also interfered with my ability to lead a normal life. I started to search for information on other alternatives.

A friend who worked for LDS Social Services in another state told me about a type of therapy that has great success with depression: Cognitive–Behavioral Therapy. I looked for everything I could find on C/B therapy. I searched for non-biased information and found reports of several research studies which show evidence that C/B therapy is as effective, or more effective, than medication over the long term. Brain scans have shown it to have similar effects to medication on the metabolism of the brain, with an effect that continues beyond the end of therapy. This is unlike the effects of medication, where the good effect often disappears with the end of the prescription. It is difficult to separate the brain as an organ of the body from the mind and its thoughts. Talk therapy can have an actual physiological effect on the brain's structure and function. Your emotional and mental health can have a real, tangible effect on your physical health, both for good and ill. The spirit is more connected to the body than I had thought possible both for good and ill.

I won't repeat here everything I found in my research; the significance of those studies to me is that I decided therapy might be the answer I was looking for. I started searching the Internet for information on Cognitive–Behavioral Therapy. I found the network of Centers for Cognitive–Behavioral Therapy that are linked, by affiliation and training, to the University of Pennsylvania, home to the development of this kind of therapy. Included in this network was an office in Columbus, Ohio, near my home. I called for an appointment.

Aaron Beck, MD, is the father of Cognitive–Behavioral Therapy. His work has been built upon by David Burns, who has written several popular books on the subject. I ordered one of these books to read before my first meeting with Dr. Kevin Arnold, the director of the Center for Cognitive and Behavioral Therapy in Columbus. I tried hard not to think about the indignity of needing therapy and just hoped for help.

I liked what I read. The basic principles of the therapy seemed to me to be rooted in truth and logic, without the determinism of therapies that concentrate on childhood traumas determining the rest of one's life. Instead, the person learns to recognize incorrect perspective in their thinking that results in unwarranted emotional and behavioral reactions. Here is an example:

I am in my bedroom when my husband gets home from work. I notice him glance at a book on the bed and interpret that glance in this way: "Well, it looks like Meghan's been reading today while I was at work. I don't know why she doesn't clean the house, rather than lying around reading all day." I immediately feel guilty and defensive, and any response I make to him from then on is rooted in these feelings, when actually his glance may have been nothing more than to see if we had a new Western in the house. However, my emotional and behavioral responses are based on the irrational belief that I can read his mind and know what he is thinking. Then I react without checking to see if my assumption is true or not. As a result, the emotions and behaviors that are evoked are based on my mind's incorrect perception of reality, or distorted thinking.

This example is greatly simplified, but it shows the kind of thought processes that can get us into trouble. This therapy is somewhat like a structured class in learning to identify distorted thinking and escape its psychological consequences. As we break these cycles of thought, there can be a change in brain metabolism; our thought processes can have a physical effect on the function of the brain that releases us from the depressive state.

At my first appointment I met the therapist, Dr. Kevin Arnold, and we discussed my reasons for coming. I told him about myself and that I felt stable at the moment, but worried about increasing doses of Zoloft. I didn't realize then how far I really was from being stable. However, compared to where I had been, I saw myself as basically back to normal. I was coping, but not happy, confident, or relaxed. Only as I look back on this period now do I realize that I was still really very near the edge.

Dr. Arnold was a good listener and sympathetic to my religious commitments. I completed some forms asking questions about myself and left with several more lengthy questionnaires that asked me to "rate your agreement with the following statements on a scale of 1 to 6." I completed these for my next session and brought them back with me.

Dr. Arnold briefly reviewed my answers, looking up at me in the process and asking, "Do you think it is your responsibility to make sure everyone around you is happy?"

I was taken aback: of course I did. Wasn't I supposed to feel that way? Isn't that the way Christ wants me to live? I felt as if I had just been informed that sentences don't end with a punctuation mark.

"I'm not supposed to feel that way?" I asked.

"No," he replied.

Later on, we discussed the misconception that I could *make* another person feel a certain way. He pointed out that while I can be kind and considerate, I cannot take upon myself full responsibility for the way someone else chooses to respond.

Dr. Arnold went on, asking me other questions that made me feel as if he were reading my mind. At times I was surprised to recognize that yes, I really did believe something, even though I had never consciously thought about it. For example, when he asked me if I thought it was wrong for me to ask others for help, I realized I did, even though consciously I had merely thought I valued self-reliance. But it actually went deeper than that—I really believed that if I needed someone else's help, I was a failure.

My answers created a pattern that he was able to read. They showed that I had certain deeply held beliefs that were contributing to my depression. I was unable to live up to unrealistic standards and expectations I set for myself.

Cognitive–Behavioral Therapy is based on the theory that there are certain automatic thoughts, or schemas, that we consistently use to interpret events around us. He suggested that one of mine was unrelenting standards for myself.

When he first said this to me, I laughed. I thought of my cluttered bookshelves, my primed and still unpainted bedroom walls, and my occasional dusting. If I could sit in a room with toys on the floor, and read a book without straightening the room first, I certainly didn't think I had unrelenting standards.

Dr. Arnold remarked that my unrelenting standards were in interpersonal relationships. For example, I was always eager to help friends, to serve them in whatever way I could, yet I absolutely refused to think that I should ask for help myself, or be the recipient of service. I felt that I needed to be self-sufficient, and if I wasn't I felt that I had failed. I saw myself as a helper, not one who needed help. This attitude colored my perceptions about myself and my relationship to those around me. It was based on a false idea of what a friendship really should be.

Another thing we talked about early on was my third grade teacher. In the patient history I filled out I wrote this:

> *Third grade teacher was demeaning—told me I was lazy and stupid. Performed poorly in school from 3rd to 11th grade when I took the ACT and scored in top 1%. Then I began to believe I was capable, but I always felt insecure in relationships, as if people didn't really want me or I wasn't pulling my weight.*

As we talked about other issues, I recognized how many times I interpreted comments in light of what this teacher thought of me, not based on my husband's or friends' feelings. If I felt I had let David down, suddenly I was feeling the same shame and lack of love that I did in third grade, when I couldn't earn my teacher's love because she had none to give—only bitterness, which she vented on me as an eight-year-old child. When I felt I had not met others' expectations, I automatically responded with the same emotions I had felt in this teacher's class. Dr. Arnold helped me see the inappropriateness of unconsciously applying those remembered powerful emotions to most everyday interactions.

I had "homework" after almost every session. Once I took home a week's schedule, where I kept track of my activities by the hour and rated them according to the pleasure or mastery (competence) I felt for each. Another time I made a list of the things I liked doing by each sense. "Taste," for instance included trying new ethnic foods and drinking cold water when I've been working outside on a hot day.

As I began to work on recognizing my automatic thoughts and

reactions, I kept track of times when I would be upset. I had a record to describe the situation, the emotions I felt, the automatic thoughts that preceded the emotions, what the rational response should be, and the outcome. One of these situations was a disagreement with one of my children, where she ended up walking off.

My emotions were *stress and frustration; urge to eat something.*

My automatic thoughts included *We've made progress so she shouldn't be falling back into this old pattern; I need a break, I need to get my mind off of it, therefore I want to eat something; I shouldn't lose my temper, so I'll eat something instead.*

The rational responses were *The evidence of my life suggests that people can make a lot of progress, yet occasionally slip up. It's not a catastrophe when a slip-up occurs. Each situation is always a little different, so the progress can be made each time when things change.*

For the urge to eat, the rational response was *The costs to eating chocolate include weight gain, extended exercise, and shortened life span. Ten minutes of classical music or going for a walk is far less costly than any of these.*

The journal shows that after thinking through the rational responses, the automatic thoughts carried much less weight. My therapy taught me how to see rational responses. This exercise helped me in recognizing automatic responses so that I could be aware of them and evaluate them to see if they were truly valid. Usually they were not.

Though this thumbnail sketch of C/B therapy might make it sound as if it is merely trying to think rationally rather than emotionally, the therapy is actually far more complex than that. I have tried to give the reader some idea of what to expect from therapy, but books by David Burns will be a much better resource.

I am not a therapist. I am, however, an expert on the value of C/B therapy in my own life. I have my life back, completely and confidently. I have hope again, and passion, and commitment, and all the other things I lacked, even when I was on medication. The medication certainly helped, but it was a stopgap measure, working from pill to pill and still leaving me with fear and uncertainty.

I started therapy in the early spring, three years into a major depressive episode. I was taking so much Zoloft that I needed twelve to fourteen hours of sleep a day. I had an underlying deep despair that I was not aware of, and I was going through life as a zombie. A few months into the therapy I began cutting back on medication, until I was able to discontinue it completely. My life wasn't problem-free from the first therapy session on, but the understanding and skills I gained helped me to change my emotional responses to the point that a fundamental change occurred in me: my brain, my chemistry, whatever.

One element of my experience may be atypical. I can see no clear precipitant or trigger to my depression. I never suffered any sort of abuse or trauma as a child (other than a demeaning third-grade teacher), so there were no lingering effects to deal with as an adult. The best guess I have, even now, for the onset of this major depressive episode is that I did experience some postpartum blues; I had several months of interrupted sleep; my husband and I were both very stressed about his work situation for nearly four years before he changed jobs (and he was serving as bishop during that time); and I have a definite biological vulnerability to clinical depression. I didn't deal well with my worries: instead of sharing them with my husband, I tried to shield him by worrying on my own and holding things in. I cut myself off from my biggest support. All these elements worked together to bring me lower than I had ever believed possible.

At one time the thought of cooking a meal was overwhelming to me. After I ended therapy I saw a gradual increase in my capacity and confidence. I became better able to tend to the needs of my family, and I cautiously started to become involved in outside activities again. Since my therapy ended a few years ago, I have been president of a local writer's group, president of the high school PTO, and active in church service. I also home-schooled three of my daughters for half a year before moving from Ohio to Michigan. Today I am active in my children's schools, serving as Relief Society president, and trying to find time to finish writing a novel. There have been times when I have started to feel wobbly, but I know how to deal with those times. My final sessions with

Dr. Arnold were spent discussing relapse prevention. One thing I have discovered for myself is my need for an adequate night's sleep. I am much more vulnerable when I am tired.

I don't know if I will always be free from the fear of experiencing another depression, but I know there is effective help. Heavenly Father didn't remove my burden, but he led me to the means of strengthening my shoulders to bear it. I'm grateful for the light that now fills each of my days and the hope I feel again.

### Balm

What weight of sin, grief, sorrow, or
Bewildered and wronged innocence
Bore down upon the Christ as
He endured our pains?
He felt the agony of victim and
Perpetrator,
Saw visions of a world so
Cruel and grim, that the
Mere sight must have
Wrenched life's breath away,
Compelled him to
Plea for Reprieve.
What quality gave him strength
To turn again,
Accept the cup,
Endure the anguish
Of a bloody victory?
Duty?
Honor?
Obedience?
Faith?
I think that only Love
Could shine with a brilliance to

*Light the dark*
*Recesses of Hell,*
*As he sought us out to*
*Heal crippling scars of telestial life:*
*Restoring the joys of innocence*
*To hard-won knowledge.*
                    —*M. D.*

C H A P T E R   T W O

# Definitions and Perspectives

*Chapters two through eight are drawn from Betsy's clinical experience. She has been a therapist for over twenty years, specializing in the treatment of women and depression.*

If I could engrave one cardinal precept in the mind and heart of every woman who experiences feelings of discouragement and loss, it would be the truth that sadness is a normal part of living in mortality. There are events and situations which truly *are* sad. These events cause the kind of suffering, adversity, tribulation, and opposition in all things which we are to experience to gain the knowledge necessary for our progression. As written in Doctrine and Covenants 122:7: " . . . all these things shall give thee experience and shall be for thy good."

Most of us understand sadness. We are appropriately sad when we experience a loss, a disappointment, an offense, or a grief. Sadness is a human feeling in response to living in a mortal world. It provides a way to distill our pain and discouragement into memories, lessons, and mortal experience; it can even draw us toward one another. Sadness is a process.

Depression, on the other hand, is not a process. Depression is a brain illness. The despair of depression is often unfathomable to those who have not experienced it. Depression isolates us from one another, and the severity of the pain is very different from normal sadness.

Yet people can confuse depression with sadness. Well-meaning friends may tell a depressed person not to be sad or recommend the things that usually would help someone who is sad to feel better. Similarly, a depressed person may mistake her own sadness for depression. Although people who are depressed *feel* sad, it is not the only emotion they feel, and it is not normal sadness. The sadness that is part of depression is not on a normal scale: it is overwhelming, unrelenting, and hopeless.

## Differences between Sadness and Depression

*Though deepening trials throng your way,*
*Press on, press on, ye Saints of God!*
*(Hymns, 122)*

One of my favorite hymns contains those lines. Sadness is exactly the kind of trial addressed in this hymn. Though our hearts may be heavy with hurt, remorse, or discouragement, we have the capacity to press on. We feel comforted when we fast, pray, and read our scriptures. Though pain is present, we are able to function—physically, emotionally, mentally, and spiritually—in spite of our distress. Sadness is time-limited: at some point, we are able to put our sadness in a context that allows us to go forward. Sadness may be quite difficult to manage but we *can* manage it.

When we are depressed we feel overwhelmed by feelings of sadness, as well as feelings of hopelessness, worthlessness, and despair. Depression causes us to doubt our abilities and capabilities and consumes us with shame, guilt, and unfathomable feelings of unworthiness. These feelings render us unable to conceive of ever being happy.

In contrast, when we are sad, we do not feel hopeless, worthless, or guilty without cause. We feel appropriately sorrowful, despondent, grieving, melancholy, or blue. While our world might not seem rosy, we do not see everything through the unrelenting gray lens of negativity that is a hallmark of clinical depression.

Sadness does not require professional intervention, such as medication or talk therapy. However, it is sometimes both necessary and prudent to consider therapy as well as an antidepressant or mood stabilizer for someone who is suffering from depression. I repeat: sadness and depression are not the same thing. Sadness is a normal reaction to life's disappointments or losses; it is not an illness. Depression is a brain illness.

## Mistaking Sadness for Depression

Sometimes depression can be challenging to diagnose. When a physician takes a medical history some of the apparent and reported symptoms and characteristics of depression may manifest themselves in ways that appear to be very similar to sadness. The difference between sadness (a process) and depression (a brain illness) can often be determined by gauging the intensity, severity, longevity, and interval of the feelings.

| | |
|---|---|
| Intensity: | How "sharp" is the despair? |
| Severity: | How does this compare to what you normally feel or how you normally behave? |
| Longevity: | How long does the despair last? |
| Interval: | How much time exists between episodes? |

This kind of gauging is important for a physician to consider when she is making an assessment, because prescriptions should not be handed out merely on the basis of someone feeling blue.

It is important to state that the "pop-a-pill" mentality to fix life's problems can sometimes exist in otherwise independent and normal people. Although it may seem convenient and attractive to find a quick, easy solution to a discouraging mood, we shouldn't confuse a bottle of

Prozac with a bag of M&M's. It is easy, but hazardous, to mistake sadness for depression.

There are many things a person can do if she is trying to determine whether she is suffering from depression rather than experiencing the sadness that is a normal part of mortality. These include the following:

- educate yourself about the difference between sadness and depression
- seek support from family and friends
- talk with others who have walked the same path
- gain perspective by helping others
- study the scriptures for spiritual insight
- pray for guidance to ask the right questions
- pray for guidance in solutions to your problems
- fast for an extra portion of the Spirit

If you are experiencing sadness—even profound sadness—rather than depression, these things will help you to move forward in healing and to feel better and happier. If a woman can learn to understand sadness as one part of her life and not her total life, she will be on the road to "pressing on."

Depression, in contrast, will be helped very little by these efforts. Depression is not a mood: it is a physical disorder with emotional symptoms.

## Depression Is Real

In a recent study cited in *U.S. News and World Report*, the World Health Organization ranked depression as the number one health problem for women and projects that by the year 2020 it will become the number two health problem (following heart disease) for people in general.[1] Depression demands recognition as a major force that negatively alters lives. Yet, depression is not invincible. It is an illness that can be successfully treated. Depression *can* be overcome.

## The Hopelessness of Depression

I do not like the word *depression*. As a practicing therapist for almost twenty years, I am frustrated by the ordinariness of the word. Depression is not ordinary: it is agonizing. In daily conversation, the word *depression* is used interchangeably with such synonyms as *sad, discouraged, blue, mournful, grieving,* and *despondent.* While depression may contain parts and shades of all of these synonyms, true clinical depression is worthy of a name which embodies all the metaphors for hopelessness described in the following poem:

> *Hopeless: descent into the prison of numbed emotion.*
> *Hopeless: the open chest wound, heart exposed and trampled.*
> *Hopeless: the incarceration of a body seemingly wrenched from its spirit.*
> *Hopeless: the isolation chamber opposite of all that is beautiful and good.*
> *Hopeless: the sentence of solitary confinement to an abyss of pain from*
> *which there is seemingly no escape.*
> *Hopeless: master despot who rules my days and rules my nights.*
> *Hopeless: Gethsemane, personal, to me.*

I wrote this poem at a time in my life when I was very depressed. The soul feels hollow to one who is depressed. Hopelessness is the daily cloak which wraps heavily around her shoulders. She is bowed down beneath its weight.

Many years ago, Pogo, a famous comic strip character, lamented, "We have met the enemy and he is us." This could describe individuals struggling with depression. We become enemies to our own selves. We feel like enemies to everything that we once believed, dreamed, or hoped.

In Joseph Smith's acutely human supplication, as recorded in Doctrine and Covenants 121:1–10, he shares with those of us who have suffered depression a mirror of our own plea, "O God, where art thou?"

In my work as a professional therapist I have heard this cry, "O God, where art thou?" expressed verbally and nonverbally many times.

## A Picture of Depression

Several years ago, I was seated in the front of the chapel during sacrament meeting when the first counselor in our bishopric sprinted from the podium, down the aisle, and through the back doors. Several moments later, the second counselor also ran down the aisle and through the back doors. A few minutes later, as sacrament meeting concluded and I walked to my Sunday School class, the first counselor walked up to me and whispered, "We have a problem." As he led me to the bishop's office, he told me that he and the other member of the bishopric "had noticed Sister Miller fall apart in the back of the chapel and run out of the meeting."

I usually have on my "therapy hat," and I am pretty good at picking up clues as to how people are doing emotionally. But Sister Miller? I was shocked. She was our Gospel Doctrine teacher. She was both elegant and intelligent. All of us thought she was definitely one of the world's best Gospel Doctrine teachers. She was always smiling, always going out of her way to help. I would never have suspected Sister Miller would have "fallen apart" in church. Neither would the bishopric have suspected. Both men were shaken by the depth of her despair. They had immediately given her a priesthood blessing. She remained inconsolable. That is why they came to get me. The counselor told me that Sister Miller had gone out to her car to wait for me.

As I walked out to join Jenny in her car, I found her doubled over in the driver's seat, head buried in her hands, shaking and sobbing as if her very breath were being forced from her by some force she did not understand. She was sobbing, "I'm going crazy, I'm going crazy! I know you are going to have to put me in a hospital. That's all right—I have good insurance. Satan has hold of me. I am a terrible person. I have prayed for help, and God won't help me. I just don't have enough faith."

All during Sunday School, I listened as Sister Miller poured out her feelings: "I am a wretched human being. I want to drive in front of a truck because I can't stand my pain anymore." Sister Miller uttered a long wailing cry followed by bursts of gasps and tears. She was sobbing inconsolably.

All of us who knew her, and I had known her well for three years, would have ranked her as a "10" on the competence scale. When she wasn't a leader in the ward, or at an event, she was one of those tireless worker bees in the kitchen cheerfully doing dishes. She was a soft, gentle soul.

But now she was in torment. "What is happening to me? I know I am going crazy. I just know you are going to put me in the hospital."

Her facial expressions and anguished voice tones augmented her words. I have learned to recognize these nonverbal cues as proof of a client's ultimate dread. "I am either going to be locked up in a hospital or my therapist is not going to realize how serious this is."

What a dilemma! A depressed person is frequently torn by an exaggerated wish to be "taken care of," her intense fear of loss of freedom (hospitalization), and the equally awful fear that the therapist, or husband, friend, or other loved one will not perceive how critical her distress has become. She feels out of control. Usually she has silently attempted to master the tempest within. Like a freshly wound Jack-in-the-box, she finally explodes open at an unexpected moment. Sister Miller had reached that moment. Her anguish was tangible.

Sister Miller carried out her depression drama in a fairly universal way. She thought she was going crazy. She intuitively understood she could not bear the unrelenting burden of this degree of pain any longer.

She did not understand what was happening to her. Her only interpretation was that she was going crazy. As an active LDS woman who followed Church teachings to the best of her abilities, she had prayed and read the scriptures and prayed some more. She found no relief, so she concluded that she was somehow at fault, unworthy. She repeated the sentiment to me I have heard hundreds of times from hundreds of depressed clients: "As a man thinketh in his heart so is he. My thoughts are so terrible. Therefore, I, Jenny Miller, must be terrible."

I gently said, "You know, Jenny, it is true that 'as a man thinketh in his heart so is he.'" I went on to explain that this scripture is about right thinking. Unfortunately, when a woman becomes depressed, she may have terrible thoughts. She may become a victim of her thoughts, but her terrible thoughts are not real. I explained to Jenny, "Your thoughts that are terrible are not the thoughts of your heart. They are the product of your depression. At this moment in time, you are the victim of your thoughts, but your terrible thoughts are not real.

❦

"However, you can learn to be the producer of your thoughts. I do not mean that we can instantaneously become the producers of our thoughts. But this will be your goal, to remember: 'We are the producers of our thoughts, not the victims of our thoughts.'"

Jenny stopped crying momentarily and said, "Write that sentence down. I want to remember it."

I wrote the quote down. Jenny began to cry again. "But these *are* my thoughts and they are terrible. I think Satan put them there. I just know I am going crazy."

"Jenny, Satan did not put those thoughts in your head. Satan only has control over us when we open ourselves to temptation. And you are not 'going crazy.' The thoughts you are describing to me are depression."

"Are you sure? You don't think I'm going crazy?"

"No, I can tell you definitely, you are not going crazy."

I came very close to putting Jenny in the hospital that Sunday afternoon. But hospitalization is the last option to consider. It is the therapist's goal to offer concrete options in lieu of hospitalization. The client must be able to make small steps and small commitments to the therapist to remain safe (free from suicide attempts or self-injurious behaviors).

Jenny's reference to having thoughts about driving her car into a truck concerned me and was a symptom of the seriousness of her condition. I kept that reference in my thinking as I continued to evaluate Jenny for hospitalization.

Jenny was suffering a major depressive break or, in lay terms, a "nervous breakdown." Nerves cannot break so there is no such illness. However, Jenny was experiencing a total breakdown of all that was normal functioning to her, including her spiritual closeness to her Father in Heaven. She was bereft. She used the word *crazy* because that is the worst thing she could imagine.

I repeated and repeated to Jenny, "You are okay. You are not crazy."

Because she continued to ruminate about her "bad thoughts," I explained and reexplained in different ways how depression causes thought distortions and thinking errors. "Jenny, your brain is your enemy right now. Depression makes you look through gray lenses. Everything you see is colored by the effects of the depression. You do not have rose-colored glasses—you have glasses with the darkest tint of gray. Your world is filtered at this moment by an ugly color. That is why your thoughts are not real.

"Today, you will have to trust me and trust all you have known and felt in the past. You will get through this and soon you will be back to yourself."

Jenny appeared relieved but still pled for reassurance. "Are you absolutely sure I am not crazy?"

I asked Jenny to tell me what had been going on in her life. I listened as her words tumbled over each other, explaining all the stresses that she had experienced in the last two months. The human spirit is amazing. As we wrote down the serious and complex issues which she had confronted within an extremely short space of time, I was astounded how anyone could have kept functioning. Any of several of the circumstances could have felled a woman to sadness and discouragement and been a trigger to depression. (We will talk more about triggers to depression in chapter three.)

However, it was clear that Jenny was far beyond sadness and discouragement. Jenny had never had what she described as "such a bottoming out" before. Patiently, I educated her further about depression. I explained to her that what she was describing to me was clinical depression, or a major depressive episode. Jenny recounted intense and daily crying for the previous three weeks, an inability to concentrate, not being able to eat for several weeks, insomnia, and morbid thoughts about death and dying. In addition, Jenny told me that all of the guilt of old sins long ago repented of had resurfaced, creating overwhelming feelings of worthlessness. Her "crash" in sacrament meeting came when the intensity of her hopelessness engulfed her.

It was apparent to me that Jenny had severe symptoms of depression. I had no doubt she needed medication, but as I am not a physician, I could only recommend that she see a doctor. I made that recommendation, and

Jenny was so desperate she did not even resist the suggestion, as many patients or clients initially do. I immediately helped Jenny make the telephone call to get the earliest available appointment for a medication evaluation. I coached her to say, "This is an emergency."

It was an emergency.

The next morning as I said my morning prayers, I prayed that Jenny would have a positive experience with the doctor. Because she had been such a healthy woman, she did not have a relationship with a primary care physician. I had encouraged Jenny to write down her symptoms so that the doctor would have in a minute what it had taken us all of Sunday School to explore. I prayed that she would be blessed so that the doctor would "hear" her depression and support me in affirming her.

Jenny went the next morning to a medical appointment. Her doctor was a female—Jenny's age. She was wonderful. She said to Jenny, "Yes, you are having a major depressive episode. And I do want to prescribe an antidepressant to help take the edge from your symptoms so that you can get enough energy to work on your depressive thinking. Your therapist is right. Your thoughts are not real. They are depressive thinking. You are not going crazy. You will be okay. Depression is very treatable. Call me if you have any side effects from the medication."

Jenny came to my office the next night bearing her little blue pills and relating that Dr. Clayton had confirmed my diagnosis. I wanted to hug the doctor. Now, Jenny had two "experts" that had both given her the same information. She didn't quite believe us yet, but she said, "It feels like the truth, but how would I know because I can't trust my thoughts right now. You and Dr. Clayton both told me that 'my thoughts aren't real.'"

"Your bad thoughts, Jenny. Your bad thoughts aren't real. You can still count on your good thoughts."

## Encountering the Ugliness of Depression

In retrospect, how did I know I didn't have to hospitalize Jenny? That Sunday, she was expressing suicidal ideas. She reported to me, "I am having thoughts about driving my car in front of a truck."

This was a serious declaration. Under some circumstances, it could have been life-threatening. However, I was able to offer Jenny alternatives to her suicidal thinking. And she was able to accept those alternatives.

I offered to her four concrete options. I first helped her right on the spot to make a telephone call to get an emergency medical appointment the next morning. Second, I made an appointment to see her in my office that next night. Third, I asked if she had a friend whom she could invite to spend Sunday night with her so she would not be alone. And then fourth and finally, I took the paper where she had asked me to write the quote about thoughts, and I asked her, "Jenny, what is the most important thing you need to know right now so you can be safe?"

Without hesitation, Jenny answered, "I need you to tell me I am not going crazy."

"I can do that very easily. You are not going crazy. You have a 'big depression.' And depression is not 'going crazy.'"

Underneath the quote "You are not the victim of your thoughts, you are the producer of your thoughts," I added, "Your bad thoughts are not real."

"Are you absolutely sure?"

"I am absolutely sure."

A month later, Jenny told me, "The single most important thing you did for me that awful Sunday afternoon was to tell me I was not crazy and that I would be okay."

Much of Jenny's story is universal to people experiencing a major depressive break. Their minds have betrayed them. Their spiritual resources appear empty. They are devoid of hope or joy or even feeling. As one client expressed to me, "Part of me feels like an old woman because I don't have the energy to fight this. Part of me feels like a frightened child because I am not in control of my emotions, and I don't know what to do about it."

I have treated hundreds of women who have walked the mournful walk of burdensome depression. I have seen the signs and the symptoms and the verbal and nonverbal language of the nine characteristics that signal this devastating brain illness. (We will discuss the nine symptoms of depression in chapter three.)

With Jenny Miller, I had encountered, again, the ugliness of depression. And I was reminded, once more, that no one is exempt. When we accepted our assignment to come to earth, we accepted the terms of a mortal probation where we can expect adversity, tribulation, opposition in all things, and the wages of sin: our own sins and also the undeserved effects of those who sin against us.

However, depression is not a normal response to the hard conditions of life. Sadness is a universal feeling and a condition of mortality. It is normal. It is temporary. While sadness may be intense, it is neither life-sapping nor unrelenting.

## Biological Vulnerability to Depression

For some people, sadness is at the low extreme of their feeling range. In contrast, Dr. Peter Whybrow, UCLA neuropsychiatrist, explains that "certainly, stressful events—the death of a loved one, for example—can trigger depression, but only in someone whose brain is vulnerable to the disease . . . [with] a 'neurobiological Achilles heel.'" Continuing his explanation, Dr. Whybrow maintains, "That's why the disease runs in families, and also why, although most people experience grief when a loved one dies, only five percent develop clinical depression."[2]

In short, some of us have a biological vulnerability to depression. Our illness of depression is just as real as diabetes or heart disease or arthritis. It is just as physical. While it does manifest itself emotionally, including feelings such as sadness, it is not sadness. It is not even on a continuum with sadness. It is a brain illness.

I think it is helpful, useful, and truthful to consider depression as a "thorn in the flesh." It is neither a character weakness nor laziness nor something to be ashamed of any more than we would be ashamed of arthritis. When the Savior counseled us on the Mount to "love the meek and humble of the earth," I believe he wanted us to mourn with anyone who has a "thorn," and that is *all* of us. We just have different thorns.

But while Jenny's depression had brought her to her knees, she was also a reminder to me that the brightest and best among us are sometimes the very ones with the hidden but serious wounds. The hymn "Lord, I Would Follow Thee" addresses beautifully both the reality of hidden sorrows and our responsibility to help one another:

> Who am I to judge another
> When I walk imperfectly?
> In the quiet heart is hidden
> Sorrow that the eye can't see.
> I would be my brother's keeper,
> I would learn the healer's art
> To the wounded and the weary
> I would show a gentle heart.
>
> (Hymns, 220)

## A Devastating Illness

Another example of a "hidden sorrow that the eye can't see" and "the wounded and the weary," is Sister Browning. Sister Browning was a faithful, devoted, and capable counselor in the Primary presidency in her ward. She was both liked and admired by the other ward members.

Then one day there was a front-page article in our newspaper about Sister Browning. She had AIDS: not just HIV-positive, but full-blown AIDS. She had decided to make it a public issue. She wanted to publicize having to fight her insurance company for continued benefits, even though her disease had been acquired through a work-related incident as a health care provider. Though this news came as a great shock, we felt an increased love and desire to support Sister Browning. Her courage and strength was inspiring to us. No one would ever have suspected she had AIDS. Not Sister Browning. Just like Sister Miller. No one would have suspected.

Two women. Two wonderful LDS women. Two women of faith. Two women carrying heavy burdens of hidden sorrow.

But there was another distinction between the two women besides the obvious difference of one having AIDS. Sister Miller was depressed; Sister Browning was not.

Sister Browning had been diagnosed six years previously and had watched this terrible disease ravage her body. The newspaper quoted her doctor as saying, "Mrs. Browning has about eighteen months or less to live." Yet Sister Browning was *not* depressed. She told me, "I have never been depressed. I can't even relate to depression. I have felt sad, but I have had such wonderful support from my husband and my children and my family. I do feel some hope. I have never been depressed."

The point is *not* that Sister Browning had a supportive family or that she had hope. Sister Miller also had a supportive family and many friends. The one, singular difference is that Jenny Miller had a biological vulnerability to depression as an illness. Sister Browning did not.

Neither Sister Miller nor Sister Browning is unique. I have served for the last three years as the Relief Society president of my ward. When it is my turn to conduct, I am always humbled, as I stand before the sisters, to know of their depth of suffering and struggles and fears, most of which are hidden sorrows.

There is a depth of human sorrow such as that expressed in the fear and ache of Sister Miller that she was "going crazy." Speaking of such penetrating feeling, Alma anguishes, "I was racked with eternal torment, for my soul was harrowed up to the greatest degree. . . . I was tormented with the pains of hell; . . . the very thought of coming into the presence of my God did rack my soul with inexpressible horror. Oh, thought I, that I could be banished and become extinct both soul and body. . . . I [was] racked, even with the pains of a damned soul" (Alma 36:12–16).

Though speaking of his conversion from sin into the fold of God, Alma accurately depicts the torment of depression. While it is requisite that we "pay the price" of repentance for our sins, in depression we are paying a debt which we do not owe.

What I have learned from a half century of being a woman, and being a therapist, and being a Relief Society president, and serving in many capacities in the Church, is that there are many "hidden sorrowers" among us. And there is much we can learn from both the sorrow and the sorrowers. We come unto Christ as we learn to help each other bear these sorrows. Surely our Heavenly Father loves the sorrowers, for he gave us a baptism covenant which commits us "to bear one another's burdens, that they may be light . . . and . . . mourn with those that mourn . . . and comfort those that stand in need of comfort" (Mosiah 18:8–9).

Another poignant scriptural writing related to the depth of human misery is the eloquent lament of Jacob: "Ye have broken the hearts of your tender wives, and lost the confidence of your children, . . . and the sobbings of their hearts ascend up to God against you. And . . . many hearts died, pierced with deep wounds" (Jacob 2:35). "Broken," "sobbings of heart," "pierced with deep wounds": Jacob has just described depression. While this scripture is speaking of sins against the sanctity of the family, most depressive episodes have nothing to do with personal "sin." Jacob's description touches my heartstrings as one who has struggled with her own "deep wounds."

## The Faces of Depression

Walk with me down a corridor with other women who share their particular sorrows and deep wounds. These are the sorrowers whom I know best—the "faces" of depression.

For eight years, my mental-health office was down a hall and around a corner from the main receptionist's desk. Many times every day, I walked that route. Twenty-six steps. I learned a lot from first-time clients while escorting them the twenty-six steps to my office.

People in pain are desperate. People in pain don't wait for introductions. They start talking before we ever enter the office and sit down. They spew their pain out as if vomiting the words, sensing that this verbal cleansing might give them relief. They are right: it does. That is why "talk therapy" is so beneficial. People intuitively know what will help them.

It's just that most of us cannot bear the burden of someone else's intense suffering. We deny it; we ignore it; we resist it. We go over it, under it, around it. That is why a good, trained therapist can help. A good therapist wades right in, knowing that depression is not contagious.

Twenty-six steps. There was Sandy, the slim, fragile-looking young woman who wept softly as we walked those steps. "My husband made me come," she said. "He is so worried about me. I'm no longer the girl he married." She began sobbing. "Being a mom to four children under eight is so *unrelenting*."

Twenty-six steps. There was Carma, who flew around the corner like a cannon ball, exclaiming, "I hope you can fix me. I'm a mess!"

Twenty-six steps. There was Kailie, my bishop's married daughter, who reluctantly followed me, protesting, "I don't want to be here. I am so embarrassed. I'm just a little sad." She had just lost a child in an automobile accident.

Twenty-six steps. There was Fran. "I can't go on anymore." Fran had a personal history that read like a raunchy novel. She was struggling to accept the Atonement in her life. She could accept the Atonement for everyone but herself.

Twenty-six steps. There was Adrienne, who was angry, and the anger was consuming her. "I hate my mother-in-law. If I just didn't have to deal with her, my life would be perfect. I feel like I'm in competition with her for her son. I just hate her." While much of Adrienne's emotional energy was expended in anger, she was thoroughly depressed.

Twenty-six steps. There was Michelle. "I feel dead inside."

Those twenty-six steps took me into the life stories of hundreds of women. I listened to their voices. I heard the pain of young, old, and middle-aged; of married and single; of every color of skin; of educated and uneducated; of wealthy and poor; of brilliant and retarded, articulate and halting of speech. I stood in the sacred place of their hearts.

And in my practice, I have heard the words of the prophet Jacob over and over again: "broken, sobbings of heart, pierced with deep wounds." Depression: a broken heart, a broken spirit.

It is important to explain at this point that the "broken heart" of depression is not the "broken heart, contrite spirit" of the scriptures. This latter "broken heart," when one becomes vulnerable and humble before God, is very desirable. The broken heart of depression is not humble. It is squashed and self-debasing. True humility is confidence in meekness, confidence in acknowledging God in all things. In clinical depression, one is full of self-condemnation and feels dead to joy, dead to the spirit, devoid of feeling, empty. And yet, paradoxically, one is filled with the most exquisite pain imaginable.

## Different Definitions of Depression

I have researched, studied, and lectured about clinical depression over the years. I have often heard the repeated themes of depression—loss, the "broken hearts" and "piercing with great wounds" spoken of by Jacob, the "harrowing up and racked with great pain" expressed by Alma. The passage in Jacob, for me, most accurately represents the "picture" of depression.

Another theme I have heard frequently in describing depression is the cumulative pains or exhaustion of unrelenting stresses over time. It was this dynamic of things ongoing over time that precipitated the depressive break of Sister Miller.

Depression often occurs when we lose something that has been very reinforcing to us. Depression always manifests itself as a broken spirit, sometimes from the cumulative stressors of life. Whether a loss is to our spirit, such as a depressive break imposed from the accumulation of life's difficulties (i.e., loss of self), or whether that loss involves a loss to our heart (a broken relationship), the operative word is *loss*.

However, *loss* is not a strong enough word to convey the sufferings of depression. Depression can kill—literally, as suicide statistics attest. But even without a literal death, depression kills joy, kills hope, kills those spiritual feelings upon which we have relied in the past.

Recently Jessica, a mother of a young family whose bishop called me because she had become suicidal, wept as she asked, "What's wrong with me? I feel like Heavenly Father has left me. Intellectually I know that's not true. But I feel like my prayers do not make it above my bedroom ceiling. What is happening to me? I have always had my prayers answered. I have always felt the Spirit. Now I feel numb and dead inside. What is wrong with me?"

Jessica's depression was life-threatening. Her pain was overwhelming. In her depressed thinking, her only escape appeared to be suicide. The magnitude of the suffering in depression cannot be overstated. The pain is real. The pain is physical. The pain is tangible to the sufferer. Not the depression itself, but the agony of the pain is what drives some to suicide.

It is important, regardless of which "picture" or definition of depression we embrace, that we remind ourselves that depression is a brain illness. *Depression* can actually be more accurately considered as the plural *depressions* because evidence from more sophisticated diagnoses, brain imaging studies, and other measurements indicates that depression is not a single illness.

For the purpose of this book, we are considering primarily the brain dysfunction commonly called "clinical depression," "chemical imbalance," or "Major Depressive Episode (MDE)." Depression initially may appear to occur spontaneously. Other times it may appear to evolve into a state of physical symptoms accompanied by depressive thought distortions. Sometimes, a depression may follow a largely somatic (physical) course with the primary symptoms being sleep disturbance, eating disturbance, difficulty focusing or concentrating, and sexual problems. Another strain of depressive illness may revolve around negativity and cognitive distortions (thinking errors) which result in the client feeling worthless, guilty, and hopeless. Depression may also occur as a combination of these factors. However depression is manifest, it is an insidious brain illness that stands shoulder to shoulder as an equal in its dangerous effects with the worst of human diseases.

## Summary

*Depression* is a colorless word for an ugly, life-altering, and profoundly wrenching brain illness which causes pain, distress, and decreased ability to function and feel any pleasure. Its closest synonym is *hopelessness*. Some people are genetically predisposed towards this brain illness, while others may experience profound emotional trauma without ever experiencing true clinical depression.

---

1. Joannie M. Schrof and Stacy Schultz. "Melancholy Nation," *U.S. News and World Report*, 8 March 1999, 56–57.

2. Peter Whybrow, quoted in Schrof and Schultz, 60.

# CHAPTER THREE

# Depression's Characteristics, Symptoms, and Triggers

Depression *is* ugly and feels ugly. As a therapist, I have a strong commitment to fight depression and to the instruction taught in 2 Nephi 31:20, to "press forward with a steadfastness in Christ [and] a perfect brightness of hope." All my clinical work is directed "towards hope." As a therapist specializing in women and depression, I am interested in four aspects of the illness:

1. The Characteristics and Symptoms of Depression
2. The Triggers to Depression
3. The Physical Nature of Depression as a Brain Illness
4. The Treatment of Depression

In this chapter, we will discuss the characteristics and symptoms of depression as well as triggers to depression. Chapter four discusses the physical nature of depression as a brain illness. In chapter five, we will learn about the treatment of depression.

## Characteristics and Symptoms of Depression

During the writing of this book, I went one night with my husband to an indoor golf dome. As he hit golf balls, I sat on a bench with my longhand notes and began to work on the draft for this very chapter.

An attractive woman, whom I judged to be in her mid-thirties, was seated at the opposite end of the bench. While I was writing, she interrupted me by asking, "Are you writing something?" Not wanting to be rude or to explain that I was working on a book, I just answered briefly, "I'm writing an article."

She obviously did not understand that I was not particularly interested in being social that night, for she continued by asking, "What's your article about?"

Because I was extremely vested in my writing and "on a roll" with my thoughts, again, I answered briefly, "Depression." As soon as she heard my response, she perked up and became very animated in her flurry of questions. I finally did admit to this total stranger that, in fact, I was collaborating with another woman on a book about depression. I said to her, "Our goal is to offer hope to women who suffer from depression."

"I'll buy your book!" she exclaimed. Then she began to pour out her heart; she had been depressed for over twenty years. "I work in the plastics factory downtown. I like the people I work with. I hate my job. But I'll never be able to do anything else because I don't have any skills. I started there twenty-two years ago at $4.25 an hour. Now I make $20.80 an hour. It's good money for a woman like me, and I have insurance benefits for my kids, but I don't get any pleasure doing what I do. I feel sad most of the time." Then, almost parenthetically, she added, "That is why I drink, you know."

During our conversation, she related that almost all her personal friends were both depressed and alcoholic. She understood that they were all self-medicating with alcohol. She added, "I think you need to write your book, because I think most women are depressed; but they don't know what to do about it, besides drink."

I did not get any writing completed that evening but I did meet a new friend. And this chance encounter with a total stranger—not even among the LDS audience of women to whom Meghan and I were writing—was a confirmation to me of all I know about the magnitude of clinical depression in women.

Three days later, I sat in a clinical session with Jennie, a young woman whom I had hospitalized two months previously because of suicidal behavior. (Her agitation and hopelessness about her life led her to drive 110 miles per hour, at night and on a back road, trying to roll her vehicle.)

I was sharing with Jennie the experience I had just had with the woman at the golf dome. Jennie observed, "I can totally relate to that woman. She drinks because she can't think of a better way, and I've always thought of suicide and dying because I can't think of a better way."

Initially, I felt horrified by my client's comparison, and her oblique disclosure that she felt suicidal so much of the time. I was mentally scrambling to know the most empathetic, insightful response I could make to her comment which had taken me so off guard, when once again I found myself amazed and enlightened by the resilience and irrepressibility of the human spirit. In a casual manner, Jennie moved directly to the disclosure that she viewed her struggles with suicide in the same way as the other women's alcoholism. She then smiled and said, "But, I only have *one* thing to get over—my thoughts about suicide; and she has *two* things to get over—her drinking and the ravages to her body."

Resilient. Irrepressible. My client who had been hospitalized two months earlier for suicidal "acting out" had just described herself as having a "lesser" problem and therefore as less hopeless than an alcoholic woman. She was beginning to heal herself with her own thinking skills. And her thinking about her *one* struggle (which may have been very different than the thinking of the alcoholic woman's *two* struggles) was, nevertheless, right thinking for her life. I must admit that this type of experience is why I love what I do. Individuals frequently find their own answers within themselves. They intuitively grasp their own meanings and their own voice. My practice is not unique in this regard; a good therapist is a skilled facilitator, "thought trainer," and cheerleader for her client's personal discoveries.

I have many examples of clients finding their own answers. Actually, I believe it is the therapist's job to ensure that a woman finds her own answers. Recently I saw a woman who is struggling with both depression and anxiety. In a nutshell, depression is the *conviction* that things are terrible and hopeless; anxiety is the *worry* that at any moment things will become terrible and hopeless.

This woman is juggling her grim convictions that things are terrible (depression) with her grim worries of impending things that will be terrible (anxiety). However, she made progress when she defined a situation for herself in a way that made it more manageable in her present circumstance. She was elated when I congratulated her on her imaginative and productive thinking. In other words, she had come to her own awareness. She had gained her own insight. She had figured out a way to make her life better. All she required was a cheerleader to say, "Go for it. You are right on track."

Usually, women recognize when something is awry in their emotional life. As with my new "golf dome friend," although she had not made healthy, active choices to improve her depression, she knew its name. Frequently women know that "something" is amiss, but they do not have the word *depression* to give their condition a name.

Many times women come to therapy saying such things as:

- I think I'm going crazy.
- I don't know what's wrong with me, but nothing feels good to me anymore.
- I feel dead inside.
- I can't get out of bed in the morning.

- I feel overwhelmed, and I can't function anymore.
- I can't cook anymore; I can't even think what to cook.
- I can't find the energy to do all the things I used to do.
- Something is wrong with my mind; I can't concentrate anymore.
- I feel so guilty.
- I have to sleep all the time.
- I want to graze through five bags of M&Ms—the large bags.
- I'm scared to tell you what my thoughts are because you'll lock me up in a hospital.
- I'm really frightened because last night I was driving home from work and all of a sudden a thought flew through my mind and told me to drive into a tree. I am so scared. I don't know why that thought came to me.
- I think about dying all the time.

These actual statements, or similar statements, have been made to me by hundreds of different clients. The themes are the same. Although those suffering from these feelings may or may not know the name *depression*, they intuitively know that something is very wrong. However, they may underestimate the seriousness of their symptoms. They may also feel hopelessness about their symptoms.

If a depressed woman happened to read William Styron's *Darkness Visible*, she would recognize herself as a fellow traveler along the byways of depression. Styron's language lays bare the bleakness of the illness: "For over seventy-five years the word [depression] has slithered innocuously through the language like a slug, leaving little trace of its intrinsic malevolence, and preventing by its very insipidity, a general awareness of the horrible intensity of the disease when out of control."[1] He describes an experience with depression as, "My brain had begun to endure its familiar siege: panic and dislocation, and a sense that my thought processes were engulfed by a toxic and unnamable tide that obliterated any enjoyable response to the living world."[2]

With such words as *malevolence, slithering, like a slug, insipid (dull), dislocation, siege, toxic, obliteration,* William Styron has painted a picture of depression. Yet professionals who treat depression are required to diagnose with less poetic, more insurance-friendly terms such as *pain, distress,* and *suffering.*

All service professionals in the area of psychiatry, psychology, and social work use the *Diagnostic and Statistical Manual of Mental Disorder—4th edition (DSM-IV)* to diagnose. According to *DSM-IV,* the following condition constitutes a mental disorder:

" . . . a collection of identifiable symptoms which cause pain, disability, distress and suffering; and an impaired ability to function emotionally, socially, mentally or behaviorally."[3]

A major depressive episode (MDE) is one of many discrete diagnoses listed in the *DSM-IV.* It is described under the general classification of Mood Disorders.

The symptoms of a major depression include (1) experiencing a change from the way the person has previously functioned, and (2) experiencing at least five of the following symptoms over a period of at least two weeks:

- depressed mood, most of the day, every day for at least two weeks
- loss of pleasure in one's usual activities
- significant weight loss or gain
- insomnia or hypersomnia nearly every day (inability to fall asleep/stay asleep or sleeping all the time)
- psychomotor agitation (inability to sit still, pacing, hand wringing, pulling skin or clothing, etc.) or psychomotor retardation (slowed body movements, thinking, or speech)
- fatigue or loss of energy every day
- feelings of hopelessness or worthlessness; inappropriate feelings of guilt
- diminished ability to think or concentrate
- recurrent thoughts of death; thoughts, ideas, plans, or attempts at suicide

## *Triggers to Depression*

Frequently, there are triggers to depression. It is important to recognize that these triggers jump-start a brain which is already vulnerable to clinical depression. This is one reason people have such different depth and breadth of response to the same events. In other words, while my body may be vulnerable to depression, another person's may be vulnerable to migraines, someone else's to high blood pressure, yet another person's to heart disease, and so on. Being susceptible to depression is not a weakness or a moral failing; it does not make me a bad person any more than a person is bad for being diabetic.

The technical word for trigger is *precipitant*. A precipitant is an event, situation, or circumstance with significant meaning to the depressed person which has occurred within a short time preceding the downward spiral into depression. Some depressions apparently occur without a known trigger or precipitant. In contrast, many times a precipitant or precipitants to depression are identifiable and understood.

Before addressing some of the precipitants to depression, I want to make it clear that most clinical depressions I have treated would be classified as major depressive episodes. It is my emphatic conviction that MDE is a brain illness which is physiological, neurochemical, biological, and medical. In other words, when you are experiencing depression it's not "just in your mind." It is a whole body illness which has a psychological component, but is rooted in physiology.

Dr. Philip Gold, a National Institute of Mental Health neuroscientist, has suggested that we give the disease a more accurate name. He suggests, "hypothalamo-pituitary-adrenal axis dysfunction."[4] While "hypothalamo-pituitary-adrenal axis dysfunction" is not bland like the word *depression*, it is also very removed from the language that has meaning to the great majority of us. It does, however, make clear the physical nature of the affliction.

The physical nature of depression can operate in two important ways:

- A clinical depression may *begin* as a brain illness.

- A clinical depression may *evolve into* a brain illness.

Depression may appear to occur spontaneously or there may be a trigger recognized as preceding an episode of the illness. In either scenario, brain chemistry is impacted and mood-elevating neurotransmitters are diminished. What lay people call "chemical imbalance" is present. While depression has psychological triggers or precipitants, depression is also very physiological (physical).

That fact being established, I would like to describe some of the precipitants to depression that I have encountered in my career as a psychotherapist and which are common in other therapist's practices as well. This list is not meant to be comprehensive or exhaustive.

## Cognitive Distortions

There is a particular cognitive distortion that will be familiar to many Latter-day Saint women. This distortion is something I have experienced in my own life. I have learned to recognize and laugh about it now; but it used to be a very weighty issue for me. It's called "inner dialogue disorder."

Inner dialogue disorder occurs when you have a conversation with yourself. In these conversations, you imagine all sorts of mental comparisons to Sister A and Sister B and Sister C. The problem with this is that (1) you grade yourself as if life were a report card, (2) you grade yourself as if the only two grades available were "A" and "F," and (3) you grade your "insides" compared with everybody else's "outsides."

If those mental comparisons were not enough to fell the strongest of women, the final insult is to add up all the combined talents of Sister A and Sister B and Sister C and then hold up yourself in comparison to the ultimate Molly Mormon, Super Mom, Fascinating Woman, and Composite Biblical Heroine: Ruth-Esther-Elizabeth-Mary-Eve.

Here is an example of an old cognitive distortion of mine. This is my own inner dialogue disorder. Many of you may recognize yourself in my musing. Listen to how I mentally compare myself and come up short in every instance:

*Yesterday, I compared my housekeeping skills to* House Beautiful.
  *I failed.*
*Yesterday, I compared my cooking skills to Betty Crocker.*
  *I failed.*
*Yesterday, I compared my physical fitness to Jane Fonda.*
  *I failed.*
*Yesterday, I compared my intelligence to Einstein.*
  *I failed.*
*Yesterday, I compared my compassion to Mother Theresa.*
  *I failed.*
*Yesterday, I compared my beauty to Julia Roberts.*
  *I failed.*

In the cognitive distortions of my inner dialogue disorder, I am "convicted" by my own thoughts. I allow myself no defense, no trial, and no jury. Just my own harsh verdict.

I have since changed my distorted thinking. When I find myself making these kinds of comparisons, I add another line.

*Yesterday, I compared my housekeeping skills to* House Beautiful.
  *I failed.*
    But . . . even though you can't get into any of my bedrooms, there
      is a small trail through my living room floor.
*Yesterday, I compared my cooking skills to Betty Crocker.*
  *I failed.*
    But . . . my kids won't eat "sautéed mushroom, anchovy, and eggplant soufflé" anyway.
*Yesterday I compared my physical fitness to Jane Fonda. I failed.*
    But . . . I did read in the *Guinness Book of World Records* that
      there was a woman who weighed 960 pounds, and I don't
      weigh that much yet.
*Yesterday I compared my intelligence to Einstein.*
  *I failed.*

But . . . while I know nothing about "relativity," I know a lot about "relationships."

*Yesterday I compared my compassion to Mother Theresa.*
> *I failed.*

But . . . I did see four out of five of my visiting teaching sisters this month.

*Yesterday, I compared my beauty to Julia Roberts.*
> *I failed.*

Well . . . what can I say?

By recognizing my own tendency to unrealistically compare myself to others, and by learning to laugh at that tendency, I was able to correct some negative thinking.

Another common cognitive distortion is "awfulizing" or "catastrophizing." Here is an example:

> *Oh, no, I missed my bus.*
> *I'm sure another bus won't be by for hours.*
> *I'll be late to work.*
> *My boss will never understand.*
> *I'll lose my job.*
> *No one will ever hire me again.*
> *Because I missed my bus.*

In this example, a simple problem is turned into a huge problem and the "catastrophizer" is riddled with anxiety by assuming worst-case scenarios over and over again. The fears that are generated by this kind of thinking are way out of proportion to the reality of the situation. If you struggle with "catastrophized" thinking, cognitive therapy can help teach you to think in more positive thought patterns.

## Psycho/Social Triggers

"Psycho/Social" is just a fancy way of saying those things which occur in the world of the self (psychology) and those things which occur in relationships between people (socially). Psycho/Social precipitants of depression include such things as:

- misunderstood or inaccurate roles
- misunderstood or inaccurate rules
- feelings of being a misfit
- cultural scripts
- the physical and emotional stress of being a woman
- "family of origin" issues (which include any of several abuses: physical, emotional, sexual, neglect, exploitation, and/or abandonment)

### ❧ Misunderstood or Inaccurate Roles

Misunderstood or inaccurate roles could include, but are not limited to, any of the following: man/woman, husband/wife, parent/child, youth/adult, teacher/student, leader/follower.

A person's expectations for, or understanding of, any of these roles could be faulty or inaccurate because the people involved may have differing perceptions or definitions of the roles. Roles also could be perceived inaccurately because of differing environments, lack of appropriate and healthy examples, or even ignorance. An example of a woman living out an inaccurate role would be a woman who physically threatens her children. Perhaps in her family, the mothers for generations had viewed the role of parent as "spare the rod and spoil the child." She may genuinely believe that harsh physical punishment is synonymous with discipline, instead of understanding that the goal of discipline is to change behavior, not to hurt or punish the child. In this example, the woman would not necessarily be guilty of intentional wrongdoing. She would have an inaccurate picture of her role as parent/disciplinarian.

An example of where the role of "wife" is both misunderstood and inaccurately portrayed, in a gospel-centered context, is in the marriage of the Bayliss family. Janeane Bayliss is a client from rural Idaho. She and her husband, Andrew, both grew up on farms where they learned to work

❧

hard. They both have strong convictions about food storage and self-sufficiency. Unfortunately, Andrew has a role for Janeane. To Andrew, "wife" equals cook, dishwasher, baby tender, homemade bread maker, "canner" of all things, home decorator, chauffeur, clothes washer, shirt ironer, dog walker, and even yard "pooper scooper" (this is the final insult to Janeane). Janeane is overwhelmed and devastated. She says, "I see my 'role' as Andrew's helpmeet and as the mother of our children. I want to have our food storage complete. I value self-sufficiency as much as Andrew. I am a hard worker.

"But I love to oil paint. I have not painted a picture for three years. And I am so tired all of the time. I must admit, although I can't tell Andrew, I am really sad. I cry every day. Nothing feels good anymore. I probably couldn't paint if I had a minute."

While Janeane and Andrew have the same Church values, their ideas on the "roles" of husband/wife are poles apart. Janeane is in agreement with the principles of the gospel which Andrew desires for their family. However, while Janeane would like the role of a helpmeet, Andrew has inflicted the role of a servant on her, and she has accepted it. This is probably unintentional on Andrew's part. It is nevertheless hurtful and demeaning. Division of labor responsibilities in the home (and in the yard with "pooper scooper") have not been agreed upon or negotiated. Andrew has not been sensitive to his wife's need to be a person as well as his wife. He has not helped create time blocks so that she could resume her oil painting.

While Janeane loves Andrew dearly, his misunderstanding of her role as "wife" is causing heartache and beginning to create resentment in their marriage.

## ❦ *Misunderstood or Inaccurate Rules*

Misunderstood or inaccurate rules are the "rules" or "scripts" we live out in our culture and our families and that we sometimes place on ourselves. For example, the family rules which govern many of us are often unspoken, sometimes unrealized, rules that have unique meaning to our particular family, though these rules might never have been discussed or articulated.

The way a certain family handles anger, for example, might be an unwritten and unspoken "rule," but each family member lives it out, as children learn from parents. The rule has become a powerful example, without anyone stopping to examine whether or not the family rule really is the best way to proceed. Here are some different ways particular families might live out their rule or script about anger:

- One family may use sarcasm to cope with anger.
- Another family may use humor to deal with anger.
- Some may fight like cats and dogs, but be ardent in the defense of each other. If an outsider attacked a family member, they would close ranks.
- Another family might sweep anger under the carpet, with an unspoken agreement not to deal with anger or its cause. Instead, they may use denial, avoidance, or even passive acceptance.
- Some families may use negotiation. They may have had family councils where rules for resolving anger among family members have been discussed and agreed upon.

Conflict about the nature of these unspoken rules may occur in families where there has been no discussion of conflict resolution. Each person comes at the problem with his or her own perceptions and expectations. Furthermore, husbands and wives come from two different families that have had their own sets of "rules." If no definition has been reached on how a family resolves a dispute, each member of that family is troubled because it appears that no one is listening, no one cares, no one wants to help.

Anger management is an example of how a misunderstood or inaccurate rule can be a trigger to depression. Frequently, a depressed person will have implicit or explicit anger as a component of the depression. If the family rule is "We don't deal with anger," the depressed person may feel there is no way to express his or her anger. The anger may then slowly boil until it explodes.

Another person may live in a "cats and dogs fighting" home, yet be personally reserved and timid, neither wanting nor having the "cats and dogs" skills. This family member may feel alienated. Anger, as well as other strong emotions, and the family rules surrounding them, may be a powerful trigger to depression.

### ❧ Misfits

"I don't fit into society. I am too shy, too afraid, too odd, too weird, too different, too eccentric, too sensitive, or any of the other 'toos.'"

We all know some of these people. They may be "difficult" or just "odd," or they may be withdrawn and isolated. A few characters from recent movies are illustrative: Shirley MacLaine has played two parts portraying "difficult" women. One was Tess, the widowed wife of a former president in *Guarding Tess;* the other was the crusty Ouiser in *Steel Magnolias*. Two other examples of strange but endearingly odd characters are Bob as played by Bill Murray in *What About Bob?* and Melvin Udall, as played by Jack Nicholson in *As Good As It Gets*. Each of these movies paints a picture of an unusual and challenging personality who neverthe-less gains sympathy and warmth from the audience.

In a word, a misfit could be anyone who might be called "eccentric," has differing styles or verbal habits, or is viewed as a recluse or hermit. A misfit could be perceived either positively or negatively by society. The key indicator for depression is how the misfit views herself. If the misfit defines different, unique, or unusual as "good," then she may live along the fringe of society in relative harmony. But if she views the different-ness as "bad," or feels unaccepted by others, depression may result.

The past few years the media has headlined the misfits of society who commit heinous crimes, such as the series of school shootings we have witnessed. Fortunately, misfits of this type are a minority. The truth is that most misfits are people so reserved, frightened, isolated, or alienated that they are far more likely to remain as those receiving pain rather than to become those causing it.

❧

## ❧ Cultural Scripts

As members of the Church, we are masters of beating ourselves up with cultural scripts. We tell ourselves such things as, "A good Mormon woman bottles peaches"—even if she and her family hate peaches. Or, "In our family the woman does 'woman work' and the man does 'man work.'" Or, "I must live the threefold mission of the Church and do everything perfectly and *simultaneously*, even though right now I have six children, a husband, a dog, a cat, a goldfish, a garden, and I'm the first counselor in the Primary presidency."

One way to recognize this kind of distorted thinking is when you hear the words, "A good Mormon always . . ." or "A good Mormon never . . ." or "A good Mormon should . . ." These are dangerous phrases.

A few Mormon cultural scripts that I have encountered include:

- We must have food at homemaking meeting.
- The sacrament bread ought to be homemade.
- High council speakers are always boring.
- My mother made those plastic grapes in homemaking about twenty years ago, but we should make them again for the new sisters.
- A Relief Society lesson with less than six visual aids, two hand-outs, a small treat, and a take-home reminder is not an adequately prepared lesson.

Frequently the very finest of Latter-day Saint women get stuck in these "cultural" traps.

Sister Winters is the homemaking counselor in her ward Relief Society. By profession she is an interior decorator. If Sister Winters is asked to be in charge of a Relief Society celebration, it will be a CELEBRATION in capital letters. The decorations will be perfect. The invitations will be perfect. The food presentation will be perfect. And if Sister Winters can control the twenty-six different women who have the food assignments, the dinner will be perfect.

❧

I will tell you that Sister Winters is someone from my past, and she is a dear friend. I have her permission to tell this story about her because she knows she is a perfectionist. But she also has a great sense of humor!

Sister Winters was in charge of the Relief Society Birthday Party. To complement the main dish, Chicken Kiev, she had chosen "Yummy Potato Casserole." She had dutifully typed eight recipes for the eight sisters who had agreed to cook this particular menu item.

As Sister Winters tells the story, on the morning of the party, she received a telephone call from Sister Flake.

"Sister Winters, what does *parboil* mean?"

"Sister Flake, *parboil* just means to boil the potatoes in their skins for about fifteen minutes. That way, the potatoes are partially cooked and you do not have to bake the casserole as long."

"Well, I don't like that. Do I have to do it?"

"No, Sister Flake, you do not have to do it. Just bake your casserole for one hour, instead of thirty minutes."

Several hours later, Sister Winters answered her telephone again. "Sister Winters, I don't have any cheddar cheese. And I don't want to go back to the store. I have some mozzarella. Can I just use that?"

"Yes, Sister Flake, that will be fine."

One-and-a-half hours before the party, Sister Winters answered the telephone at the church. "Sister Winters, this is Sister Flake again. I don't want to dice the potatoes. I want to mash them. I think it will taste better."

"Okay, Sister Flake. You may mash your potatoes."

Thirty minutes later—and one hour before the party was to begin—Sister Winters was called to the hall telephone again. "Sister Winters, I do not want to put the corn flakes on the top of this potato casserole."

"Sister Flake, I would *really* appreciate if you would please put the corn flakes on the top of the casserole. We have seven other casseroles coming, and I'd really like them to all look alike. When we are serving the dinner, we would like all the sisters to see they are being served the same thing. I didn't mind if you didn't want to *parboil* the potatoes. And I didn't mind if you substituted white cheese for yellow cheese, and I didn't mind if you mashed your potatoes instead of dicing them because none of that 'shows.' But, Sister Flake, please put the corn flakes on top of the casserole."

"Sister Winters, I don't want to put the corn flakes on the top of my casserole!"

My good friend, Sister Winters, and I have told this story and retold this story. Now it is funny. Sister Winters did not think it was so funny that day. But we have both come to see a false "cultural" script.

Who made the rule that all food at a ward dinner or a Relief Society party must be *uniform*? Culture did. Not even "positive culture" but "perfectionism culture." It might be a preference to have all the food items look identical. But is it necessary? Is it even desirable to have all the food look identical if having the food look identical is a hardship to a sister, either a financial or skills-based hardship? Is it necessary for food to look identical for it to taste good? That day Sister Winters was genuinely distressed because one potato casserole did not match the other seven potato casseroles.

The mismatched potato casserole that was not topped with corn flakes is a marvelous example. Sometimes we get ourselves caught up in the thick of thin things. In our flurry of perfection, we choose a "cultural" expectation over what might be infinitely more important. Sister Flake *was* difficult and resistive. But, perhaps there was an alternative explanation to her behaviors. Perhaps she did not have the money to buy yellow cheese or corn flakes. In any event, she did do her assignment, although in her own way. Sister Winters and I both learned a lesson about "cultural scripts," and both of us are far less likely now to require "uniform" food contributions.

## ❧ Stresses Associated with Being a Woman

Even *being a woman* has implications that may sometimes make a woman vulnerable to depression. I have seen this concept best illustrated by Anne Morrow Lindbergh in *Gift from the Sea*:

"'My cup runneth over.' Is this then what happens to a woman? She wants perpetually to spill herself away. All her instinct as a woman—the eternal nourisher of children, of men, of society—demands that she give. Her time, her energy, her creativity drain out these channels if there is any chance, any leak. Traditionally we are taught, and instinctively we long, to give where it is needed—and immediately. Eternally, woman spills herself away in driblets to the thirsty, seldom being allowed the time, the quiet, the peace, to let the pitcher fill up to the brim."[5]

As women we naturally tend to give and serve to the extent that we may not take time to replenish ourselves, physically, emotionally, or spiritually. If this is the case over a long period of time, it can eventually lead to a depressive break or depressive episode.

## ✾ Stresses Associated with Family of Origin Issues

Shortly after I had accepted a job as a new therapist in a mental health center, one of my senior colleagues was having a discussion with me. He mused, "Have you ever thought about how many *adults* walk into our center, but it is the wounded *child* who sits in our offices?"

When my colleague said that to me, I was too new and too inexperienced to know what he was talking about. However, it took me only a short time to understand why the prophet Jacob anguished about the unrighteous ways some people treat their loved ones. Family of Origin issues (called "FOO" in psychobabble) include all the multiple abuses inflicted on people by members of their own family: physical, emotional, and sexual abuse; neglect; exploitation; and abandonment. National statistics fairly consistently demonstrate, for example, that one out of every four women has experienced some type of sexual betrayal, ranging from fondling, to molestation, to rape, to incest, to any other perversion of the sacred powers of creation.

In a job interview with two exceptionally competent female psychiatrists in Richmond, Virginia, I was asked if I had experience working with AMAC victims (Adults Molested as Children). When I replied that I had worked with AMAC issues, the senior female psychiatrist, who was thirty-five years old, nodded sadly and stated, "When I went into this field, I had no idea how many women would come to me with this as their presenting issue, or one of their presenting issues." (Frequently a woman will initially make an appointment to see a psychiatrist for her depression, and then the Family of Origin issues will emerge.) Continuing her thought, this young female psychiatrist added, "I have begun to believe that when I scratch the surface, 80% of my patients will report some type of sexual abuse." While certainly not every woman suffering from depression has been sexually abused, it is all too common, even among LDS women.

One cannot practice as a therapist for very long without confronting the betrayal, violation, injustice, and horror of abuse, no matter what form it takes. And along with the abuses through physical, emotional, and sexual perversions come the equally life-altering traumas of neglect, exploitation, and abandonment.

I want to emphasize that although these events *have been* life-altering, they do not need to destroy the future. As tragic and savage as these abuses may have been, the sufferer has claim upon the Atonement of Christ to assist in the healing. This is well illustrated by the personal accounts in chapters ten and eleven. While one may not be able to alter the *fact* of being a victim, one may choose to not *remain* victimized.

## Situational Triggers

Situational stressors are those losses we could classify as adversity, tribulation, "opposition in all things," and living in a mortal world. This is the category where many people might begin with a genuine grief or sadness related to a death, divorce, accident, injury, natural calamity, or some other emotionally life-altering event, and then that initial "normal" sadness would descend into a true clinical depression.

## Physical Triggers

Some types of depression do run in families. This indicates that a biological vulnerability can be inherited. I am a genealogist, and I am thankful that I did not learn my family medical history information before I was ready to handle it. I was a solemn, serious child. I grew into a solemn, serious adult. I have worked to develop a warm, enthusiastic, and animated side to my personality. Inside, I am still a serious, solemn child.

I had known from childhood that I was extremely sensitive and that I tended to "take things very hard." As I grew into young adulthood, I experienced several episodes of depression.

I became a practicing psychotherapist in my thirties. At about the same time, I was doing genealogical research on my mother's paternal line. I discovered that my mother's grandfather had committed suicide at the age of fifty-six. He had been a prominent member of his community, and I found many newspaper articles that were in his local paper about his death. I was devastated by this discovery. While still pondering that information, I further discovered that his father, my second great-grandfather, had been diagnosed with "melancholia" and had spent the last twelve years of his life in a "lunatick [sic] asylum."

At that juncture, I talked to my mother about her siblings and discovered that I had an aunt who had been hospitalized in St. Elizabeth's, Washington, D.C., for one year on a psychiatric ward for a severe depression. I further learned that my very favorite uncle whom I had adored as a little girl had suffered several psychiatric admissions for deep depression.

On one hand, this new-found "genealogical" information was devastating because of the implications to me. On the other hand, I felt relieved that what I had experienced for many years was a part of my heritage. Not necessarily the part I would have chosen, but it made my ancestors very real to me. It also provided insight into my personal struggles with depression, as I realized my genetic endowment.

In addition to genetic predispositions, there are also other biological implications to depression. There are ties to the endocrine system, the thyroid gland, sleep patterns, and neurochemistry. There are disease processes which seem to be especially tied to a coexisting depression such as heart disease, arthritis, alcoholism and diabetes, to name just a few. Sometimes, aging processes appear to create susceptibility to depression. Many women who suffer from PMS have episodic depression. Certain medications also may cause depression as an undesirable side effect.

Finally, there are physical injuries, such as spinal cord damage, traumatic brain injury (TBI), or cerebral vascular accident (stroke) which may trigger a clinical depression, because of the physical damage to the brain, not merely as an emotional reaction to the injury.

## Developmental Crises

Dr. Erik Erickson is one of the leading writers on the subject of developmental crisis. Popular authors Gail Sheehy and poet/essayist Judith Viorst have also written about some of life's passages. A quick definition of a developmental task is a "passage," or stage of life. It is similar to the scriptural concept of "line upon line, precept on precept." Just as no one jumps into calculus without first understanding the basic mathematical functions of addition, subtraction, multiplication, and division, no one truly masters higher emotional developmental skills until she has negotiated the foundation skills.

For example, the developmental task for adolescence is "identity versus identity diffusion." Sometimes your teen has the very nicest of identities and then it diffuses. *Diffuses* is a synonym for wanders, deviates, rambles, "waffles," and drivels. An adolescent is part child and part adult. At any given time a parent may face the "six-year-old" version, the "rational adult" version, sometimes even the "regress to toddler tantrums" version of their teen. This is identity versus identity diffusion.

At age fifteen, my middle daughter wore "pouffy" hair, more makeup than her mother liked, and was the high school trendsetter of St. George, Utah. She was a wonderful, prize-winning artist who wanted to be a fashion designer. Her identity at that age was hair, makeup, and fashion. She even worked in the nicest beauty salon in our community. She had me convinced that she really would be a fashion designer, and I have no doubt she had the talent to do that.

At age eighteen, she decided she wanted to be a doctor in a third-world country, so she attended the University of Utah as a pre-med major. She loved her anatomy and physiology classes and, again, I was convinced she was going to be a doctor—in a third-world country, of course. "Pouffy hair" and makeup were out. What she called "granola" was in.

At age twenty, as a second-semester junior, she announced she was going to Patagonia (Chile and Argentina) with the National Outdoor Leadership School. To sell me on the idea, she informed me that John-John Kennedy went on the NOLS adventure. I was not impressed, as he was a gazillionaire and I was a middle-class mom. Nevertheless, my enterprising daughter got a scholarship and left for Chile for four months of bushwhacking through the jungle, glacier climbing, and sea kayaking. When she returned, she informed me in a casual conversation that she almost died from hypothermia.

She is now an environmentalist. Her evolving interests and values and commitments are the developmental process of "identity versus identity diffusion," or searching for identity.

To develop into mature adults, adolescents need to learn "who they are and what they stand for." Adolescence is well known as a time of experimentation and rebellion as the child/woman struggles to learn about and define her self, her values, her boundaries, her "separateness."

Most people seem to have a pretty good understanding of adolescence as a developmental stage because adolescence is a colorful time of life. Of course, the colors may range from all black to all bright to monochromatic to outlandish. And the behaviors of the adolescent range from the outrageous or rebellious to the dramatically emotional, all thrown into a mass of contradictions called "teenager." Less well understood is the next developmental stage where the emerging character and personality seek meaning through connection with another.

Continuing with the ideas of Dr. Erik Erickson, the developmental task of young adult life is "Intimacy: to lose and find oneself in another."

At one time I served as the Laurel adviser in Young Women. I became very close to these girls, particularly one of them I'll call Carlie.

When Carlie was nineteen years old, she found "the one." She was so excited to be married—and so excited to be married in the temple. Two months before Carlie's wedding, I was asked to be a presenter at a stake women's conference. My assigned topic was marriage. Carlie was in my audience that day as I spoke about love and commitment. I told my audience that Carlie was getting married in about two months, so I didn't think she would pay attention to me about this. I said that if you really want a marriage to endure, you have to believe that commitment to your spouse and to the institution of marriage and to your temple covenants is even more important than "love." Love can be like a tide that waxes and wanes with the trials and tribulations and adversities of a mortal life. But commitment is the glue that keeps a marriage together even in those hard times. I quoted President Boyd K. Packer, who admonished, "Even a rickety marriage will serve good purpose as long as two people struggle to keep it from falling down around them."[6]

I could tell that Carlie was amused by me and that she fully expected her marriage would be different. Her love would be a constant, shining thing. She had "lost herself in another."

Carlie moved away after her marriage. We stayed in touch. And then one day, Carlie called. She was crying with those desperate, hopeless tears of a person who is on the brink of losing her dream. When she could manage her tears, she said to me, "I did listen to your talk but I didn't believe you. I thought you were wrong about John and me. I just knew we'd be exceptional. I loved him so much." Then Carlie told me tearfully that she had decided she needed to get a divorce. "We are so different! How come I didn't realize that?" How grateful I was that Carlie called me.

I mentally retrieved my old women's conference talk, only this time Carlie really listened. I reminded her of all the wonderful qualities she had told everyone that John had. I reminded her of her temple covenants. She and John were discovering that their personalities and interests were very different. He was no longer so excited to take her to the musicals she loved, and she had gotten bored with computer basketball, football, golf, and baseball. But their values remained the same. They were both good people. They just needed some of that "glue" called commitment to get them past the disenchantment that occurs when you discover you are living with a "real" person, with all of the quirks of another personality.

The good news is that the second part of the developmental crisis of young adulthood is "to find oneself in another." I am happy to report that Carlie and John "found" themselves. The romance which had ebbed for a brief while became a great wave upon their renewed commitments to each other and acceptance of their differences. Carlie and John are now happy, content, and committed to each other and to their marriage. I would call them a little "Zion" family. They continue to have the same kinds of mortal life challenges we all encounter, but they are choosing to build relationship skills that nurture pure hearts.

Dr. Erickson identifies the task of young adult life as finding a balance between individuality and intimacy. Consider the amount of energy just these two words evoke: *individuality* and *intimacy*.

Maintaining a balance between both these developmental tasks requires a Herculean effort. Sometimes, the tension between these tasks precipitates depression. Women and men are more vulnerable at different "developmental times." Unfortunately, women are more at risk, developmentally, for depression when they are young mothers with preschoolers and other small children than at any other time. However, understanding a few basic developmental ideas can be a passage to "feeling better." It is true that knowledge is power, and gaining the maximum self-knowledge empowers you to gain or regain your own personal self-mastery. Consider the following information about young mothers raising young children.

The developmental stage which includes young mothers raising preschoolers is the period named by Dr. Erik Erikson "generativity versus stagnation." In simple terms, the stage of generativity means where adults meet their need to achieve through their work. Usually, a man seeks achievement through his career, while his wife's focus, if she is staying home with young children, is on child-rearing.

I remember a cartoon where a man is proposing to a woman with the words, "I'd like you to be the co-star in the melodrama that is my life." Emotional drama: That is an apt description of the particularly stressful stage of a young mother with preschoolers.

Sandy is a good example. Her husband, Mark, called me at work one day. "I am really worried about my wife. I am the junior high coach, plus I teach special education. I am also a counselor in the bishopric. I know I am gone a lot. But Sandy is such a competent person. I just can't understand what has happened to her." Mark continued, "When I married Sandy, she was an excellent student, held down a part-time job, took an aerobics class, decorated cakes for me for every special occasion and played the violin in the university orchestra.

"Now she cries all the time, the house is a mess, she acts like the kids are too much for her, and all she does is complain that I am never home. She's in the Primary presidency but she keeps pressuring me to tell the bishop to release her. I don't know what to do. Sandy has always really enjoyed serving in the Church. Now she acts like everything is a burden."

I met Sandy the next day for an emergency therapy session. This was a young woman crushed under the weight of clinical depression. It was so serious that she and I discussed hospitalization. I called Mark at work and he met us in the office. They both agreed that we would try two alternatives before hospitalization. They made an immediate call to Sandy's mother, who lived about eight hundred miles away, and asked her to come support Sandy for at least a month. I also had Sandy evaluated for medication by a psychiatrist. The psychiatrist prescribed a medication regimen immediately.

I had asked Sandy what her number one pressure was. With great effort and tears of "mother guilt," and as if saying these words were the most grueling admission she could make, Sandy haltingly said: "My children are just so unrelenting. Being a mother is just so unrelenting. My responsibility is *unrelenting*. I just can't do it anymore."

Sandy and Mark had four children. The oldest was a little boy of seven. She also had two preschoolers and an eight-month-old baby.

Most young adults go into marriage anticipating some of the larger sacrifices of raising a family: time, money, and emotional resources. What comes as a complete surprise is the endless number of little sacrifices. Sandy perceived these as "unrelenting." In her words, "Every day I fix nine separate meals, ranging from bottles to junior food to our family meals; I have three children in diapers at the same time; I never have the time, energy, or money to do the things I used to enjoy; I am tired of having to cook 'things the kids will eat'; and I cry every third month when it is my turn to do Sharing Time for Primary. I used to love going to the beach to swim and collect shells or take a nap, but now it is just one more responsibility to monitor four busy children under the age of seven and keep them safe *and* entertained. And on top of all this, I feel guilty for how I feel."

In addition to the array and complexity of these demands on the mother, frequently the young husband and father is "launching" his career. He is likely to be preoccupied with proving himself in his new responsibilities. He also has the stresses of being the provider for his growing family. Frequently, the couple began as a two-income family and now that the children are coming, the man sometimes has the sole responsibility of being the provider. Not only does he bear an increased responsibility for the financial support of a growing family, his wife may desire more praise and attention from him, as she adjusts to the role of mother. Their differing responsibilities and needs may result in communication problems and additional stresses.

Although the whole stage of development for child rearing is included in "generativity" (or those motivations to achieve which come through child rearing and work in one's career), the specific time of raising preschoolers is called "The Authority Period: Ages 2–5."

Dr. Kathleen Berger explains that "when children become preschoolers, the issue of authority, over the child and within the marriage, becomes crucial. This is often the period of greatest confrontation between husband and wife, due to the mounting pressure from increased financial burdens, multiplying household tasks, and shifting roles, as well as the child's growing need to assert his or her independence, sometimes in strident, destructive ways. In addition, couples often have a second child while the first one is still small, in effect doubling the stresses related to child care during these years."[7] Children are wonderful; they give deeper purpose to life. But saying that each additional child doubles the stress level in a home may be a conservative estimate. Stresses increase exponentially, as additional children come.

A woman is likely to be more vulnerable to depression when she is the mother of preschool children than at any other developmental time. Conversely, her husband is likely to be at a thriving emotional point in his life as he begins to realize success in his career. The disparity of "low" and "high" emotional tension between husband and wife complicates and intensifies an already challenging passage for both partners.

I would encourage anyone struggling with depression to consider reading a book about developmental psychology. Even if your depression is largely shaped by another precipitant, it may be that a developmental crisis is an added factor. Knowledge is power, and understanding the process you are experiencing can assist you in successfully negotiating a developmental passage.

## Major Changes in Life Values—Negative or Positive

While it is both logical and common sense that negative events and losses can trigger depression, it is less well understood that very positive events can also trigger depression. Some common examples I have seen in my practice include the following:

First, postpartum depression. Most women cherish the experience to be a mother and have planned this very personal, exciting choice. And yet when this new little seven- or eight-pound person arrives, many mothers develop the "baby blues." The combination of the hormonal shifts following the birth, in addition to the amazing responsibility, sleep deprivation, and a myriad of other factors combine to produce a true postpartum depression. I have worked with many women who have experienced this problem. It is often complicated and often exacerbated by the tremendous guilt the mother experiences for not feeling the joy and satisfaction she had expected with the birth of her child.

A second common positive life change that sometimes precipitates depression is when a person, usually a spouse or a child, becomes clean and sober (alcohol or drug free). Sometimes, the "enabler" (the rescuer and caretaker) spirals into a major depressive episode. Though her loved one's recovery is what she has always wanted, when it does occur, the enabler has lost her job. Caring for the addict gave her life purpose and brought her a significant measure of personal fulfillment. Who will she watch over and take care of now?

Another common event that is positive, but can result in a depressive episode, occurs when a person makes a large career move or changes jobs. Everything about the change may be totally positive, but sometimes the cumulative stresses of the change and the losses attributed to the former job or position combine to elicit depression. The same idea holds true for moving to a new neighborhood. The move may be welcome and anticipated. However, the combined stresses of the relocation and losses attached to leaving familiar neighborhood, schools, jobs, church, and friends may combine to evoke depression.

## *Summary*

Clinical depression, or a major depressive episode, is a group of identifiable symptoms which impact mood in a way that causes pain, despair, disability, and a reduced ability to function. While clinical depression is rooted in biology and neurochemistry, there are often psychological "triggers" that push a biologically vulnerable brain into the episode.

---

1. William Styron, *Darkness Visible* (New York: Random House, 1989), 37.

2. Styron, 16.

3. *DSM-IV*, (1994), xxi.

4. Philip Gold, quoted in Joannie M. Schrof and Stacy Schultz, "Melancholy Nation," *U.S. News and World Report*, 8 March 1999, 57.

5. Anne Morrow Lindbergh, *Gift from the Sea* (New York: Pantheon, 1955), 39.

6. Boyd K. Packer, *That All May Be Edified* (Salt Lake City: Bookcraft, 1982), 291.

7. Kathleen Berger, *The Developing Person through the Life Span* (New York: Worth Publishers, 1988), 454.

# The Physical Nature of Depression as a Brain Illness

As anciently as 400 B.C., Hippocrates believed that "black bile" was the cause of "melancholia." Even at that early date, common sense seemed to dictate that there was a physical element to depression. Today, one of our greatest unsolved mysteries is the intricate relationship between the neuroanatomical framework of brain structure and the resulting behaviors, including the behavior and mood of depression.

## The Role of Biology

In 1980, while I was in the graduate school of social work at the University of Utah, we were taught that there was "endogenous" depression and "exogenous" depression. Endogenous (derived from the

Greek word for "arising within") was biologically determined depression. Exogenous depression reputedly occurred as a reaction to loss.

This theoretical distinction has now evolved into the understanding that biology plays a significant role in all major depressive episodes (MDE). Depression is complicated and unfolds itself in many ways. Most researchers now think of it as more than one disease process. One primary category of disease process appears to be the somatic (bodily) or "melancholy" variety where the afflicted person finds it difficult to sleep, eat, concentrate, or be interested in sex. The other primary category is manifested by the client who reports feeling like a "zombie" with numbed feelings. While this distinction is not always present nor are the two mutually exclusive, there is some evidence that depressions may follow one of two courses: Either a course which primarily interrupts normal physical functioning such as eating, sleeping, and sexual functioning or a course where the primary symptoms revolve around negative thinking, cognitive distortion, and pronounced feelings of worthlessness, guilt, and hopelessness.

Present thinking indicates that moods appear to flow from complex tributaries which include some or all of the following:

- heredity
- neurochemistry
- psychiatric and other medical illnesses
- the endocrine system
- the thyroid
- upbringing
- social environment
- the company we keep (or fail to keep)
- life situations which we either create or find ourselves in

While these tributaries are complex and intertwined, those of us who have been caught in the turbulent rapids of a major depressive episode have no doubt that we have been plummeted into something that is exceedingly *physical*.

Depression is classified as a "mood disorder." This is simplistic, at best, because mood is only one of more than a dozen bodily functions that are interrupted by a depressed brain. As mentioned in chapter four, Dr. Philip Gold, a neuroscientist at the National Institute of Mental Health, coined the term "hypothalamo-pituitary-adrenal axis dysfunction." It's not very catchy, but it certainly gives a distinct signal that depression is physical. This is news to rejoice over for all the depressed people who have been stigmatized as lazy or weak-willed. Dr. Gold maintains, "It takes an incredibly strong person to bear the burden of the disease."[1] I am encouraged and gratified by Dr. Gold and his contributions to humanizing a disabling illness by giving it an unmistakably physical label. Depression itself is difficult enough without having to bear the added burden of believing it is "all in your mind."

## Depression in Women

Dr. Bernadine Healy, current director of the National Institute of Health, reported in a May 1999 interview with *Newsweek* magazine that "depression is very much a women's disease. [Women are] more likely to experience it at any given age, and more likely to experience it as a crushing physical torpor [doldrums]. And unlike depressed men who are more prone to alcohol abuse or suicide, [women are more likely to] suffer silently."[2]

Under the auspices of the National Institute of Health and Dr. Healy's leadership, the Women's Health Initiative was launched in 1993. The largest clinical study ever undertaken, it will span the next fourteen years. Its target is the devastating diseases afflicting women, such as depression.[3]

Finding and interpreting the multiple causes for depression is still in its growing stages.

The *Diagnostic and Statistical Manual of Mental Disorder—4th Edition* (*DSM-IV*) states, "No laboratory findings that are diagnostic of a Major Depressive Episode have been identified. However, a variety of laboratory findings have been noted to be abnormal in groups of individuals with

Major Depressive Episode compared with control subjects. It appears that the same laboratory abnormalities are associated with a Major Depressive Episode [MDE]. . . . Sleep EEG abnormalities may be evident in 40%–60% of outpatients and up to 90% of inpatients with a Major Depressive Episode. . . . [Additionally] neurotransmitters implicated in the pathophysiology of a Major Depressive Episode include norepinephrine, serotonin, acetylcholine, dopamine, and gamma-aminobutyric acid. [Physical] evidence that implicates these neurotransmitters includes measures of their levels in blood, cerebrospinal fluid, or urine and platelet receptor functioning. Other laboratory tests that have demonstrated abnormalities include . . . other neuroendocrine challenges, functional and structural brain imaging, evoked potentials, and waking EEG."[4]

In other words, although a specific laboratory test does not yet exist that can singly diagnose a major depressive episode, there are significant laboratory results which are evidence of the physical components of depression.

Additionally, hormones and brain structure itself appear to influence depression. This is just a brief synopsis of some of the research areas that are currently being studied.

The National Alliance for the Mentally Ill (NAMI) has a strong position statement about the biological bases of severe mental illness, including major depressions. "Severe mental illnesses are biologically based brain disorders that can profoundly disrupt a person's ability to relate to others and to their environment."[5]

Dr. David Burns, a psychiatrist pioneer in the field of cognitive therapy, postulates, "First, the physical (somatic) symptoms of depression support the notion that organic change is involved in at least some depressions. These changes in body function include, among others, agitation (increased nervous activity, such as pacing or hand-wringing), or retardation (motionless apathy—you feel like a ton of bricks and do nothing). You may also experience a 'diurnal' variation in mood (this refers to the worsening of symptoms in the morning in some depressions), changed sleep patterns (insomnia is the most common), constipation, abnormalities in appetite (usually decreased, sometimes increased), an impaired concentration, and a decreased interest in sex."[6]

Dr. Burns then addresses the second argument which supports a physiologic basis for depression. Some types of mood disorders do appear generationally in families, thus indicating a genetic factor. As with other known genetic disorders, an inherited abnormality would likely be caused by a disturbance in brain chemistry.[7]

This book is focused on bringing hope to women who suffer from depression. A major contribution, we believe, is to educate women that depression is a physiological illness. We do not intend to present an exhaustive overview of this fact. However, as many lay people are now familiar with such terms as "serotonin," "dopamine," and "norepinephrine," a brief explanation of their function might assist the reader in understanding the assumptions about neurochemistry in brain function.

## Brain Function

The brain has an elaborate electrical system. The neurotransmitters are like chemical "mailmen" or chemical "messengers" that transmit electrical signals from one nerve cell to another across the synapse (the space between nerve cells). This chemical signaling, or the neurotransmitters at work, sets in motion the complex neural interactions that affect our feelings, thoughts, and behaviors.[8]

Brain cells, called neurons, communicate by way of chemical reactions and the transfer of electrochemical energy. As brain cells or neurons communicate, they create neural pathways within the brain. Every time we learn information, we form new connections between neurons. Another name for learning is cognition. *Cognition* is a scientific word that means thinking or thoughts. Here is an analogy of how our brain can be impacted by transforming thoughts:

Think of yourself as an actress in a play. You have been cast as the villain and you learn all the villain's dialogue. You rehearse and rehearse and rehearse your dialogue until you can speak it by memory without stopping to think.

This is exactly what occurs in depressive thinking. Your neural pathway (thinking) has grabbed hold of a script. That dialogue is always negative, distorted, and/or untrue. But it is running freely down your neural pathway, creating havoc in your brain chemistry. Unfortunately, your thoughts get rehearsed and rehearsed and rehearsed. Pretty soon, you "believe" your distorted thoughts and, because your dialogue has been rehearsed so often, it now "feels" true. Thus, the goal of talk therapy is to change the dialogue or script from negative to positive, from unhealthy to healthy, from irrational to rational, from survival-reducing to survival-enhancing.

While anyone who has suffered depression clearly recognizes the effect on mood, less well understood is the effect depression has on other body systems. Depression is a "whole body" illness, involving your moods (feelings), your thoughts, and your body as it expresses itself, both in physical complaints and in behaviors. Dr. Burns theorizes that "depression might result from decreased levels of certain brain substances known technically as 'amines' . . . chemical transmitters."[9]

A simplistic analogy might be baking chocolate chip cookies and leaving out the baking powder. The cookies would be edible, but the leavening ingredient that makes the cookies rise would be absent. The cookies would not rise and they would taste "flat." In a similar way, mood-elevating chemicals help our mood to elevate or "rise." And the absence or decrease of mood-elevating chemicals makes our brain chemistry "flat." A stronger analogy is to imagine a loose wire in the tuner of a radio, which creates "static" (fixed) sound. Faulty connections in the brain result in mental and emotional "static." These connections can be changed by creating new brain connections or new neural pathways.

## New Research

Exciting research in brain functioning is ongoing using sophisticated brain imaging techniques with MRI (magnetic resonance imaging), SPECT (single photon emission computerized tomography), and PET (positron emission tomography). Another recent tool is the use of a fiber optic laser. These sophisticated tools are used by research scientists who continue to study and assess neuroanatomy, neurophysiology, and other brain functions.

As just one example, Dr. Mark George, a research scientist at the National Institute of Mental Health, and a pioneer in brain mapping, has established that the left prefrontal lobe and the anterior paralimbic region are centers of emotional response. In an interview in *Newsweek* about his work, Dr. George gives convincing evidence that depression is physical. He reports: "Researchers can actually see the shadow of the monster. It's visible on the PET scans of depression sufferers: a chilly blue blob of reduced blood flow on the left prefrontal lobe, along with apparent metabolic abnormalities in the anterior paralimbic regions."[10]

To those of us who have experienced severe depression, that "chilly blue blob" gives evidence to what we have intuitively known: depression is a physical, as well as an emotional, illness.

## Summary

Most people understand and acknowledge the psychological basis of depression. But it is crucial that those who suffer from depression—and the people who love them—also accept the physical nature of depression. The actual somatic (physical) symptoms, the generational patterns in families that confirm genetic predisposition, and the overwhelming new research studies all attest to the physical nature of a major depressive episode.

---

1. Philip Gold, quoted in Joannie M. Schrof and Stacy Schultz. "Melancholy Nation," *U.S. News and World Report*, 8 March 1999, 57.

2. Bernadine Healy, "A Medical Revolution," *Newsweek: Special Edition, Health for Life* (1999, Spring/Summer), 65.

3. Healy, 64.

4. *DSM-IV* (1994), 323–24.

5. *NAMI Advocate* 17.2 (September/October 1995): 13–14.

6. David D. Burns, *Feeling Good: The New Mood Therapy* (New York: Signet Book, New American Library, 1980), 375–76.

7. Burns, 376.

8. Burns, 376–80.

9. Burns, 376.

10. Mark George, "The Hidden Anatomy of Sorrow," *Newsweek: Special Edition*, 71.

C H A P T E R  FIVE

# The Treatment of Depression

There is no magic wand to cure depression, though we all wish for one. Some people suffer depression unknowingly for years, never having a name for this malady that saps their will and happiness. Recognizing and giving a name to the illness is the first step to managing it.

It is possible that a depression may last for years, if untreated. It is also true that depression may be self-limiting: that is, in some cases it may remit (go away) without intervention. However, there is no guarantee that if you just "wait it out" your depression will cure itself. Indeed, in some cases depression gets cumulatively worse over time. Professional assistance in diagnosing and understanding your depression, as well as in treating it with talk therapy and/or medication, is certainly the most effective treatment for your depression.

In this chapter, we will help you to understand the options for treatment, both physical and spiritual, that can help you to find relief from this burden.

# Talk Therapy

The goal of talk therapy is to speed up the recovery process and hopefully to make it a learning and life-enriching process. I believe it is critical for the client to learn to listen to her own voice; but sometimes that voice has been so shut down, it requires a nurturing guide to lead it through the labyrinth of the depression cave.

"Talk therapy" is a powerful tool used to derail depressive thinking. Cognitive distortions, self-loathing, negative self-talk, and negative perceptions may all be confronted, managed, and even done away with through the power of right thinking and self-talk. Healing words and healing actions may follow. The following is a mini-course on how talk therapy can actually transform or change depressive thoughts.

The goal of talk therapy is threefold:

1. The first goal is to form a connection between the client and the therapist (this is called the therapeutic alliance), so that a relationship of trust exists.
2. The second goal is for the therapist to assist the client in learning "healthy talk."
3. The third goal is to provide a feedback loop so that the therapist is providing healthy and appropriate feedback to promote the client's positive life changes.

## ❦ The Therapeutic Alliance

The therapeutic alliance is the trusting relationship that is formed between the client and therapist. The personality and methods of the therapist can be of less importance than the confidence and trust the client feels in the therapist. This trust is vital to enable the client to accept her therapist's suggestions and insights. It is also important that

❦

the therapist and the client share the same values, or at the very least, that the therapist has an understanding of and respect for the values and belief system of the client.

I have worked for twenty years with people who see me for the first time when they feel most vulnerable and fearful. I personally think that the therapeutic relationship itself may be a major change agent. A good therapist will serve as a guide who is willing to share her client's burdens that they may be light, mourn with her as she mourns, and comfort her as she stands in need of comfort. In the light of kindness and empathy, the depressed person is able to rethink her distorted assumptions and move out of the cocoon of depression into an environment where it is safe to grow.

## ❧ *Healthy Talk*

It is the job of the skilled talk therapist to help the client to recognize and confront negative and distorted thinking. He or she helps the client learn "healthy talk." Remember, every time you learn, you are creating new connections or neural pathways in your brain. This is more than the power of positive thinking. While it is certainly advantageous to look at your challenges in a positive way, the goal of talk therapy is to promote physical changes in brain functioning and to effect change in your mood, your thoughts, and your behaviors. The goal of talk therapy is to have you become a "change agent" over your own life.

When we gain new understanding about old experiences, we can reinterpret these harmful experiences. The painful experiences lose their power to harm us. These changes may occur through an increased ability to transform, interpret, explain, redefine, and even alter or cast off old information that has harmed us. For some people, it is not the past that needs to be reinterpreted, but the present. Their need is to change harmful or negative ways of thinking about new experiences.

## ❧ *Feedback*

The third goal of talk therapy is to provide objective feedback and direction. A woman may discuss her current functioning, her past history,

❧

the gaps between what she wishes to achieve and her current achievements, her body's response to the depressive illness, and the effect of her actions on others. The therapist can help guide her thinking so her perceptions are more clear and balanced. The therapist may provide an objective point of view to help the client recognize and confront distorted thinking, as the client develops her own skills in self-evaluation. Therapy provides an environment which seeks to encourage a person's healthiest thoughts, feelings, and behaviors.

A therapist with LDS Family Services, Amelia, had an experience with a client that illustrates the power of a change in perception. Amelia was working with a teenage girl, Kate, who had attempted suicide multiple times. In spite of good grades and a beautiful singing voice, Kate felt that she was worthless and incompetent. Her perception of herself was shaped by very low self-esteem.

Amelia asked Kate to bring in pictures of her life. In one photograph, Kate was playing soccer—one of the sports in which she excelled—for her high school soccer team.

"In this picture, Kate, you look strong," Amelia commented. "You look competent. What are some good points about you and the way you play soccer?"

"Well, I'm a good team player. I try hard, and I work well with the other girls on the team. I stick with it—no, that's not right, it's more than that," Kate replied. "That's not a strong enough way of saying it."

Kate and Amelia spent some time trying to come up with the right word for Kate to describe her attitude toward the game. "No, it's not *persevere*, either—I need a stronger word than that."

How about *tenacious?*" Amelia suggested. "That means you keep at it and never give up until you're done—like that picture of a cat hanging onto a branch, who is never going to let go."

"That's exactly right!" Kate exclaimed. As she wrote the word down, she started laughing. "I am such a hypocrite! I've described myself as a person who never gives up—as tenacious—but I gave up on life. Why did I do that? That's not me. That's not who I am. I am tenacious."

This moment of recognition of her real self gave Kate the under-standing and courage to begin transforming her thinking about herself. Eventually she came to the point where she valued her own life again. This shift in perception and healing are the goals of talk therapy.

## Examples of Healing

While there are many examples of how learning can shift a depres-sive thought connection to one of hope, I will share a powerful example I have seen repeated many times in therapy. This particular transformation was demonstrated recently as I watched a moving episode of *Oprah*. She had five guests who had all been victims of sexual abuse, ranging from incest, to abuse by neighbors, to rape. There were two common reactions that all five women spoke about. These are two responses that I have also heard numerous times in my therapy office.

The first reaction occurs when a little girl becomes sexualized at a tender age, so this experience becomes her worldview of sexuality; she initially believes childhood sexual experience is normal. As she becomes older and learns this worldview is not normal, and instead perverse, she becomes very confused. She begins to believe that she is somehow to blame. Depression, guilt, and personal disgust follow. She may numb her-self to any sexual feelings.

The sexual abuse victim sometimes has another, different response. Because she has been sexualized so early, she may become promiscuous. She will continue to act out in sexual ways, without understanding why she feels so "out of control." Her behaviors heap more guilt and more depression and more self-disgust on her already fragile ego.

In both cases, the victim is troubled by guilt, depression, and self-disgust. In her talk therapy the goal is to help the woman *learn,* or create new brain connections, based on accurate information about early sexu-alization. She can begin to understand the reasons for her acting out (or in other cases, "shutting down" sexually) and for the crippling depression she has suffered. This knowledge gives her power to understand and adjust her behavior. She now has the opportunity to choose behaviors that will lead her to contentment and hope. In working with adults molested as children, it is the power of healing words and accurate perceptions that begins the shift in their distorted thinking. As with other emotional illness issues, it is possible through discussion to view and interpret an event in a differing way.

As another example, a woman who has gone through a terrible divorce has usually also had her self-esteem shredded so that she no longer recognizes the person she once was. She is likely to be left in a significantly reduced financial, social, emotional, and spiritual situation. Her anger toward the offending spouse may initially be her survival skill.[1]

But what she or those around her may not realize is that anger is actually her depression defense. That is, her anger is like a shield she holds out to ward off more hurt. She has the right idea but the wrong solution.

Eventually, an angry woman and/or a depressed woman needs to confront the wrong thinking, negative thinking, and thought distortions which keep her soul clenched in agony.

Several years ago, I had a client who was involved in a prolonged custody fight. This was during the horrendous civil wars in Rwanda. This woman was consumed with rage towards her ex-spouse. During her ordeal, we had a refugee family from Rwanda move into our stake. The husband was the only member of his family of origin to survive the massacre. He lost father, mother, and eight brothers and sisters to the war in his homeland. He and his wife gave a fireside for the stake. My client was in attendance.

She heard this story of massacre and survival, of leaving everything behind, of coming to a new country without "purse or scrip" and of losing every family member to the brutality of war. The magnitude of the suffering stood before her, not on a tiny television tube, not with a disembodied voice on the radio, but in the person of a heroic man.

This drama changed her negative thinking. This story shifted her distorted thoughts from her innumerable victimizations (she *had* been victimized, but she had magnified and distorted her plight) towards empathy for the many other people who suffer cruel and unusual brutalities and injustices. In her mind and in her heart she became a fellow sufferer with the man from Rwanda. By thinking of someone else's plight and the magnitude of it, she was able to begin putting her suffering into a perspective that would allow her to accept it and move on.

The astonishing point to this story is that all the change took place in her mind as she changed her perception and thoughts.

A therapist's ultimate goal is to teach emotional self-reliance so that the client can access her own healing words to soothe herself. When confronted with negative thoughts and negative self-talk, the client develops skills to confront that negativity through focusing on her true strengths and goodness. Because this healing self-talk is different for each person, it is important to work with a therapist to learn the positive self-talk you need to overcome your negative thoughts and emotions.

Remember: new learning = new thoughts = new brain connections = new neural pathways. You build a new road that can be chosen instead of the old depressive one. Your brain holds the connections. But you're in the driver's seat.

## Choosing a Therapist

I have worked as a therapist in state social services, mental health services, vocational rehabilitation, a hospital, a private family counseling center, a day treatment facility for the developmentally disabled, school systems, a huge managed-care corporation, and LDS Family Services. From my twenty years experience in almost every clinical setting, I would choose to work with LDS Family Services the remainder of my career. The plan of salvation is the best base I know. Being able to use a spiritual paradigm to complement the emotional, mental, social, and physical domains of life is the balance most people need to give "meaning" to their suffering and to their lives. As an active LDS woman and a practicing Mormon psychotherapist, I have a fervent testimony of the efficacy of combining the theoretical truths of psychology (and *not* everything in the field of psychology *is* truth) with scriptural counsel to "press forward with a perfect brightness of hope" (see 2 Nephi 31:20).

Many women live in areas that do not have satellite offices of LDS Social Services. Or there may be a satellite office, but not a clinician experienced and successful in the treatment of clinical depression. Occasionally, an active LDS therapist and an equally active LDS client may not be a "fit." As a client of mental health services, it is critically important to feel safe, valued, and in harmony with your therapist. *In harmony* does not mean you have to think alike. It means you have to think together. Therefore, if you are unable for any reason to find an active LDS therapist, choose someone who is spiritually and religiously based, sensitive to your value system, and respectful of your beliefs.

For example, I have a friend who had a very good therapist who did not at all agree with her position that "No success can compensate for failure in the home." However, he did not try to dissuade her from her beliefs nor belittle her adherence to making every effort to promote this theme within her home. My friend had distorted this teaching and felt that because she had wayward children, she had failed in the home, as a mother, and as a human being.[2] Her therapist tried to help her understand that her success was not dependent upon the choices of her children. He tried to help her understand that she could control only her own choices. This therapist also accepted my friend's beliefs about the eternal nature of the family, though he did not share those beliefs. Therefore, though he did not share her LDS views, he did treat her very successfully for depression.

There are a variety of theoretical approaches to talk therapy, as well as personal styles on the part of the therapist. There is no "right" method, just as there is no one "right" therapist. It is important to find someone you can trust, who is supportive of your personal beliefs, and who is experienced in helping clients recognize and confront their distorted negative thoughts.

There have been many studies aimed at determining which modality—talk therapy or medication—is more effective. Because of the variety of talk therapies and medications, when compared as a whole against each other the results have been mixed and inconclusive. However, some types of talk therapy are more effective with depression than others. Many therapists believe that the best of all possibilities in treating depression is a combination of talk therapy and medication. And one element that a scientist will never quantify is that you also have spiritual choices.

## *Medication*

"The most widely used treatment for depression are the many antidepressants and mood stabilizing drugs. . . . Most patients will get some relief from one of these drugs or a combination of them. All have proven more or less equally effective in controlled test: 65% to 85% of patients improve, compared with 25% to 40% of those taking a sugar pill instead."[3]

An experienced therapist has seen enough clients to be confident in the ability to recognize the intensity and duration of symptoms that would warrant an evaluation for medication. Whether or not the therapist makes that recommendation, I would always encourage the client to err on the side of caution in making the decision to medicate and recommend that they consult with a psychiatrist or other physician experienced with psychotropic medications.

A psychiatrist is a medical doctor whose training is specific to the human psyche, human dynamics, abnormal psychology, and psychotropic medications (mood stabilizers, mood elevators, mood tranquilizers, and all other drug classifications which are used to manage brain chemistry for psychiatric purposes). There may be times and places where a psychiatrist is not available to you. There may be circumstances where you have a family doctor whom you trust. The most important thing to remember is that only a physician—a medical doctor—can prescribe medication for the relief of your depressive symptoms.

There are both sensible and necessary times for someone to have an evaluation for medication. These times would include but not be limited to:

- when the depression is long-standing
- when the depression is so severe the person is nonfunctional

- when the predominant symptoms are somatic or physical (such as sleep disturbance, eating, psychomotor, sexual dysfunction, etc.)
- when the person is unable to stop crying
- when the depression has an identifiable beginning and the person has begun to function in a significantly different manner than before the trigger
- when there is a family history of depression
- when medication has been effective in a previous episode
- when the person is obsessing (can't stop unwelcome thoughts)
- when the person is sleep-deprived
- when the person has poor or exaggerated responses to other medication

Many psychiatrists treat severe depression with medication because they have found that the medication takes some of the "edge" from a sufferer's anguish. Medication may be necessary to restore sufficient bodily and cognitive ability so that the depressed person has enough energy to change the thinking errors which accompany the illness.

In my practice, although I am not a physician, I have seen a number of people who could not do the work of talk therapy without the support of medication. Their bodies, moods, and thinking were impaired to the degree that they were non-functioning. I have welcomed the consultation and expertise of competent, caring psychiatrists.

Ultimately, the decision of whether or not you are a candidate for medication resides with you and your medical doctor. You may ask your therapist to assist you with words to describe your symptoms; sometimes a treating doctor may even want you to sign a release so that he or she may consult with your therapist. However, the bottom line is that medication is the exclusive domain of a medical doctor.

You should never, under any circumstances, take medication prescribed for another person. Medications should be used only with the supervision of a doctor.

As you talk with your psychiatrist and/or primary care physician about evaluation for medication, you may want to ask such questions as these that might guide you to a more successful experience:

- *Will this medication take away my "true self"?*

While I can assure you that the medication will usually assist you in feeling more like your true self, this question ought to be asked of your doctor.

- *How many different kinds of antidepressants are there?*

Your doctor will be able to discuss the various large categories of anti-depressants with clinical implications for each. The important thing to remember is that your doctor has a significant number of medication choices; if one is not effective, another may well be. Sometimes it is a process of trial and error to find the best medication.

- *Will I definitely benefit from medication?*

Most people will benefit from drug therapy, with results ranging from feeling profoundly better to mildly better. There are a few individuals who do not experience relief from their symptoms through medication man-agement. Sometimes, these individuals are truly refractory—their bodies do not respond to medication. However, in my experience as the thera-pist working in partnership with psychiatrists, a few people do not have a good response to medication either because they do not accurately follow their doctor's recommendations, or because they resist giving the medica-tion a fair trial. Many antidepressants require weeks to become completely effective.

- *How long will I need to be on an antidepressant?*

Trust your physician with this decision. Your part of the process is to keep your doctor informed of how the medication is performing for you. Never stop taking the medication on your own; it is usually necessary to decrease dosages gradually according to a set schedule. If you are the kind of person who likes clear guidelines, ask your physician to give you a range of time that you might need to continue the medication to achieve and maintain the most effective therapeutic results.

## Transformations

Depressed people frequently express the thought that they feel "like a worm." We can associate the "worm" with a caterpillar. What better place to become a butterfly than in the light of another's warmth? I think it must be very painful for the caterpillar to shed the worm skin and unfold its new wet wings, still to be tested. Think of this poem by Margot Baker:

### The Chrysalis

She started out
in a chrysalis state,
taking time
to develop,
be nurtured,
allowing herself
a healing growth.
I watched as she emerged
from her cocoon,
to stand,
and slowly stretch,
tipping her face up
towards the sun
receiving of its light,
its warmth
while gaining in strength.
Then,
I saw her as she stood
poised for flight,
her wings spread.
I gloried at their elegance,
and watched
as she gracefully
soared upward.

In this poem, the caterpillar has spun itself into the dormancy of the chrysalis. This is much like the numbing that frequently shuts down a depressed person. Like the chrysalis in the poem, this numbing may be the time for "healing growth." But in order for the transformation to be complete, the new creature or emerging butterfly must strain against the chrysalis wall to release her new beautiful self. Likewise, the depressed woman strains to find meaning. And when the suffering takes on meaning to the sufferer, the task is nearing completion.

I agree with Mary Pipher who wrote in *Reviving Ophelia* that most clients come into therapy seeking "meaning" for their lives, and more specifically, meaning to their suffering.[4] It may not be essential that a woman find meaning in order for her depression to be alleviated. However, in my experience with Latter-day Saint women and other women of faith, finding meaning is almost always a component to being healed from the ravages of clinical depression.

The goal of talk therapy is transformation. The transformation looks like this: When a person can objectively examine and transform her emotions and feelings, she is finally free to change her perceptions about herself and her life. Taking a deeper step into transformation, when she can change her thoughts and attitudes, she can impact the way she feels and acts. When she can improve her thoughts and attitudes, she will be led to improved feelings and actions.

I do have a bias that the most important assistance anyone can render to help a clinically depressed person recover more rapidly and more effectively is to assist her to get appropriate diagnosis and treatment. I personally do not think talk therapy is the only viable solution. I have, however, found it to be a life raft to the other side of the raging rapids within one's own brain. I have experienced this beneficial effect both as a therapist on behalf of my clients and as a person who has suffered from clinical depression.

## Spiritual Choices

As members of the LDS church, we understand that people are dual beings: a physical being and a spiritual being. Depression is an affliction of the mortal body. That is not to say depression does not affect the spirit: it does.

With clinical depression, we frequently benefit from both the interventions of man (talk therapy and medication) and the interventions of God. The spiritual man may receive a transcendent blessing which we call the Atonement. Depression is an amazingly heavy burden, and when we embrace the Savior we invite him to help us carry it. It is important and significant to recognize that Christ suffered and died not only for our sins, but also for our pain. In Doctrine & Covenants 45:5, Christ advocates the cause of those who believe in him: "Father, spare these my brethren that believe on my name, that they may come unto me and have everlasting life." The key here is that as we do our best, the Savior's grace is sufficient for us. He pleads our cause; he helps carry our burden. His mercy is tender; his love is infinite. He makes up the difference: not just for everyone else, but for *you*. He tells us that his was an infinite Atonement, for every man and woman, and he does not lie. Accepting this truth is one way of confronting negative and distorted thinking.

## Blessings of the Spirit

In the darkness of a depression, it can be difficult to believe that we are worthy of the cleansing, healing blessings of the Spirit. Nevertheless, the Lord desires to heal our wounds and lift our spirits. There are various spiritual resources which may also help in our healing.

Counsel from a nurturing priesthood leader may enable us to believe more strongly in our own worthiness. He may also be able to give recommendations for therapists or other professionals, based on other ward members' experiences. Unless your bishop has only had his calling a week, chances are he has counseled other ward members suffering from depression, though not all bishops share an awareness of clinical depression or a sensitivity toward this type of affliction. In our experience, however, most bishops and branch presidents are eager to know how to assist members with these issues.

Your bishop may also be able to put you in contact with other sisters or brothers who have experienced similar trials, and who may be a support to you in yours. If it is necessary, he will be able to help you through the repentance process. However, a depressed person often feels unworthy even when there has been no sin committed. Don't be fearful, as others have been, of disappointing your leaders, of being released from callings, or even of being excommunicated. Your depression itself is *not* a reflection of your worthiness. This may be hard to believe when you are under the influence of depression, but it is true. All your feelings and thoughts may be telling you that you are unworthy, for some unfathomable reason. Don't trust those feelings and thoughts. They are distorted. Do trust your priesthood leaders, as they reassure you of your worthiness and of the love Heavenly Father has for you.

Prayer, fasting, and priesthood blessings may help to buoy you up, or they may not. Do not despair if they don't. You will again feel the Spirit, though now its comfort seems far away. This is the result of a physical condition, not unworthiness. Try to recognize the other ways the Spirit directs you, through priesthood and Relief Society leaders and through your own intellectual promptings, which can still come, though often without the emotions of joy or peace which previously accompanied them. Though prayer and scripture study may no longer be as rewarding as they once were, they are still essential and can bring greater understanding about the purposes and blessings of tribulation.

In all ways, seek to discover that Christ is your personal Savior and that he suffered your pains so that you would not have to carry their weight alone. As your thoughts and feelings become balanced again through treatment, this testimony will become more profound and precious. Isaiah writes that the Lord will give "unto them that mourn in Zion . . . beauty for ashes, the oil of joy for mourning, the garment of praise for the spirit of heaviness" (Isaiah 61:3). Deep gratitude for the tender love of the Savior will be the gift you retain from your depression.

## Summary

The most effective treatment for depression includes a commitment to utilize both the best "interventions of man," which could include talk therapy and/or medication, and the blessed "interventions of God."

Talk therapy is a powerful tool to derail depressive thinking. Cognitive distortions, self-loathing, negative self-talk, and negative perceptions may all be confronted, managed, and even eliminated through the power of right thinking and self-talk.

Medication may be necessary to restore sufficient bodily and cognitive ability so that the depressed person has enough energy and awareness to change the thinking errors which accompany the illness.

The truths of the gospel are vital to our true perceptions of ourselves. Counsel from leaders and scriptures, prayer, fasting, and priesthood blessings may help us to understand the love and mercy the Lord extends to each of us.

---

1. Good sources for further information on the role of anger in abuse, depression, and healing are *The Anger Book* and *Feeling Good*.

2. Lehi, Adam, and Heavenly Father are all good parents, with children who made wrong choices. Agency is an essential part of the gospel plan, and children who are of the age of accountability are responsible for their own choices. Teaching correct principles is the parents' responsibility, which must not be neglected. But success in the home is not dependent upon children's choices.

3. "Mood Disorders: An Overview—Part II," *The Harvard Mental Letter* 14.7 (January 1998): 4.

4. Mary Pipher, *Reviving Ophelia: Saving the Lives of Adolescent Girls* (New York: Putnam, 1994), 34.

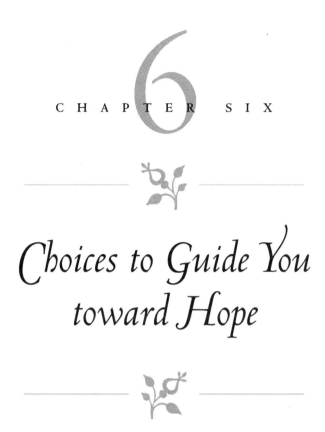

CHAPTER SIX

# Choices to Guide You toward Hope

Many, if not most, of the clients I have seen over the years come into therapy expressing hopelessness. It is impossible to talk someone into having hope. Hope is not achievable in the midst of her affliction. Knowing that asking a depressed person to "seize hope" is futile, I ask for something infinitely smaller. I ask her to have a *desire* to have hope. I have named this desire a glimmer.

Hope is necessary to an act of faith. Faith is only an abstract concept to someone in severe depression. One of the greatest challenges to depressed people is that they feel unworthy and isolated from the comforts they had previously felt through spiritual channels. Usually in an initial session (before any relief from therapy or medication), a depressed person will say, "I feel no hope. I feel no light. I feel no spirit. I feel nothing."

It is common that a well-meaning but uninformed person will have instructed the depressed woman "to fast and pray and read the scriptures." Although this advice may help someone who is struggling with sadness or discouragement, it will not help the clinically depressed person. In fact, this advice will only succeed in making the depressed person feel worse—more guilty, more unworthy, more hopeless. When depression takes over the brain, one's thinking becomes distorted, negative, and non-responsive to the platitudes of life. We do not know all the reasons why this is true, but we do know that one cannot expect a depressed person to take comfort from beautiful words, even the inspired words of the scriptures.

Usually an active LDS woman has already tried, mightily, "to fast and pray and read the scriptures." In the past, this will often have helped her. Yet, this time it has not helped. In fact, she may feel worse. She is already confused because doing this *has* helped her feel better in the past, but now the experience is bitter, because she does not feel the usual comfort or guidance. "Fasting and praying and reading the scriptures," though essential, is not the treatment to manage the medical and physical symptoms of a brain illness. It is like telling someone with a brain tumor or broken leg to fast and pray and read the scriptures to get better, without any medical treatment.

## A Glimmer of Hope

When a client tells me of her hopelessness, I find it useful to ask the following: "You may not feel there is any hope, but could you imagine even a 'glimmer' of hope?" Sometimes that glimmer is even a lifeline.

I have carefully chosen this word. A glimmer is just the smallest of small. A glimmer is the size of a mustard seed. People in pain are in such agony that they will reach for something small, something manageable. In all my years of practice, I have had only a very few patients who would not buy into imagining a glimmer.

*My light is dim*
*My light is naught*
*Bitter draught.*
*Life has broken my spirit*
*Life has broken my heart.*
*A glimmer is a phantom flame*
*A glimmer is a tunnel light*
*It is not large*
*It is not bright*
*Tiny end on a firefly*
*There is no hope*
*There is no "I"*
*One small glimmer shines alone*
*In Christ, a tiny*
*Hope is shone.*

This poem illustrates how very tiny a glimmer is. During the closing in of depressive illness, the most a person can usually hear or feel of healing is a small glimmer of hope. My definition of "glimmer" of hope is healing words, or healing music, or healing actions, or a healing blessing. The healing is only a brief break in the depression. It may last only one minute. It may last ten minutes. It may last an hour. It may last a day. But each time there is a tiny recovery, there is a tiny success of healing.

Years ago I was the co-facilitator for a women's group comprised of displaced homemakers just returning to college after many years' absence or, in some cases, after having never been to college at all.

One night a woman in my group came with a tape recorder and tape. She shared her story: She had come home from work a few nights before and found her seventeen-year-old son trying to "cook" methamphetamines on her stove. She erupted into a rage as this was, for her, the final straw in a painful saga related to her son's substance abuse. She evicted her son from her house and told him not to come back until he was ready to accept help and remain drug-free at home.

Several nights later, a penitent son returned to his home and said to his mother, "I want you to listen to this song." The song he played for his mother was Michael McLean's "Hold On, The Light Will Come." This young man, who was not LDS, had "crashed" at a friend's home after he was thrown out of his own home. His friends were playing a Michael McLean tape when he heard this particular song. It moved this tough, truant, amphetamine-cooking teen to tears.

He told his mother that he went out and bought himself the tape. He had experienced a prompting. An unsolicited, unbidden prompting. A song from a composer who is earnestly LDS to a teen with no discernible faith. A glimmer of hope.

As my friend played "Hold On" for our group, fourteen women had tears streaming down their faces. The next week we all confessed we had gone and bought the tape. This has become my favorite piece of popular music. I have played this song in many lessons and workshops over the years. People in five states have been introduced to Michael McLean through the way this song has touched me. I was introduced to it by a scruffy drug-abusing boy who heard the lyrics and found a glimmer of hope. Glimmers can come in unexpected ways and times.

## To Loved Ones of a Depressed Person

Glimmers of hope most often come into the life of a depressed person through her loved ones. You, as a spouse, a relative, a friend, even the therapist, may have to say the same things a thousand times. It is difficult and relationship-stretching to be with a depressed person.

Your warmth and your concern will be felt in small increments. Your loved one is not able to feel lovable, valuable, worthwhile, and important to you during a depressive episode.

To encourage warm, appropriate, healthy, and loving responses, I love to use a quote that I've kept in my wallet for many years, because it explains the nature of depression in a way that is uniquely meaningful in my life. It comes from the weekly *Parade* magazine column of Marilyn vos

Savant, who was asked to address this query in her column: "You once answered a question about a broken heart, but what does one do with a broken spirit. Can it be repaired?"

She answered, "To me, the major difference between a broken heart and a broken spirit is that people break hearts and time mends them; but time breaks spirits, and people mend them. My suggestion is that you take any broken spirit you know and expose it repeatedly to the light of as many warm personalities as possible."[1]

This is where the therapist, spouse, and friend alike are called upon to "love our [depressed] neighbor as ourselves" and to walk that "second mile." To me, showering the light and warmth of our love on a depressed person is taking up the call Christ gave us to "bear one another's burdens, that they may be light" (Mosiah 18:8). Depression is a mighty burden. Our love is not a cure, but it is a help.

## Spiritual Choices

The covenant we all make at baptism is, to me, a pinnacle of spiritual choice. In Mosiah 18:8–9, Alma entreats us to be "desirous to come into the fold of God, and to be called his people, and [be] willing to bear one another's burdens, that they may be light; yea, and [be] willing to mourn with those who mourn; yea, and comfort those that stand in need of comfort."

The Apostle Paul struggled with his own suffering, which to us he identified as his "thorn in the flesh." In Romans 12:15, the Apostle Paul wrote, "Rejoice with them that do rejoice, and weep with them that weep." In other words, when we are in the company of a depressed person, it is not wise to say, "buck up."

I once had a young wife tell me that if her husband told her one more time to "buck up," she thought she might kill him. Dr. Carlfred Broderick has given us a consummate "one-liner" in *One Heart, One Flesh*. He says, "I have tried to make it a rule that nothing I am doing at the moment outranks my wife's claim upon me when she is joyous *or despondent*" (italics added).[2]

It is important to recognize that when someone is truly clinically depressed, it is very difficult for that person to access her spiritual understandings. The despair of depression is a pall over her; it will be necessary for her to regain some glimmer of hope emotionally before she can once again "draw on the powers of heaven."

While there is no spiritual formula to "cure" the ravages of depression any more than there is a spiritual formula to cure heart disease, or cancer, or diabetes, there are some spiritual choices a sufferer can follow once she has received that "glimmer" of hope.

## Choosing the "Big Picture"

In Doctrine and Covenants 122:7, we read, "that all these things shall give thee experience, and shall be for thy good." In times of despair, that is not very comforting; in fact, it can be maddening! Different scriptures will help different people find that big picture perspective.

In Doctrine and Covenants 121, the Prophet Joseph Smith's cry "O, God, where art thou . . ." was very comforting to me. For one of my friends, that scripture just made her feel more guilty, because she wasn't in Liberty Jail, yet she felt such despair. Search for scriptures and inspirational passages that speak to your own heart. As you find scriptures that help you discover the big picture for your life, your suffering will gain the personal meaning that allows you to abide its pain.

Another important part of choosing the big picture is to recognize that sometimes you can see your big picture ahead of you, but you have to advance toward it with baby steps.

I once had a client named Mary Blair who had come home early from an appointment to find her husband and best friend engaged in a sexual encounter. The multiple betrayals devastated her. The husband and friend refused to stop their relationship, so Mary Blair left her job, her community, and the secure future she had planned and returned the three thousand miles to her mother's home, where she had not lived for twenty-some years.

When I met her, she was actively suicidal. She was unable to work.

Our initial sessions were Mary Blair sobbing quietly from the desperation and loss of everything she had cherished. Parenthetically, I want to note that Mary Blair was the perfect example of dignity in anguish. She had temporarily lost her composure, her sense of self, her sense of hope. But beneath the despair of a broken heart and a broken spirit, I could sense a part of Mary Blair that I knew was invincible. I like to think of that part as her spark of divinity—that measure of each woman that allows us to call ourselves daughters of God.

Mary Blair had been a religious person her whole life. As a member of the Church, she had always tried to live her life in harmony with the gospel. Her "big picture" was that she saw herself involved again in service and commitment to the Savior. Listen to Mary Blair's own words as she shared with me the baby steps she had to take to move herself back into the big picture of church activity.

"When I arrived back at my home, I initially moved in with my mother. I did not tell her what had happened to me and why I came home because I was so horribly embarrassed and bereaved. Fortunately for me, she did not press me. It was also awful because I could not go out and get a job even though I had held a professional position for many years in the community where I had lived with my husband and raised my children. Basically, for a number of months, I wrapped myself in a blanket, sat in a hard wooden rocking chair that wasn't comfortable—it matched how I felt—and cried.

"Yet every Sunday I had a ritual. Every Sunday, I required of myself that I get up and get dressed for church. My worship had been a cherished part of my life for years, and I wanted to go to church. Yet I couldn't. I had returned to a community where I had been a convert twenty-five years earlier, so I didn't know anyone, and I was too traumatized to reach out to my old ward. But I got up and got dressed. That was the best I could do, and I usually cried while I got dressed. Then I would sit in front of the television and watch a local broadcast of a church service my mother enjoyed. I did my 'get dressed ritual' for several months.

"Next I decided to drive to the church building. My new ritual was that every Sunday morning, I got dressed, got in my car, and drove to the church. I couldn't drive into the church parking lot because someone might see me. Fortunately there was a dental office across the street, so I would drive into the one parking space where the tree branches hung over my windshield and sit and watch through the leaves as the busy Mormons I used to be like scurried into the meeting house. I did the 'parking ritual' for about three months. It was the most I could do. And as I watched the people live a life I used to have, I wept softly, but with loud anguish.

"Three months later, I was ready for an act of real bravery. I still was unable to work. I would read the newspaper employment section and break down. I did not feel I would ever work again. But I was still trying to get myself into the church building. No one knew I was back. I didn't even know if there was anyone who would remember me. I had been the lone convert from my family so many years previously. But, oh, how I wanted to go back to church! So I came up with a new baby step. The very next Sunday, I got up, got dressed, drove to the dentists' parking lot and this time nervously waited until I believed the sacrament song was being sung. I entered that church building with more courage than it would take an FBI agent to enter a building holding hostages. I was absolutely afraid. I longed to be back in the sanctuary of peace I had always felt in church, but this time I felt I was pushing forward a leaden shell-body where I used to live. The pain was exquisite, the fear palpable.

"I did it. I made it to the foyer during sacrament. Thank goodness that my old ward still sent deacons to the foyer, because I actually got to take the sacrament. Victory. I felt so comforted by taking the sacrament. Then fear and pain washed over me yet again, and I fled the building.

"But I had done it. I had gotten the wounded creature into the building. I thought of how God created the lights in the firmament and said, 'It is good.' I had spent five or ten minutes in the building of my old ward of twenty-five years ago and taken the sacrament in the foyer, and it was the greatest act of Christian courage I had ever rendered. 'It was good.' It was my widow's mite. It was all I had in my very depressed soul. But I did it!"

Mary Blair shared with me the progression of the baby steps she was able to take until she finally was back at church for "three *whole* hours," as she put it. Shortly after, she was noticed by a kind counselor in Relief Society, her records were requested, and she was called to be the Spiritual Living teacher. She reported that giving her first lesson was almost as grueling as her first mini-visit to the church foyer where she had taken the sacrament, then fled.

Mary Blair's depression was profound. Not only were the tragic events which precipitated her depression life-altering, the depression itself was life-altering.

But Mary Blair held the "big picture" in her heart. And her way to the big picture was paved with baby steps and small victories.

## Choosing Change or Acceptance, Not Fear

In 2 Timothy 1:6–7, the Apostle Paul wrote, "I put thee in remembrance that thou stir up the gift of God, which is in thee by the putting on of my hands. For God hath not given us the spirit of fear; but of power, and of love, and of a sound mind."

Fear is not God-given. Love and a sound mind helps us seize the power of our agency. We are free to choose fear. We are equally free to choose the changes and acceptances that propel us toward healthy living. As a young woman I had a wonderful experience that showed me the positive power of acceptance.

When I was twenty years old, I worked for Aspen Grove Family Camp, BYU's camp for alumni up near Sundance in Utah. My job was the "Kitten Korral Director." My two friends and I were responsible for the daily activities of the primary age children. Each Wednesday, we took these little children on a kind of picnic "trek."

One sunny Wednesday, we "trekked" the children up to a beautiful meadow on Mt. Timpanogas where I asked a little four-year-old girl named Tammy to offer a blessing on our food.

This is Tammy's blessing:

*Dear Heavenly Father,*
*We are in the meadow today,*
*And we have sack lunches,*
*And I have a tuna fish sandwich,*
*And I HATE tuna fish sandwiches.*
*But help me to eat it anyway.*

*Amen.*

What a practical prayer! And what a wise little girl. Tammy already understood the principle of change and acceptance. Tammy could not change her sandwich filling under those circumstances in the meadow. So she chose to accept her plight. Note that acceptance does not mean we have to *like* something. We only have to accept it.

In chapter two, I referred to my friend who has AIDS, which she contracted as a health care professional. As of the time of writing this book, she most likely has less than two years to live. She is a young mother with young children. She does not like her circumstances. But she accepts her circumstances. Her acceptance has brought her serenity.

Acceptance is familiar to all who embrace the Serenity Prayer:

*God grant me*
*Serenity to accept the things I cannot change,*
*Courage to change the things I can,*
*And wisdom to know the difference.*

I am encouraging one of two positive choices: making a change or accepting those things over which we have little or no control. In life, we always have three choices in any given circumstance: change, accept, or be miserable. Being miserable is where we sometimes get "stuck." It is far better to change or accept certain circumstances. We also sometimes get stuck in the notion that accepting something means we have to like it. Acceptance only means we have to *accept*. To accept something does *not* mean we have to like it. Remember my friend with AIDS. She does not like her distressing illness nor does she like the fact that she will die at such a young age. But she has accepted her illness and her future. She moves on with her life by taking charge over the many things she can control.

I had a good friend in Salt Lake City, Utah, whose seventh child was born with Down's syndrome. I frequently heard her tell people, "I can dwell on the thousand things Jeannie will never be able to do, or I can appreciate the ten thousand things she can learn to do." In other situations, where we have been sinned against, the recognition that we must leave judgment to God allows us to go on with our lives without worrying about the punishment of others.

These choices all remind us of Tammy and the tuna fish sandwich which she hated. Life may sometimes give me a tuna fish sandwich when what I really wanted was peanut butter and jelly. But, again, I am in charge. I can be miserable. Or I can change my sandwich if possible. Or if I'm on a picnic and change is not possible, I can accept that this time I have a tuna fish sandwich and, like Tammy, "eat it anyway." And if I really want to embrace the whole principle of acceptance, I can even eat it graciously without complaint, whining, or anger—grateful to have something instead of nothing.

## Choosing to Laugh

In Proverbs 17:22, we read: "A merry heart doeth good like a medicine."

One of my all-time favorite clients was a young single parent raising four children, working, *and* attending nursing school. Macy was overwhelmed with "mother guilt" for having to leave her young children so often for work and school. Her mother guilt, fatigue, and heredity all caved in to one major depressive episode. I had her evaluated for medication and was following the usual regimen for treatment: weekly therapy sessions and quarterly medication evaluations. She was not getting better rapidly. And then, one week, Macy came to her appointment with a giant smile. She informed me that the previous week in her nursing class they had discussed "Laugh Therapy." I was familiar with the groundbreaking ideas written about this method in *Anatomy of an Illness* by Norman Cousins. I had read the book and thought his effort to immerse himself in humor to fight the pain and suffering of his illness was a great idea, and I had frequently recommended the book to clients.

However, Macy used the information even more proactively. She went out that night and rented two funny videos to show her children. Every night for the next week she rented a comedy and sat with her children with her primary goal being "to laugh." Interestingly, Macy received three benefits from her own therapy task. She did laugh and feel better; she felt less stressed; and she started feeling better about her relationship with her children.

I have been grateful for Macy because she increased my inventory of therapy techniques. She also made me become personally aware of the humor all around us.

Recently my client Gaylynn, who has suffered from depression for many years, went to see *Parent Trap*, a comedy. She went with a group of friends. They all laughed hysterically through the whole movie. In Gaylynn's words, "*Parent Trap* did not 'cure' my depression, but laughing that hard took my mind off my gloomy thoughts for the night. I even felt better the next day."

One Sunday a good friend of ours sat in his Dutch Reform congregation reading the church bulletin. As he read the bulletin, he began to laugh out loud, thoroughly embarrassing his wife. When our friend showed his wife the bulletin, she had to laugh out loud, too.

| *Sermon: 9:00 A.M. Service* | *"Jesus Walks on Water"* |
| *Sermon: 11:00 A.M. Service* | *"Searching for Jesus"* |

It is good to laugh. When a depressed person can laugh, "even a little," it is one of those glimmers discussed earlier. When we can laugh, even a little; when we can serve, even a little; when we can strive, even a little; when we can feel happy, even a little; when we can believe Christ, even a little, then we are on the right path, going in the right direction, and beginning to "press forward with a steadfastness in Christ, having a perfect brightness of hope" (2 Nephi 31:20).

## Choosing Christ

"I can do all things through Christ which strengtheneth me" (Philippians 4:13).

"And he said unto me, My grace is sufficient for thee: for my strength is made perfect in weakness" (2 Corinthians 12:9).

I have witnessed some powerful changes occur in people's lives as they have accepted the invitation from Christ to give him their pain. It is my experience that those who are suffering do not have a clear perception of the magnitude of Christ's sacrifice. Most people accept the Atonement as Christ paying the debt for their sins. Less well understood is the fact that Christ also suffered and died for our pains. Jesus died for our pain, our sicknesses, and our sorrows, as well as our sins: "And he shall go forth, suffering pains and afflictions and temptations of every kind; and this that the word might be fulfilled which saith he will take upon him *the pains and the sicknesses of his people*. And he will take upon him death, that he may loose the bands of death which bind his people; and he will take upon him their *infirmities*, that his bowels may be filled with mercy, according to the flesh, that he may know according to the flesh how to succor his people according to their infirmities" (Alma 7:11–12; italics added).

Also, in Doctrine and Covenants 88:6 we are taught of Jesus that "he that ascended up on high, as also he descended below all things, in that he *comprehended all things*, that he might be in all and through all things, the light of truth" (italics added).

Dr. Wendy Watson, BYU professor of marriage and family therapy, has movingly written about the Atonement: "The ultimate change agent is the Savior, although he, himself, never changes. Don't you love that seeming irony: The only true change agent never changes! And he loves you. And he loves your desire and your efforts to change. He wants you to change, to have a change of heart, a change of nature, [a change from depression], and, over time, to completely cast off the natural man. He did all he did so you could change! We need to actively, persistently plead for the power of his infinite and atoning sacrifice. And as we do, his ultimate healing will bring to each of our lives the ultimate change."[3]

Early in my practice, I had a powerful encounter with a young woman who finally embraced Christ as her personal Savior.

Ross Ann was a twenty-eight-year-old woman who had suffered horrific sexual abuse from several brothers and some cousins. Though she had served a full-time mission and was teaching special education when I met her, she was filled with self-loathing. She compensated for her self-hatred by going about fifteen extra miles in everything she did. Because of what had been forced upon her, she was convinced that she could never be worthy of the celestial kingdom. But because she loved children, she contented herself with what she described as "helping my kids to get the self-esteem I never got."

She wrote her special education children notes of encouragement. She attended every extracurricular activity each of them had. In short, Ross Ann tried to do for her kids what no one had done for her.

One day Ross Ann sat with me in a therapy session and repeated her old refrain, "I am just a black sheep. I will always be just a black sheep. I will never fit in with the 'normal people' of the world. I am too damaged."

This particular day, I remember praying silently and fervently, "Give me the words that Ross Ann needs to hear to begin healing from the abuse."

I heard myself say, "Ross Ann, tell me about the black sheep."

She began to cry softly and answered. "My black sheep is a lost sheep."

"Ross Ann, who is the lost sheep?"

*"I am the lost sheep."*

And again, I heard my voice ask, "Ross Ann, who did the Shepherd leave the flock to find?"

Silence. Pondering. Tears. "He left the flock to go find the lost sheep."

"And Ross Ann, who is the lost sheep?"

Sobbing. "I am the lost sheep."

This dialogue cannot begin to capture the power of that exchange. The witness of the Holy Ghost to Ross Ann and to me was unmistakable. But the story does not end here. I am a great believer in making the therapy experience "tangible." I do many paper and pencil kinds of tasks: I draw pictures for clients. I write quotes. I encourage them to write their feelings in a journal. But on this day, I asked Ross Ann to do something very unusual, something I had not done before. I asked her to go buy a lamb. I told her to find the best and prettiest stuffed toy lamb she could find in Salt Lake City, Utah. I told her, "This lamb will help you hold on to the witness you have felt this day. The Shepherd [Christ] went to look for you; he knew your pains. He died so you don't have to hold on to them any longer."

People are so amazing. The next week Ross Ann came to her therapy session carrying a shopping bag. She was so proud as she brought forth the lamb she had chosen to remind her of her new thinking. She had bought the softest, most beautiful fleecy lamb. And best of all, it was not a black sheep; it was a snow-white lamb. She had gotten the picture. She no longer felt she was damaged and different and dirty. Ross Ann was the lamb found: clean and white as snow.

## Summary

Choose the "big picture." Choose change or acceptance, not fear. Choose to laugh. Choose Christ. Choose just a glimmer of hope, if that is all you are able to do. These spiritual choices will assist you to choose hope.

Hope is there for you. Believe Christ when he promised that

"whosoever stands at the door and knocks . . . it shall be opened unto you" (Luke 11:9).

---

1. Marilyn vos Savant, "Ask Marilyn," *Parade Magazine*.

2. Carlfred Broderick, *One Heart, One Flesh* (Salt Lake City: Deseret Book, 1986), 42.

3. Wendy L. Watson, "Family Focus," *Brigham Young Magazine* (Spring 1999), 67.

# CHAPTER SEVEN

# How Do I Help Myself When I'm the One Who Is Depressed?

For years I have known that it takes me six and a half minutes to do my makeup.

One Sunday, while I was serving as the Relief Society president of my ward, it took me two and a half hours to do my makeup. You who are now in the throes of depression will immediately understand my challenge.

I had just begun the descent into another bout of raging depression. This particular Sunday, both my counselors and my secretary were out of town. It was Easter Sunday. I knew I *had* to go to Church and conduct Relief Society. Even if I could have mustered the energy to think of how to call another sister to do this, what would I say? How would I explain this unusual situation of why I was stepping outside my presidency duties, asking someone else to conduct Relief Society in my place? Besides, how could I even let someone else know what was going on with me? And so, long before church started,  I sat on the carpet in my bedroom in front of the full-length mirror, with my makeup scattered in front of me, trying valiantly to make myself function. Putting on my makeup seemed an insurmountable task. Two-and-a-half hours later, my makeup was on my face and by some Herculean effort I managed to get dressed and to get myself to church to conduct.

I cannot fully explain why everything just slows down for the depressed person or why everything takes so much effort and so much time. But that day, sitting in front of the mirror, I felt as if I were slogging through molasses: every effort was against the current of natural, normal life.

However, the larger message I wish to convey with this example is that I *did* something. I put on my makeup. I *did* a very tiny thing—six minutes was all it usually took. Although my six minutes dragged to two-and-a-half hours—and even so many people at church that day told me how "pale" I looked—the point is I *did* something. And you need to do something, too!

In May 1999, *Larry King, Live!* presented a program on clinical depression. One of the guests was Dick Cavett, who has publicly shared his struggles with depression. He offered a useful analogy.

To paraphrase Mr. Cavett, this is depression: You are lying on a couch in your living room feeling weighted down with a horrendous burden which renders you immobile. Ten feet away, there is a credenza and on the credenza is a magic wand. You know that if you could just get to the magic wand you could wave it and the magic would immediately restore you to health. But you are absolutely incapable of getting yourself off the couch.

I believe this analogy is compelling for two reasons. One, it shows the complete opposition in the rational thinking of the depressed person's brain: *I see the magic wand and my brain realizes it is only ten feet away. In opposition to that, I am completely unable to force myself to go get the wand.*

*This opposition is perplexing to me, for I desperately want the wand, but I am utterly incapable of making what I know is a minimal effort to get it.* (The apparent easiness of the solution is probably a major reason it is so difficult for a nondepressed person to relate to a depressed person.)

The second reason I really like Cavett's analogy is that it points to the necessity of *doing* something.

Recently, I had a young, depressed mother as a client. I saw her on a Tuesday. On Saturday, her husband went out of town for a few days and left her home with three young children—two were preschool age. On Saturday, she made a desperate crisis call telling me she was feeling out of control with her depression. After talking with her for a while and assuring myself she was not suicidal, I concluded our conversation by reminding her of two concrete facts. First, she was welcome to call again if her symptoms did not abate. Secondly, I reminded her that I would see her again on Tuesday. I then challenged her to *do* something.

I took my cue from the fact that she had repeatedly told me that her children were begging to go outside and that at the moment, she felt like a "bad mother" because she made them stay inside. She felt she couldn't leave the house. I asked her if she thought she could drive somewhere. That she felt she could do. So I suggested that she tell the kids they were going on a picnic, then drive them to McDonald's and if she could do nothing else, go through the drive-up window.

I did not hear from my client for the rest of the weekend, but on Tuesday, as I ushered her back to my office, she asked, "How did you know I would feel better if I got out of my house?" and this question was quickly followed by "Do you have any idea how hard it was for me to do?"

Small steps slogging through molasses. Do something small, but *do* something.

The operative word for you who are suffering is *do*. President Kimball said, "Do it." If you are struggling with clinical depression, *do* something— take a baby step.

I will list some concrete things that have worked as baby steps for me and for others. This is not an exhaustive list nor are there any guarantees one will work for you. Experiment with your own small steps.

- Consider choosing a therapist, if you have not already done so
- Consider medication
- Exercise, even if it is a walk around your block
- Get out of your house, apartment, or living space, if only for five minutes
- Call a friend, maybe even go to lunch
- Watch a funny movie or video
- Write your feelings in a journal, including possible options to help you feel better
- Do something you usually enjoy
- Keep a commitment even if it is agonizing for you to do it
- Do some gardening (that is, if you like it!)
- Go window shopping

As a gentle reminder of my basic premise, I would like to review and conclude these suggestions with the "Parable of the Beeper."

For many years I was a mental health therapist working in a rural community. Those of us with at least five years' mental health experience were required to carry a beeper one week per month from 5:00 P.M. when our agency closed until 8:00 A.M. when it reopened. This was a difficult challenge for me even in the best of times because it meant going out alone into the community to assess mental health crises, which were frequently police-related issues or involved mentally ill transients. I am a 5' 1" woman who has frequently been told that her looks are round-faced, apple-pie America. This is not exactly a description that commands authority! But it was my job, and I did it. My husband worked for the same agency and he, too, had the beeper one week per month.

There came a point during my tenure at this agency that something happened to me that was the most terrible and life-altering event of my life. This was the second time I personally experienced a major depressive episode. I slogged through my work life while maintaining an image that should have earned me an Academy Award for Achievement in Best Acting. I kept on "keeping on."

But the one place that I felt terrorized was carrying the beeper—I did not believe I had the emotional strength and resources to function in this arena. Because my husband and I both had "beeper duty," he usually just made my outreach calls for me. This was no small feat, as we averaged about 30 or more calls per week.

But then, one Saturday, my husband had a blue ribbon golf tournament. He teed off at 7:00 A.M. and would be finished with the round about noon. He asked me to take the beeper and said, "You know, we never have any calls before three, and you can drive to the golf course and hand off the beeper at noon."

What he said was true. So I took the beeper and as he left for the golf course, I got on my knees and said, "Heavenly Father, I don't know if this is a righteous prayer, but please don't let anyone have a crisis until noon. I can't handle it today."

This was a sincere and heartfelt prayer. I was still on my knees when the beeper went off. Our answering service called to tell me a hysterical mother was on the telephone. Her fourteen-year-old daughter had run away Friday night.

I took the call, talked with the mother, gave her some support, offered options she had not known she had, gave her the social services number for runaway teens, and welcomed her to call back.

I felt okay. I had not had to go out in the community. And I was quite amazed that I had been able to be so calm and professional in the midst of great personal suffering of my own.

Literally five minutes later, the beeper rang again. The hospital needed an assessment of a transient who had been picked up by the police. I got dressed, went to the hospital, and did my job.

While I was in the hospital, I was beeped again. This time it was the police on I-15 who had picked up one of the well-known mentally ill persons in the area. The police were requesting mental health backup.

I was deciding that my prayer must not have been righteous as I pulled onto the highway to meet the police. My chest felt heavy, and I had a sensation of not being able to breathe. The offensive beeper was attached to my purse, and I was attached to my sense of duty.

Within those five hours, I was "anxiously engaged" in being a good therapist. I was treading water emotionally and functioning way beyond my capabilities. I called it my adrenaline-push beeper duty, but in retrospect, I do believe I was "borne up on eagle's wings" (see D&C 124:18).

The seventh beep of the day was another call from the police. A mentally ill woman had driven to a residence with her car packed full of belongings. She was moving into a house, but the house was occupied— by the rightful owners, who had never seen this woman before. She had carted an overstuffed armchair from the top of her car and was belligerently arguing with the homeowners to "let me move my chair in!"

The police wanted me to "stop her." As I rounded the curve from our residential neighborhood to drive into town, I realized it was 12:15 P.M. I drove right to the golf course, handed my perplexed husband the beeper as he walked off the eighteenth green, and burst into tears.

There's a moral to the Parable of the Beeper. And it is a true principle which I have had to learn and relearn—for myself. To beat depression (or even to have an impact on it), it is necessary to *do* something. Answering that beeper seven times in five short hours was way beyond my abilities that day. Taking care of my professional business was like going through molasses that day. Trying to be empathetic with others that day was like trying to reach the magic wand that was only ten feet away. My prayer to be protected from that beeper was as fervent as any prayer I have ever pled. And yet, there was no divine intervention for me that day. Or was there? Perhaps there was divine intervention, but in a different manner than I had envisioned.

I have no words to describe how gut-wrenching that day was for me. You who are fellow sufferers know. But what happened to me can happen to you. In my situation, the *doing* was forced upon me by my job. But the *doing* was the answer. Was it the cure to my depression? No. Was it the end of my depression? No. Did I cease to struggle? No. Did the success last longer than three minutes in my depressed brain? No. Did I feel better the next day? No.

But, what did happen was that I got through that day, and it was better because I had the success of *doing*. And while my small steps that day were as tottering as a one-year-old's first steps, like the fledgling walker I did manage to stay up. Those five hours of duty may seem impossible to you. Perhaps making a peanut butter and jelly sandwich right now seems impossible to you. But doing some small thing—taking a baby step, no matter how tiny—is still a step forward.

Now I have learned to "beep" myself. I have taken the experience of external beeps and learned to find a beep by myself, for myself. The fancy word is "self-soothing."

For me, there are two beeps that can usually jog me from the molasses morass of my depression. One is to physically get out of my house and meet a friend for lunch. I usually do not share my depression, although I think it would be fine to do so. The second thing I do is to watch funny movies or videos. If I can get past the soul weariness to laugh a little, it usually jogs the depression.

Though many women will never have a second episode of major depression, some will experience a relapse. Learning skills to prevent or minimize these symptoms will give these women greater control over their own emotional well-being.

I sometimes wish there were a magic wand to cure depression. But, for me, I have to look at this thorn in the flesh which I have been given to refine me, and reflect on all the lessons of humanity I have come to realize through its instruction. My life has been heavy for me. But the heaviness of heart has also enriched my heart towards others and made me acutely aware of my personal need for a Savior and Redeemer who extends his grace to fill in my hollow places.

I like to remind myself of the eternal perspective spoken by Elder

Neal A. Maxwell: "God, who knows our capacity perfectly, placed us here to succeed."[1] I think that by "doing" I am becoming. On those days when your depression seems most insurmountable, there is a small, even thirty-second "do" within your grasp. The smallest step you can manage is one more claim upon eternity where a loving Savior welcomes every effort— even baby steps.

## Summary

On days when it seems to take your most supreme effort to make a peanut butter and jelly sandwich, know that every effort is one of the small steps which will help you slog through the depression. Even a baby step is a victory, because it moves you forward.

--------

1. Neal A. Maxwell, *But for a Small Moment* (Salt Lake City: Bookcraft, 1986), 102.

C H A P T E R   E I G H T

# What Can I Do for Someone Who Is Depressed?

*This chapter is a collection of essays written by individuals with first-hand experience with depression: either as a depressed person or as a family member of one who is depressed.*

All of these essays reveal very powerful and personal experiences. It was not easy for us to expose ourselves so completely. However, our hope that these stories would bless your lives gave us the needed courage. It should be noted that when we were suffering from depression, no one understood the strain we were under, not even our closest friends. As many depressed people, we put a great deal of energy into hiding our pain, and we were quite successful.

We hope that these essays will help you—as a spouse, a child, a parent, a brother, a sister, a visiting or home teacher, or a friend—to support your loved one in what can be a life-or-death battle.

# Meghan

It is not easy to see someone you love going through the ravages of depression. You suffer together, yet alone. The depressed person may be unable to see beyond the dark mist of hopelessness which surrounds her and threatens to destroy her. From the outside, none of this may be apparent. As hard as you may try, you cannot understand what the depressed person is experiencing. What she sees is visible only to her eyes, and it is as real to her as the earth beneath her feet. It is invisible to you and makes no sense. It seems to be a mood that could be brushed away with exercise or scripture study, or by a decision to be happy. You cannot understand the depth of her despair: but you must accept it, or you will damage her even more.

What she is experiencing is a brain illness. It is physical in nature, though its manifestations are emotional and spiritual. You would not tell a person with heart disease to stop thinking about herself so much, or a woman with diabetes to get over it. As with these afflictions, depression is not something you can just "get over." Sheer willpower is not enough to cure it. It is a damaging disease which needs treatment.

Many men and women have asked me what they can do to help someone who is depressed. Recognizing the physical nature of the ailment and helping the victim to find professional help are vital steps.

I remember vividly the lifelines that kept me going. A woman in the temple told me my "aura" was white. I don't even know if I believe in auras, but this stranger, who didn't know me and was therefore an objective observer, gave me hope that maybe there was still some goodness in me.

Renee, my friend, came over to bring me lunch one day. We hadn't seen each other for a while, and I assumed she had heard I was having a hard time and was coming to cheer me up. I was touched, but in an ashamed, resigned sort of way. Soon after she arrived, she announced she had come because she needed a "Meghan fix." Slowly I realized she was there, not for me, but for her. What a shock! Did I still have something to offer others? Apparently I did, because there she was. When I could feel no worth for myself, I trusted in the worth she saw in me.

My husband's fear at my suicidal intentions surprised me. Wouldn't it, after all, be a relief to him? In my distorted thinking, I had believed so. His shock and raw fear reassured me that he still loved me. Love always surprised me—I had none for myself and so was sure no one else did. Love was a lifeline. Renee's respect, equally surprising, was a lifeline. The woman in the temple, seeing goodness in me, was a lifeline.

I tried so hard to shut everyone out. I didn't want to contaminate them with my darkness. I presented a smiling face that would allow them to ignore the reality of my suffering. Some people never knew anything was wrong. Many knew something was not right, but I kept their concern at such a distance that they didn't dare intrude. A few—a very few—pushed their way past my defenses to offer me the love and compassion I was sure I couldn't deserve, but craved like water in the desert. A touch on the arm could sustain me for days.

Pushing past the walls a depressed person erects around herself takes great compassion and courage. She will resist you at the same time she is desperate for your love and concern. If you are easily rebuffed, she will see that as proof of your insincerity. In my last major depressive episode, none of my friends persevered in breaking through the barriers I set up, though I prayed with all my heart that someone would force her way past my evasions and reassurances. I pled in tears with my Heavenly Father to touch someone's heart, inspiring her to call me or come over and disbelieve my lies of well-being. I couldn't make the call. I couldn't impose my despair on someone else's life. But if a friend had walked into my house, insistent to know what was wrong and to help and listen, or hug me, or break through my lonely despair in any way, it would have been a blessed light shining in my darkness.

Where were my friends? Were they callous? Or indifferent? Or unaware? When I began to recover—began to wear a real smile instead of the pasted-on one—many people said to me, "It's so good to see the real Meghan again. I was worried about you. I didn't know what was wrong, but I'm glad you're back." I thanked them. I didn't ask the questions burning in my mind: "Why didn't you come to me when you saw I was suffering? Why didn't you help me? I needed you."

I think I know the answers. Much of it was my fault; some of it was theirs, or our culture's. The one thing I did vigorously during that time was hide my troubles. I had been taught to be self-reliant, not needy. What was happening to me was bad enough already, but to be pitied would have been even worse. I forgot the distinction between pity and empathy, compassion, and love. I didn't make it easy for anyone to come close.

And why did they give up so easily? They respected my privacy. They didn't want to intrude. They didn't know what was going on: perhaps it was a problem with my husband (their bishop) or something else I wanted to keep private. I'm sure they assumed that if I wanted to talk, I would. How could they understand the distorted thinking of clinical depression that made it impossible for me to approach them, or even respond to anything but the most determined and insistent friendship? I didn't believe I was loved, or respected, or anything but a burden to those around me. I had to be convinced over and over and over again that this was not true.

What is my advice to the visiting teacher, the husband, the child, the mother, the friend? This depressed woman whom you love is not well. She isn't thinking clearly. She will misunderstand so much. Be persistent in helping her feel your love, your respect, and your confidence that she will get through this. Reassure her that there is hope. Help her to find help.

## David

Family members of those who suffer from depression are also casualties of this disease. My wife Meghan's account of her experience with depression presents me as a better husband than I was. Often I was so preoccupied with my responsibilities at work or at church that I failed to give

Meghan the love she needed. Because of the long duration of the illness, I was exhausted. I sometimes found I had no reserves left to carry the family.

As Meghan's depression continued over years, I withdrew from her emotionally, probably both because of a lack of emotional fulfillment and also as a defense mechanism. Commitment to the welfare of our children, concern about the example I was setting for others, and personal commitments to marriage and keeping promises kept me in our marriage and usually kept me trying. Without doubt this was the most difficult time in my life.

It was impossible for me to talk with anyone of the near despair I felt at times about our marriage. I felt as though everyone looked at me as a role model, and I questioned my ability to measure up. How could I, as bishop, successfully counsel a brother or sister on his or her marriage relationship when I was struggling to keep my own from failing?

When I found I could take no more, very specific direction from Heavenly Father would come to comfort Meghan and encourage me to hang on. Late one night, when we had both bitterly expressed our disappointment in each other and our relationship, I left her upstairs and went to go to sleep on the proverbial couch below. (This was very rare for us. In our nineteen years of marriage I can think of only two other times.)

We had not yet prayed that evening, either personally or together. I had no desire to pray. Always before when I prayed, I would reflect upon my responsibility as a priesthood holder to comfort and to protect: of my duty to take the lead in apology and repentance. But this time I was through. I was done with a blighted marriage to this woman I was no longer sure that I loved. I could hear Meghan quietly crying above me in our room, but I did not care. I sat for half an hour or more in darkness.

Finally, because I know the Church is true, because I know God lives, I knelt and asked for help. I admitted that I was tired, that I wanted to give up.

After reviewing my frustrations, and still feeling self-righteous for my past efforts to keep our family afloat, I asked for guidance. While asking I felt an impression to go to Meghan's side. Though irritated, even resentful that once again I was having to make the first overture of peace, I went. As I quietly put my arms around my wife, she turned to me and sobbed. Her tears soaked my garments as she clung to me like our youngest child.

Later she told me of the answer to her prayers: while I sulked downstairs, Meghan prayed in despair for comfort. She knew that she could no longer sense the sweet peace of knowing she was loved by our Heavenly Father. She longed for the warmth of the Spirit, but because of her depression, she could not feel it. And so she prayed that God would show his love for her by causing me to return to her side and hold her. Considering the state of our relationship at that moment, she was praying for a miracle.

I, too, have been given a miracle in answer to my prayers. God hears prayers. He grants miracles: depression can be healed.

This is an intensely personal experience. I'm not at all proud of my behavior. I am grateful that I obeyed the subtle promptings of the Holy Ghost. I share this experience out of my love for my wife and daughters, out of my gratitude that we are still together despite my weakness. I also share it because I want other husbands and wives to seek help where I did not. I share it to caution bishops and home and visiting teachers of the impact depression has on the "healthy" members of the family. We need your help. We need your encouragement. We need you to "comfort those that stand in need of comfort" (Mosiah 18:9). While I did not cause Meghan's depression, I certainly contributed to it. I wish instead that I had done more to contribute to her recovery. Because I was worn down by years of failing communication and an unreliable emotional relationship, I was finally at the point where I was willing to quit.

I was blessed with greater understanding in my responsibilities as bishop because of Meghan's depression, and many members of my ward benefited as a result. Our only reason for writing our account is that others might be blessed with even greater compassion and quicker response on the part of priesthood leaders, with a better-equipped support network for family members, and most of all with hope. Hope that depression can be conquered; hope that you can be yourself again; hope to change and become whole through the Atonement of Christ, and feel the sweet sure knowledge that you are loved by God. He hears your prayers. With his help and the help of those friends, priesthood leaders, doctors, and counselors he provides to assist you, you can be healed.

# A Child's Perspective

I was ten years old when my mother first exhibited signs of depression. I am seventeen now and still gaining insight into my experience.

This was an extremely difficult period in my life, and I continue to feel some of the after-effects. The person I knew as Mom disappeared and was replaced with someone else who was frequently sad and angry. I felt that most of this anger was directed at me and wondered what I had done wrong. I became worried that because I was such a horrible child, my parents would divorce, and no one would want me.

I felt that my mom didn't love me. I worshipped her and thought that everything she did was right . . . and that if she didn't love me there was something wrong with me. I felt that if she couldn't love me, no one could. I began to hate myself. Things were on a downward spiral. If my mom didn't care, I didn't care.

I became even more withdrawn, bottling up everything inside of me, staying out of my mom's way, and crying myself to sleep. This went on for a long time. Eventually I began to blame my mom for the way I was feeling, and I started to dislike her. I felt no pity for her at all. I think I made the situation much worse than it could ever have gotten on its own.

Today I understand what went wrong, that my mom's condition was a result of a chemical imbalance and not something I did. In everything I have read about depression, although my reading has not been extensive, the focus is on the effects on the spouse. I feel that this is not altogether fair to the children. If one of their parents—especially the mother—is struggling with depression, the children are basically robbed of that parent. To make matters worse, this person upon whom they depend is replaced with a stranger who is angry, sad, and a variety of other emotions incomprehensible to the child. My experience resulted in the feeling that I was at the root of the problem. I felt like I was a mistake, that no one, not even God, could love me. It took me several years to realize that my mom's depression had nothing to do with me. As a ten-year-old, I was completely unable to comprehend this. Perhaps therapy is necessary not only for the depressed person and the spouse, but for the children as well.

## *Betsy*

As a licensed clinical social worker, as well as someone who has suffered from depression, I think there are a number of things one can do to help someone who is depressed.

I used to wish I could wake up and have bright blue polka-dot spots all over my body or have my hair turn bright pink. I wanted people to be able to "see" my depression. One of the things that is so difficult is that depression is not a visible illness. I once worked at a hospital where I ran a series of groups for people suffering with arthritis pain. They felt the same way. I think the common denominator with those illnesses which are "invisible" to the eye is that those of us who suffer from them want to have loved ones recognize and respect the reality of the suffering.

An important thing you can do is to let your loved one know that you understand that he or she did not "choose" to feel this way. I can assure all of you who have never been depressed that no one would choose this affliction. For several years I felt that a bowling ball had been shot through my heart. I experienced a constant crushing throbbing in my chest that matched pain for pain the psychic, emotional torture of my mind.

A healing connection may occur if you are able to affirm the reality of your loved one's illness. Many times, you, as a loved one, will have the healing words or healing actions which may soothe a troubled heart. This alone cannot cure the depression. However, loving, healing, affirming words and actions may penetrate the barrier of thought distortions of the depressed person's brain.

Never, never, never give up. If your loved one's depression seems heavy to you, imagine the leaden shoes the afflicted person wears. The heaviness I felt was so overwhelming to me that I did not want to impose it on anyone else. I isolated myself from family and friends. I became a master at creative excuses. In retrospect, I realize that I was skilled at hiding what was really going on with me. Later, several of my friends told me they had not understood what was going on but I had conveyed to them that I did not want help. This is a difficult balance both for the sufferer and the loved ones. There was a part of me which really did shut down and shut off. This was not the healthy part of me. The other part of me, the tiny fragile part, yearned for someone to break through my self-imposed emotional exile.

Remember, the depressed person is not thinking like a rational human being. Her brain chemistry is wreaking havoc. But within her steel cocoon, the creature that used to be her is fighting a battle to get "her" back. It is a battle so intense that it takes every ounce of strength to go through the motions of life.

Another perplexing and shocking thing to the depressed woman is that the spiritual strengths which had formerly guided and comforted her life are gone. I had been a religious person my entire life. I had felt great comfort in things spiritual. But I couldn't feel those feelings anymore. Intellectually, I still believed the gospel was true, and I still believed that Christ was my personal Savior. But I couldn't *feel* the truth. It was as if I could believe the Atonement was true for everyone but me. I don't even have the words to describe the awfulness I felt. But I know that many, many women have tried through the years to find words to explain this same loss.

Believe that your loved one wants her life back. Believe that your loved one would never choose to feel this inexorable suffering. Believe that you might hold the healing words or healing actions to penetrate her depression. Know that you might need to repeat those healing words a thousand times. Believe that she will return to the Light of Christ. Believe that she is trying so hard to stretch herself back into life. I was constantly trying to lengthen my stride but my emotional shoelaces were tied together—tightly.

The depressed woman is striving with a heaviness in her mind and in her heart and in her chest and in her shoes. It is like walking through cement, and depression is just that gray and unyielding. It is this very heaviness which does drown some of us in suicide.

I want to conclude by saying to you, as loved ones of depressed persons: This is not your fault. And it is not your responsibility to "cure" it. It is a personal illness and the sufferer bears much responsibility for her recovery. However, your responsibility, if you have a genuine love and loyalty to the sufferer, is to follow the admonition contained in our baptism covenant to "mourn with those that mourn; yea, and comfort those that stand in need of comfort," and "to bear one another's burdens, that they may be light" (Mosiah 18:9, 8).

Several years ago, the daughter of a prominent family in my ward committed suicide. I received about twenty-five telephone calls from concerned ward members who asked, "When I go to visit the family, what should I *say*?"

My response to them was "It is not what you say, although words can be healing. What matters the most is what you do—the outpouring of your heart, your love, your positive regard, your compassion, your empathy, your sorrow, and your sincere desire to help. Years, months, days later this family will not remember very many specific words. But they will remember behaviors: you visited, you called, you came to the viewing, you reached out when it was hard for you and hard for them. One of the bravest acts of courage is to 'go' into the space of suffering, to 'go' to the physical or emotional place of the sufferer."

While I gave this advice to friends of a family who had just endured the tragedy of suicide, the advice is equally as applicable to loved ones whose family member is immersed in depression. Healing words are excellent. Sustained healing actions are more excellent.

A good way to know how to help is to ask questions of the depressed loved one. Offer to let her talk, but don't be discouraged if she doesn't take you up on it right away. If you keep offering, it may open the door for her to talk later. Let her know she is not alone.

Another good way to help a depressed loved one is to follow your own spirit of personal revelation. It will help you know how to best serve her in her depression. It may take two weeks of healing words and healing actions, it may take two months of healing words and healing actions, it may take two years of healing words and healing actions. It may take a mortal life of healing words and healing actions. It may be the hardest service you ever render.

In a way, you may be a "type" of a savior. There is no better model than Christ, as the Shepherd, who went out to find the lost sheep. No matter how lost the sheep was, the Savior was ready to bring him back, to carry him back if need be. When someone is truly depressed, the greatest gift you can give is to offer your tender mercies, even a thousand-fold.

# Gene

As a doctor of social work and a husband whose wife (Betsy) has suffered from depression, I think there are many things we can keep in mind to help our loved one through this painful illness.

When a family member has a physical illness, including clinical depression, there is an impact on the entire family.

If a wife has an accident resulting in a debilitating physical condition, family members can clearly see the condition. In contrast, when a wife and mother suffers from depression, family members are limited in their ability to see this condition. The suffering of a woman from either an obvious physical disability or a not-so-obvious depression impacts the family. She becomes less able to continue expected responsibilities and roles, there is a need for assistance and support from others, and there may be changes in the attitudes and behaviors of the suffering spouse.

An obvious physical disability generally demonstrates a course of action. That is, some disabilities have a clear time frame to heal. Other more chronic disabilities may not have a timetable to heal, but in these instances, such as cancer or heart disease, family members appear to find acceptance of the illness because there is an observable or understandable condition.

A woman experiencing severe depression is less easily understood by her husband and children. Frequently the causes of depression are beyond the understanding of the family. The symptoms or demonstrated depressive behaviors are all the family has to relate to. They often see a wife or mother who "changes." She becomes withdrawn, failing to interact, love, support, and assist other family members. She has a loss of interest and energy, thereby giving up hope, motivation, and sometimes her goals. Even if the woman is able to carry on with usual goals, it is plain that she is sapped of energy and life force. She becomes preoccupied with herself, but in a destructive manner. For example, she believes she has failed family and friends and others. She looks at herself with dark eyes, seeing only blackness, sadness, and unhappiness. Her range of emotion is despair. This dark view of self promotes a sense of guilt for not being there for her family, and this further deepens her self-depreciation.

No one can "fix" a depressed person. A husband may, first, want to fix the problem but he soon finds the wife resists being "fixed." Why? Because, in her distorted thinking her depression serves a purpose. It is her punishment for every perceived failure she can possibly remember. Also, once the depression begins, a certain sense of reality is lost (not usually losing touch with reality, but instead viewing reality as negative and distorted). Thus, the "fixing" envisioned by the husband is not hitting the target.

A husband who has a spouse with a serious depression needs to recognize what depression is and what it is not. It is not a calculated withdrawal from the husband and family. It is not something that sheer force of intellect can control. It is not a condition to be ignored. It is not about the husband and the children. He needs to remember it is about his wife.

It *is* a condition that can be, at the least, managed, and at the best, healed. The husband needs to temporarily place his own needs aside and adopt a position of support for the spouse.

Our support through this illness can be demonstrated in very practical ways:

- Listen to the spouse (without trying to "fix" her) and encourage her to express her feelings

- Without criticizing her personally, kindly point out reality when the spouse engages in distorted thinking
- Pray with the spouse and call upon God to guide and bless you both
- Render a priesthood blessing or administration to the sick (remember, depression is an illness)
- Engage with the spouse in exercise, such as walking
- Spend time together: talk, become involved in special projects, go for rides, see a funny movie, and so on
- Be patient, kind, helpful, and hopeful
- Remember that your efforts are valuable, even if you can't see a difference right away

For serious clinical depressions, the spouse may need both medication and counseling. As husbands, we must avoid looking upon depression as a weakness. We must see it for the catastrophic illness that it is.

CHAPTER NINE

# *Ecclesiastical Perspectives*

*This chapter includes the thoughts and experiences of one bishop and one stake president in counseling Church members with depression. It is meant to offer support, suggestions, and insights from their own experiences; it is in no way intended to serve as official Church practice or procedure.*

## Bishop

As a new bishop just starting to grasp depression's devastation, I wondered why the Church did not provide specific instruction to bishops on counseling members suffering from depression. Few bishops are called that have clinical experience in dealing with depression. But for that matter, few are called with extensive experience in working with the myriad of other types of problems that wash like a flood over newly called bishops.

I realize now that it is more important for bishops to rely upon the guidance of the Spirit than it is for them to know the clinical theory of the day. But a bishop's ability to recognize the more common symptoms of depression will be a great blessing to the members of his ward. My intent in writing this is not to endorse any particular therapy or prescribe methods. It is to communicate what little I have learned about recognizing the spiritual symptoms of depression unique to members of the Church, and to stress the importance of supporting the depressed member and the member's family. From this end of what was a very dark and lonely tunnel, I am grateful that my wife experienced depression, because of the greater sensitivity I developed in my service to the members of my ward. I hope that I have also learned to be a better husband.

I make no pretense of speaking for the Church or from any position of doctrinal authority. The conclusions I draw are my own. While clinical depression is common, not everyone who is sad is depressed. Most people experience some discouragement periodically. Depression is much more profound and it doesn't go away with the improvement of circumstances or after a normal grieving period. Depression strikes across the entire socioeconomic spectrum and across all activity levels in the Church. As a bishop it was helpful for me to learn the symptoms and signs of depression, make referrals when necessary, assist in treatment if needed, but leave diagnosis to competent medical professionals.

For clarity and simplicity, I have used feminine pronouns rather than both "he" and "she." While the majority of the depressed members I met with were women, I also met with several men who were struggling with clinical depression. "Depression" is certainly not an exclusively feminine illness.

Bishops in the Church have a unique opportunity to comfort and encourage the multiple hostages depression takes in a family. The family is the basic, essential building block of society and of the Church. Members of healthy families can depend on one another. The interdependence of family members, which serves as glue and a source of strength in healthy families, deepens the poignancy of this illness. Family members often exhibit emotional withdrawal and resentment in response to another family member's depression. We all have our limits, and the family members of the depressed person need encouragement as they bear the brunt of unpredictable or unreasonable behavior and emotions they do not understand.

A prime concern of priesthood leaders should be to protect the marriage of the depressed member and her spouse. Depression affects judgment. Because of the nature of the illness, major decisions made while suffering from clinical depression are frequently flawed—particularly those that involve complex emotions and relationships as marriage does. All of us interpret the actions of others based on our own personal experience and understanding. We ascribe motivation and intent to others based on our perception of reality. A person suffering from depression will frequently interpret the words and actions of others to her own detriment. She may assume that others don't like her because she sees herself as unlikable. The actions of others that support her perception of being disliked are accepted—even magnified—in her eyes. In contrast, friendly overtures of others are minimized, ignored, or even seen as two-faced. She believes she is under attack and responds accordingly. Further aggravating the problem, her spouse may be ready to give up because he does not understand what is wrong or how to make it right. His own emotional resources may be exhausted from the whipsaw effect of unpredictable behavior and emotions.

Common symptoms of depression are widely published. However, an additional symptom is unique to members of the Church: a perceived loss of the companionship of the Holy Ghost. Because of the respect and trust members of the Church usually have for their bishop, he may be the first one, possibly the only one, the depressed brother or sister confides in. The interview with an active member who is suffering from clinical depression might begin with something like the following:

"Bishop, I don't know what's wrong with me. I don't think I'm worthy to serve in my calling anymore." Further discussion will frequently reveal that the active member has not committed a sin, but no longer feels promptings of the Spirit. Prayers seem to go unanswered where answers were once relatively constant. Unable to recognize the loss of the ability to feel the Spirit as the result of a physical condition, the depressed member attributes this change to some failing on her part, or to the mistaken belief that God no longer loves her. Knowing the doctrine of the gospel, and believing that the Spirit of the Holy Ghost will be the constant companion of confirmed members who keep the commandments, the depressed member may consider this perceived abandonment by the Spirit as evidence that she has committed some sin and therefore is no longer worthy of the Spirit.

As a naive but very sincere new bishop presented with this enigma, I asked members, "Are you studying the scriptures daily? Are you having daily personal prayer? Are you serving others? Are you keeping the commandments?" After lengthy discussion where the member searched her soul, and I struggled to understand why a good person was so miserable, we would end our interview. The member seemed to be encouraged, and I was hopeful that my admonitions would help her to regain the Spirit. Scripture study, prayer, service, and obedience were the keys to my being happy and feeling the Spirit. When I personally felt the absence of the Spirit, it was invariably because I had become lax in my personal devotions or obedience. Time and time again I observed the same connection in the lives of other members. If the laws of happiness and spiritual guidance were obeyed, the blessings would be received—wouldn't they?

For whatever reason, with clinical depression it doesn't exactly work that way. Guidance by and blessings of the Spirit are still given, but they may not be recognized. Ironically, at a time when the member most needs to feel the presence of the Spirit and know that she is loved, depression injures the ability to feel this comfort. Without question, depression colors the perception of the member. Heavenly Father loves all of his children, including those with depression, and he still answers their prayers. The presence and influence of the Holy Ghost can still direct their lives.

However, because the ability to feel the presence of the Spirit is impaired, the depressed person may perceive there is no answer and cease to believe in her own worthiness.

A sensitive bishop can be of tremendous help in this regard. Because of the love and respect members have for their bishop, and because the bishop has the responsibility to receive revelation on behalf of the members of his ward, the depressed member may believe the bishop when she cannot believe in herself. Hope is literally given to the hopeless when a bishop can tell the member, under the inspiration of the Spirit, that he knows that God loves her. If he can confidently tell her that she is not guilty of some grievous sin, so much the better: but he must tell her that God loves her.

Additionally, the bishop may seek the member's permission to alert the Relief Society president and/or quorum leaders to the member's struggles. Assigning sensitive home and visiting teachers, especially those with an understanding of the unique challenges of clinical depression, can be a tremendous support both to the member and to the member's family while they are trying to carry this heavy burden.

Many depressed members feel unwarranted guilt, and these brothers and sisters need to be reassured that their feelings of self-condemnation are baseless. This is especially common where there is a history of sexual abuse. It is vitally important for the member to understand that a victim of sexual abuse bears absolutely no guilt and has committed no sin. This may be hard for her to understand, as her feelings tell her otherwise. She must come to understand that victims of sexual abuse are still clean before the Lord.

However, depression may be a major complicating factor when assisting members who actually *have* committed a serious sin. A member who is used to the companionship of the Spirit may experience depression as a natural consequence of sin. This, however, is not the same as clinical depression. It is important to note that a member's clinical depression does not excuse sin nor does it lessen the spiritual or natural consequences of sin. I do not wish to imply in any way that depression reduces our responsibility to live all the commandments. But depression, like any other cognitive disability, does affect mental judgment. I personally found this to be a significant element in the promptings I received in administering Church discipline.

Depression impairs judgment just as certainly as alcohol or illicit drugs. A key difference is that intoxication or drug abuse begins as a choice. Depression does not. Yet depression complicates repentance tremendously because it is more difficult for a person with depression to believe she can change. For example, it may be nearly impossible for her to conceive of herself as ever being sufficiently worthy to attend the temple. Because she may feel that no one has ever loved her, she may not be able to imagine that God could or ever would love her. Helping the member to recognize the reality of God's love for her is vital to her healing and quite possibly to saving her life.

There are tremendous differences in circumstances under which God's children live, and I have limited ability to understand how those circumstances shape understanding and agency. This is one reason why I am profoundly grateful that I will not be the final, eternal judge.

Without the encouragement and support of priesthood leaders and loved ones, a depressed person may not be capable of mustering sufficient hope to try to repent or sufficient grit to complete the process. In my experience, the member involved in serious sin, who was also suffering from depression, made much greater progress in repenting of the sin when the depression was also being treated successfully.

When the assistance of a professional therapist is required, having an excellent therapist who is also an excellent member of the Church would be ideal. However, membership is not essential for the therapist to be effective. Initially, I felt constrained to recommend only therapists available through LDS Family Services. I learned over time that the competency of the therapist, and the confidence the member had in his or her skills, contributed more to the member's recovery than did the therapist's church affiliation. Let me emphasize that unless the professional therapist's clinical guidance complements the doctrines of the gospel, the therapist's efforts will be futile at best and possibly injurious. The therapist does not need to believe the gospel, but it is vital that he or she supports the religious beliefs of the member and is able to understand the dynamics of Mormon life. If this minimum is assured, a skilled non-member therapist can help in the healing process much more than an inept or inexperienced member therapist.

Depression often accompanies serious sin, though there is not necessarily a cause-and-effect relationship between them. Both are frequently associated with an abusive childhood. I have found that the assistance of a skilled professional therapist, along with the ministrations of a loving bishop, is necessary to help the member deal with the complex frustrations and emotions that surface while sorting through abuse, subsequent sins, and associated depression. A professional therapist can be an invaluable help to both the member and the bishop, because a therapist has the skills to assist in healing from abuse and depression. More importantly, the bishop has the priesthood keys to apply the healing principles of the Atonement and the gospel of repentance.

I wish to underscore the importance of going to the bishop. The bishop is always an essential component in these complex situations involving abuse, sin, and depression. Whether he is young or old, inexperienced or a veteran, he can help to make a life clean again, because he is the authorized representative of the Savior. However, in the rare event that the bishop cannot be approached, the member should seek the guidance of the stake president.

It is essential that a member with clinical depression have someone in whom to confide. Home and visiting teachers who have gained the trust of the member will be an important asset. They are able to provide long-term gospel-oriented support and love. In their stewardship, they may receive direction through the Spirit to help the member. Ward members who have experienced depression may be able to give support and hope, as well. Professional help is often required to achieve a "normal" life, especially if the problem is long-standing. I have seen best results when the depressed member, and eventually her spouse, met with a therapist, rather than relying upon medication alone.

As a final note, there are some good resources written from an LDS perspective available to assist and enlighten priesthood leaders about depression. *One Heart, One Flesh* by Carlfred Broderick is one that I found beneficial. I have also found it enlightening to reflect upon the frustrations faced daily by sisters in the Church who follow the prophets' counsel to remain at home with their children, getting little thanks and appreciation. But the most important tool for a bishop to use in counseling a member with clinical depression is the same one he uses to counsel members dealing with other issues: he must rely upon the Spirit.

The existence alone of LDS Family Services should be testimony enough that the First Presidency and our Father in Heaven quite literally support the use of professional therapists. With the authorization of my stake president I felt impressed to use the sacred fast offering funds of the Church to assist with the cost of therapy and of medication on a number of occasions. Seeking professional help for depression shows no greater lack of faith than going to the emergency room for a severed limb.

Modern medicine, including medication and therapy for depression, is not a replacement of priesthood blessings and healings by faith. The priesthood and the best professional resources God has made available to us should be used together so that all God's children may be blessed. God lives. He loves all his children, and he always, always keeps his promises.

## Stake President

One of the key responsibilities of stake presidents is to provide training for bishops. On occasion we have discussed how to help members who suffer from depression. Bishops can and do receive guidance from the Holy Ghost in behalf of their members, even though they may not have professional training in treating depression.

Many people have experienced the smile and silent nod that comes while reading a familiar verse of scripture and receiving a new understanding for different situations in life. That scripture takes on greater significance as it provides answers in a new context. The following scripture provided such an "aha!" experience for me: "There is a law, irrevocably decreed in heaven before the foundations of this world, upon which all blessings are predicated—And when we obtain any blessing from God, it is by obedience to that law upon which it is predicated" (D&C 130:20–21).

At the time I read this scripture, the Olympics were in full swing and spectators around the world were treated to the remarkable physical feats of athletes from many nations. The thought came to me that these athletes had been obedient to the laws of physical conditioning and training, and they were blessed as a result with the ability to excel in their respective athletic events. The athletes were able to perform at world-class levels because they were obedient to specific health and conditioning laws related to those events. It did not seem to follow that just because these athletes were obedient to laws of physical fitness and conditioning, they would excel in musical ability, or social skills, or science.

In this context, the verse of scripture in Doctrine and Covenants 130:20–21 took on significance relating to depression. Just because a member of the Church prays, reads scripture, pays tithing, keeps the Word of Wisdom, and attends the temple, these do not necessarily remedy the problems associated with depression.

Let me provide a few examples to illustrate this.

There are faithful members in good standing before the Lord who still suffer from diabetes and require insulin injections. There are faithful members who suffer from allergies who require regular medication. There are good members who require medications to compensate for thyroid glands that do not function properly. There are members in good standing, with limbs that have restricted mobility, who require therapy. In each of these cases a bishop would probably not suggest that paying tithing would remedy diabetes or heal the allergy. These are problems not related to the law of tithing.

We need to apply this principle to the treatment of depression.

Personal and public worship are vital to our spiritual growth. The practices or habits of regular scripture study, praying, keeping the commandments, and partaking of the sacrament are fundamental. Though these activities remain essential, they may be inadequate in dealing with depression. Similar to the other physical maladies noted above, depression might require additional intervention including therapy and medication.

We learn from Doctrine and Covenants 130:20–21 that blessings must be predicated upon obedience to the laws associated with that blessing.

How do we know what actions or remedies we need to take to help someone with depression? John 14:26 teaches us, "But the Comforter, which is the Holy Ghost, whom the Father will send in my name, he shall teach you all things, and bring all things to your remembrance, whatsoever I have said unto you."

We know that many truths have been revealed to good people seeking to help mankind, whether or not they have been members of the Church. It does not seem plausible that God, who is the Father of all mankind, would withhold revelation and truth from any of his children who were sincerely seeking to help mankind, just because they may not hold membership in his Church. If a sincere researcher, physician, or therapist (member or not) is seeking a better way to treat depression, and is obedient to the laws of research and inquiry, it seems consistent with revealed doctrine that such a person could be blessed with the answers to assist those who suffer from depression.

When we see a body function imperfectly, such as noted above with diabetes, allergies, a defective thyroid, or stiff limbs or joints, we are seeing the effects of the fall of Adam. Our physical organs, muscles, bones, eyesight, etc., were not designed to be perfect or without impairment throughout mortality, nor were our mental or emotional capacities. The state of perfect functioning must wait until we are free from the effects of the fall of Adam, even until the Resurrection. Until then each mortal must live with various imperfections.

As we ponder the significance of the doctrine of blessings being predicated upon obedience to specific laws, we need to keep in mind an eternal perspective. When we consider this mortal existence of a relatively few years compared to eternity, we may look upon the maladies of this life as less overwhelming and definitive.

To those who suffer from depression, I recommend you counsel with your bishop and be consistent in personal and public worship. These actions may be inadequate in dealing with depression, but are still essential to your spiritual welfare. You will probably have an experience similar to many others who have read the scriptures before but discover deeper significance when reading them as part of a prescribed course of action from a bishop. Being obedient to such counsel assists the revelatory process. Avail yourself of other resources including therapy and medication if needed. As difficult as it may be, it is important for you to keep an eternal perspective about this challenge. One day each of us will be free from all negative effects of the fall of Adam. Until then, we need to exercise faith in the knowledge that God knows us and is with us even if it may not seem so. God has promised each of us blessings beyond our comprehension if we are faithful now.

To those who are married to someone suffering from depression, remember that unconditional love is needed, but may not be enough. If your spouse suffered from diabetes and required insulin injections, you probably would not say: "Just pull yourself up by your bootstraps and get over it!" (A response made by a man to his wife who suffered from depression.) Neither would you expect that saying to your spouse, "I love you," would cure the illness. Your spouse does need your love and support, but the support of a loving bishop and the help of a trained professional may also be needed.

To bishops who have members with depression, your counsel to pray, read scriptures, and fast is essential, but may be inadequate. Seek guidance from LDS Family Services and other qualified professionals. Many members who suffer from depression do not feel worthy, or they may feel beyond the blessings of the Atonement. You will need to provide frequent reassurance that the Atonement of Christ is effectual for that person specifically.

Remember that "If in this life only we have hope in Christ, we are of all men most miserable" (1 Corinthians 15:19). Our hope in Christ extends beyond the veil of this life.

I can envision that one day, when we pass on to the other side and see those who have suffered from depression in mortality, we will see them as glorious beings full of light, love, and strength.

# CHAPTER TEN

# Childhood Traumas: Personal Accounts

This chapter contains stories about childhood abuses: physical, emotional, and sexual abuse; neglect; abandonment; and exploitation. Childhood traumas often result from sin on the part of an older person that holds a position of trust, such as parents, foster parents, grandparents, siblings, or some other trusted adult. This betrayal of trust is a significant part of the trauma.

These are not easy stories to hear. In my professional career, there have been many times I have struggled to maintain professional composure while hearing the heart-stopping life stories that courageous women decided to share. A few times, I have been unable to prevent silent tears from falling, because the magnitude of "man's inhumanity to man" has been so grotesque. Meghan and I feel blessed that these valiant women were willing to take the risk to share their stories. It is our hope—and theirs—that through these stories others might be blessed and enlightened.

# I Just Want to Be Loved

My name is Hyun Joo, and I am Korean. They tell me I was born in Korea at seven months, a preemie who only weighed two pounds. I guess this accounts for some of my later medical problems, but those are the easier problems.

I did not learn this information until I was eighteen years old and living in a large midwestern city in America. My father told me that when I finally left the hospital, the nurses called me "The Miracle Baby" and "The Fighter." It seems funny to me that I should still be needing miracles and still have to "fight" a lot. I am twenty-eight years old now. My Dad told me, "Hyun Joo, you have a purpose in life." I just didn't know how much energy it would take to find that purpose.

When I was just an infant, my mother ran off to the United States to become a doctor. No one knew where she went, but my father left Korea, too, to try and find her. I was left with my maternal grandparents, who frequently told me how bad a man my dad was.

I lived with these grandparents until I was four years old. Just as my grandparents put me on the plane to fly to America to be reunited with my parents, my grandfather strongly reminded me of all these bad things about my dad. I admired and respected my grandfather so when I got off the plane, I ran to my mother and into her arms, but I said to my dad, "I don't like you 'cause you're a mean man."

That's a regret I still have today. I really hurt my dad when I said those things. I believed them then and my later life made them appear to be true, because my mom continued to tell me bad things about my dad. But I've learned a lot through the years.

My dad did have a really bad temper. There were days when I'd pull on my dad's leg and beg him to stop hitting my mom, but he wouldn't stop. He beat my mom. They divorced when I was five years old.

The first really strong memory I have was when I was five and my parents took me to court. I think they don't do this anymore, but the judge asked me who I wanted to live with. I started to cry. I couldn't pick, so the judge picked my mother.

So when I was five years old, I lived with my mother for one year, and I never saw my father.

Then I lived with my father for a year, and I never saw my mother.

Then I lived with my mother for a year, and I never saw my father.

When I was eight years old, my mother went back to court. She told me that my dad didn't want to see me anymore. She said the court decided I couldn't see my father anymore until I was eighteen years old.

I was very confused and hurt. I was already a latchkey kid and took care of myself. Both my parents left for work very early and often did not return until late at night. I already had too many responsibilities, and I had to grow up fast.

When I was nine years old, my mother said to me one day, "Hyun Joo, you are just in my way because I want to be a doctor." So she took me to my father's doorstep and left me there.

She moved then to the Northeast and I've never seen or heard from her again.

I couldn't understand. I loved my mom. On the day she dropped me off at my father's, she drove me to the beach first. Then she gave me a "Simon" game and sang me a song in Korean. I still remember the song she sang.

In retrospect, it is very weird. The Korean song is a love song to a husband. Anyway, I guess I'll never understand because I don't even have any idea where she is, or even if she is a doctor somewhere.

For the first six months that I lived with my father, I was kind of happy. I had been so scared that my father would send me to foster care, but he had accepted me. I was grateful for that.

I cooked for him. I cleaned for him. I did all the laundry. I would give him back rubs. I tried to be the perfect daughter. For a short while, I was as happy as I had ever been.

My life started falling apart when my stepmother came from Korea. My dad had returned to Korea shortly before my mother deposited me on his doorstep and had remarried. Of course, when he married her, he told her he had an eight-year-old daughter, but that I lived with my mother.

By the time all the paperwork had been done so my stepmother could come to the United States, my dad had inherited me. At the airport, I wanted to be like a "real" family, so I ran up to my new stepmother and I hugged her. The first words I ever heard her say to me were "I don't like kids. I don't like you."

Even though she only spoke Korean, those words are as harsh in Korean as they are in English. Things went downhill from there. I kept trying to be nice to her to welcome her. But she always hit me and said to me, "Hyun Joo, you're so stupid," and "Hyun Joo, you're so fat" (I wasn't), and "Hyun Joo, you're so ugly," and "Hyun Joo, your dad doesn't really love you." After you hear it enough, you believe it.

I really hated the fact that in front of my father, she would act nice, calling me "sweetie," but as soon as my dad left, she became her normal, routine self, which was a mean person. She was always threatening me and telling me that if I told my dad how she really treated me, I would "live to regret it."

Because of her, I really lost my self-esteem. I was already mad at my mother for leaving me, and now my father was gone all the time at his dry cleaning business. All I had left was her, so I started to believe her.

Later in my life, my father told me that he thought the only reason my mother put me on his doorstep was that she had heard that he had remarried, and she wanted to make his life miserable. I will never know all the truths about my three parents, but the "miserable" part was right.

From when I was ten years old, all my memories are of my father and stepmother fighting about me. One day, she was beating him (he never laid a hand on her), and my dad yelled at me downstairs and said, "Hyun Joo, call 911!"

Then she screamed at me, "Hyun Joo, if you call the police, I'm going to kill you tonight."

❧

I was so scared. She'd never said anything like that before. Ever after that, I was scared to go to sleep. I slept with one eye open.

I tried to put on a happy face at school. But once I did a terrible thing. I don't know what got into me that day, but I told the social worker at school. I spilled my guts. She promised me she'd never tell anyone.

As an adult, I understand that it's the law she had to tell that I was in danger, but the law wasn't very kind to me that day.

That day when I got home from school, I saw all these extra cars at my house. They were the cops, and there were some social workers. They were there to take me. I still don't know what my dad and my stepmother told them but it was probably that I was a liar.

I knew I'd get beaten when they left. My dad mostly yelled, and he did a little spanking. With my stepmother, it was not a spanking—it was a beating. She hurt me—she hurt me a lot.

My dad and my stepmother—they fought every night about me. I remember hearing them yell and argue. My dad had always had the bad temper, but then he got some counseling and it worked because then he got better on his temper. But then my stepmother began to beat him up.

Then she forced him to put me in foster care. She told him he had to choose her or me.

He chose her, and I had to go to foster care. I was eleven years old, and I was a Korean child living in a white American society.

My foster care experiences are a nightmare in and of themselves, but as terrible as the abuse was, nothing could ever again hurt me the way it hurt to have my mother leave me on a doorstep, my stepmother hate me so much when I tried so hard, and my own father choose her over me.

I had no self-esteem left. And I didn't know the word then, but big feelings overcame me and as I entered my junior high school years, I felt suicidal. By then, the State had returned me to live with my dad and stepmother. Though I was only twelve years old, I was very depressed, and I wanted to end my life.

I did have one Korean girlfriend I had grown up with and her mother sort of knew my family situation, so she kept on trying to take me to church with their family.

But, at this point of my life, I felt empty, full of hate and loss. I kept telling her, "I do not want to go to church with you because if Jesus loved me, my life would not be so bad."

I remember a Sunday she came to my house and took me to church even though I didn't want to go. As I stepped into the church building, I felt a sense of warmth and love I'd never felt before, and I can remember I started to cry. (Now I understand it was the Spirit!) Soon after, my friend's mom had the missionaries—Elder English and Elder Beck—teach me the lessons.

At first my dad and stepmom were against me being baptized. But then I think she figured out I'd be gone more and my dad figured out he'd have less fights. So, even though my dad first told me, "Hyun Joo, I will disown you if you join that church," he did finally give his permission. And I couldn't turn away after the sixth discussion because I felt such a sense of love and peace. As much as I tried to fight it, I felt so good during these lessons that I was baptized three days after my thirteenth birthday.

On Sundays, I felt lonely sitting with no family and no support. I'd look around me and see happy families and wish I could have that. How I ached for that. And so I went inactive.

And then a good thing happened. Her name is Lillie.

Lillie is the bright star of my gospel experience. In August of 1985, I received a phone call from a woman who said she had just been called as the Young Women's president. She said, "I want to try to get you out to the Young Women's activities." I don't remember this but Lillie tells me that I was very closed and hesitant. It took three phone calls for me to finally say, "Okay, I'll try again."

Looking back now on this experience, I realize that Heavenly Father answers prayers. Lillie told me that she had been praying for strength and answers. She had just sent her only daughter away to college and she felt alone, in the sense of needing to take care of a daughter. And I was needing to be loved by a mother. So I got a Young Women's president.

Lillie was an awesome role model to follow. She was such a spiritual leader. I know her life was not perfect. She lost her husband in a car accident, and then when her only son was ten years old, he was hit by a car and left with permanent physical and mental disabilities. Then her daughter who she loved so much went two thousand miles away to college. Inside, she was still dealing with these experiences, but through her awesome spirit and strength, she made it; so she made us—the Young Women—believe we could make it.

Lillie is strength, spirituality, love, care, and understanding.

She has great love for all, but I don't have the words—I can't explain how I feel about her. I am so grateful she came into my life. I feel so blessed and loved. I would even die for her.

I don't have a "real" mom in this life, but I finally got a mom. I call her my "Church mom."

Before my birth mom left, and later with my father and my stepmother, I was locked upstairs every night, and I was eating by myself. Most of the time I had to try to cook something by myself.

But with Lillie, I had my first experience with a "real" family. Lillie loved me for who I was. We had family dinners at her house. And we did talking—even sometimes we argued. I felt like a real teenager. I didn't even mind the sometimes arguments because I understood that Lillie loved me. I learned how to bake cookies with Lillie. And I learned that I could mess up her kitchen. And it was okay to eat on the kitchen table and not have to be locked upstairs in my bedroom to eat. I spent all the holidays with her.

Later, Lillie told me that sometimes she felt guilty, like she was robbing my parents of the joy she felt with me. But over the years, as she got to know my parents, she stopped feeling guilty because she said, "They made a choice." Lillie has also told me that she believes we knew each other in the preexistence and that we made promises to be there for each other. I truly believe that we were supposed to meet and help enrich each other's lives. Sometimes it is hard for me to believe it, but Lillie says I have blessed her life, too.

When I was eighteen years old, I had not started my period. My stepmom would not take me to a doctor because she said, "Korean women all start late—you are just fine."

Lillie, who is also a nurse, was the one who went with me to the doctor. It was there that I found out that my bone density was poor and also my ovaries had never developed. I remember the doctor telling me I would never be able to have children. I thought, "Another thing has just been taken away from me—I had wanted to have a lot of children."

Lillie was the one who comforted me and told me that someday a man would love me enough to marry me even though I could never be a mom in a biological way. And Lillie was the one who encouraged me to serve a full-time mission when I had just turned twenty-two years old.

On the day I received my envelope from Church headquarters, I waited to open it until my bishop got home from work. I was kind of scared that I might go to Korea. I was so afraid that if I found my grandparents, they would reject me because I looked Korean but I had lost my language and customs. But as soon as I reached the bishop, he told me that he had had an inspiration all day at work that I was going to get my call and that it would be to Korea. When I opened my envelope, it was a call to Korea. All I could do was cry and cry. I did not want to go back to Korea. But it really helped me to accept my call and that my bishop had received his inspiration. And with the faith in my Heavenly Father, I trusted and went. It was the hardest achievement in my life.

Towards the end of my mission, I received permission to locate and visit the grandparents who had raised me as a baby and little girl. I began to believe that I could find my grandparents and have a "real" family again. I remember being both excited and scared. I felt they expected an awesome granddaughter with lots of achievements, and I felt very inadequate. I feared I would be rejected.

It is sad to say I was right. I remember the look in my grandfather's eyes—of disappointment. When I went to see them, my grandmother's first words were "Why did you join that awful Church? And Hyun Joo, what has happened to you? You are so fat. And what has happened to you, you used to be such a brilliant little girl!"

But of all the hurts of my life, the next was the biggest devastation of my life. While at my grandparents, I saw a little five-year-old girl. I can remember how beautiful she was and how well she spoke Korean and American. My grandparents told me that she was their granddaughter, and she was visiting from America. She was my half-sister, the daughter of my mom, and I didn't even know I had a sister.

I told her I was her sister and she said, "No, you are *not* my sister."

I tried again to explain to this little girl that I was her sister.

And this time, she said to me, *"How could you be my sister? My mom told me I am the only daughter she has."*

I felt replaced by this little girl who I saw was everything I wanted to be. She was receiving the praise and love of my grandparents, and she had a real mom, *my* mom. But I was without her. My half-sister's words confirmed my worst fear and my greatest nightmare. To my mother, I had never been born.

I was devastated. I lost my dad. I lost my mom. My stepmother hated me. Now my grandparents rejected me. And my sister wouldn't believe she was my sister.

I went back one more time to say good-bye to my grandfather who I did love and respect very much at one time, and I knew I would never see him again. So it was very sad for me. I remember also, as I was saying good-bye to my little half-sister who was on my lap, she asked me, "If you are my sister, how come you never come to our house? And how come my mother told me I was her only daughter?"

Right there, I could have died. But I told her, "I am your sister, and I will always love you and hope the best." I know she will be a success and have a lot of achievements, because my mom was that kind of a woman and liked achievements and success. But I left Korea with my heart sad, knowing I would never have this side of my family in my life. When my little sister said, "How could you be my sister? My mom told me I am her only daughter," I couldn't blame this little girl. But all my hopes of ever reuniting with my real mom died, and I have not still, to this day, talked to her.

I try hard not to think about it. I feel very hurt, depressed, and lonely for a mom. I feel abandoned. I wonder why she had me. I will never know, I guess. Does she love me now? Did she ever? Or was it good-bye forever when I was nine and she dropped me off on my dad's doorstep? I will never know why she could tell my half-sister she was the only daughter. Did she totally regret marrying my father and having me? Why did she want to erase me out of her life? Why did she want to hurt me, when I never hurt her? Sometimes, I wish she never was my mom because this pain will never be eased or gone. I only hope I can learn from it so I can help others.

One small thing has happened as I began to write my story. A new Korean neighbor moved into our apartments. As I told her about the song my mom sang to me when she left me, I had always thought it was a romantic song, like a husband would sing to a wife as they parted. But my new friend tells me that actually the song is a sad song about saying good-bye to someone dear—someone that you really love. That gives me a little hope that my mother did love me once.

As Lillie helped me face my darkest pains, she told me, "Whenever God closes a door, he always opens a window," and that is exactly what happened to me.

I had always dreamed about being an elementary school teacher and I planned to return to the USA and begin school. But when my mission president released me, he prophesied a rather unusual thing:

"Hyun Joo, there is a young man at this time who is taking the missionary discussions and he will be a newly-baptized member when you meet him. You will find him and you will be married. You need to help him develop in the Church and in his priesthood."

And so it happened. I did get another good thing in my life—my husband. Three months later, when I met him at a New Year's Eve party after I returned from my mission, we figured out that the missionaries had begun teaching him the discussions just as my mission president had been delivering his prophecy to me!

So far, we have been able to adopt one little boy, who is the joy of my life and receives lots of love everyday. The one thing I did not get, my children will always get: Love from their parents. And someday, I would like to have a home where unloved, unwanted children come to feel love. For all I ever wanted was just love.

Though I had the gospel and my husband and my son, my old depression kept creeping up. And finally, I had to go to my bishop because I became suicidal again. The pain was still there. My bishop recommended I see a therapist.

On my first appointment, my therapist asked me what I wanted. I said, "a better life."

She asked me to define what a "better life" meant to me. I found myself pouring out my heart. "I want a mother. I want a father. I love my dad to death, but I don't even know him because my stepmother won't let me see him or talk to him. I want my son to know his grandparents and his great-grandparents, but I don't even know them. I hate my stepmother and I know I'm not supposed to hate anyone. I just want a parent—even one parent. I want to be loved by a parent."

I cried and cried and cried. I feel such hurt. And even though I have a good husband and a wonderful son and my Church mom, sometimes I can't feel the happiness from it like I'm supposed to because my self-esteem is so low and my depression is so deep.

My therapist teaches me to focus. She tells me I cannot deny what has happened to me, but neither can I let it swallow me up. She says I cannot let my past ruin my future.

I know she is telling the truth, but sometimes I feel kind of mad when she says it. I wonder if she has ever hurt this way?

But she says something else that really makes me think. She tells me that when I can give my suffering meaning it will be easier to bear. When I'm doing okay, I can thank the Lord for all my trials as well as for my blessings—especially my little boy, my husband, Lillie, and the Church. I understand that it's my trials that have helped me to be strong because the Lord does not give us more than we can handle. And I truly feel that my hardships in life have helped me be a better person with lots of positive goals for my own family.

I work on my attitude every day so I will not treat my son the way I was treated. And I only hope and pray I will help many kids and all the people I come in contact with. I want to help others learn that we are all children of our Heavenly Father and we are all very special and unique. I am thankful for the woman in my life who taught me that lesson. Through Lillie, I have the Church as my foundation. I love the Church. I love its beliefs. I love the idea of Heavenly Father. I love prayer. And I truly do know Jesus is my Savior.

How I want my story to end is that I hope and pray I can help someone like Lillie has helped me. I was not an orphan by death. But I was an orphan five times by rejection—my birth mother, my birth father, my stepmom, and my maternal grandparents all threw me away.

I am grateful for my Church mom who helped Heavenly Father bring love to me.

President Kimball said, "Usually when God answers a prayer, he does it through another person."

It is through my Church mom that I have understood the love of Christ. It is through my Church mom that I have any "real" experience with a parent. It is Lillie who loves me for who I am—not just the easy ways all the time. She has loved me enough even to argue with me, but even then I always know she loves me. I like to think that I have been through these hard experiences so that someday I can really understand and help somebody else.

I know the Savior lives for me. And I know this mostly because of Lillie. It is through her goodness first and later through my husband's goodness that I could see myself in a positive way and believe in *me*. I want to learn to love myself unconditionally. I know the commandment says, "Thou shalt love thy neighbor as thyself." I've always struggled with the part about *"as thyself."* I want to thank Lillie, for helping me dare to believe I can someday really love myself. And my husband, Jason, for adding upon Lillie's work.

*Hyun Joo was abandoned, not only by her birth mother and her birth father, but also by her grandparents and stepmother. When placed in a foster home, she suffered further abuse and consequently another abandonment when the state returned her to her birth father. Yet despite these unspeakable crimes against an innocent little girl, Hyun Joo triumphed to become an amazing young woman. There are times that Hyun Joo gets pulled back into "old" feelings, as most victims of childhood trauma do. A movie, a book, a television program, a chance remark—the smallest thing can trigger powerful memories again. But like Hyun Joo, victims of trauma can learn the skills to not remain victimized. People who have been fragile can become strong. And people who have suffered the most afflicting depression, as Hyun Joo, can triumph with dignity and grace.*

# The Love of God

*I have just come home with pictures of my family's summer vacation. As I look at them, I see a young mother, playing on the beach with her children, having a great time. She is happy, smiling, and looks so good: these pictures must be from an LDS infomercial about families. I look closer and harder at the pictures, analyzing every detail of her expression. Yes, I conclude, it is the ideal LDS mom. Tears form in my eyes as I take it in, realizing who that woman is. It doesn't seem real. Is this possible? Is that really me?*

*I wipe the tears from my eyes and see that I appear to be who I have wanted to be ever since I was a little girl. This is my dream come true. I dreamed of having a righteous priesthood holder for a husband, having happy, healthy children, and a real house with a backyard. I always wanted a family that would pray together, eat together, have family home evening together, and go to church and sit together. All I wanted was to be happy—and everyone around me to be happy. Now I appear to have it. The picture projects the fairy-tale ending: "And she lived happily ever after." But it doesn't tell the story of my struggle up to that point.*

It still amazes me that Steve wanted to marry me after meeting my mother. I talked with my mom and agreed Thanksgiving weekend would be a good time to take my fiancé to meet her. When we arrived on Thursday, she had little to eat in the house. It was apparent by the bathrobe and pajamas she was wearing that she had no intention of preparing or eating a Thanksgiving dinner. She told us to go out to eat. When she did get "dressed," she put on sweats. She spent little time visiting with us that weekend. She stayed in her bedroom. She watched TV. And she kept calling Steve "Sean" (a former boyfriend). I was embarrassed and humiliated. How could she do this to me? But at the same time I wondered why I had expected her to act like a normal mom in the first place. I wanted to explain to Steve that my mom was sick. But sick with what? It wasn't like I could say she had the flu. How could I explain something I did not yet understand?

Six years later, Steve held my hand as I asked the bishop to help me get an LDS therapist. Our bishop listened silently, almost incredulously, as I explained that time and distance could not separate me from my mother's voice. Her loud, critical, demanding, demeaning, ridiculing, rough-sounding voice. She told me how I was supposed to feel, what I was supposed to think, what I was supposed to do, what others thought of me. She changed the past to suit her mood. Her harsh and irrational words from my childhood became a part of me and began to affect every aspect of my life. No matter where I was or what I was doing, I could hear her negative comment about it. Even as I write this, I can hear my mother's voice intruding, saying "That is NOT the way it was! *I'll* tell you what happened!"

After only a few sessions, my therapist said to me, "Madeleine, you need to accept the fact that your mother is mentally ill."

My husband said, "Madeleine, did you really need to pay someone to tell you that? I could have told you that for free."

The evidence of my mother's mental illness was there all my life. Unfortunately, I didn't recognize it because I did not have the experience to know what was normal. Now I know she has severe, chronic, incapacitating mental illnesses, which have never been treated, in spite of her years on total government psychiatric disability and her daily inability to function in the most basic ways. My mother struggled to do housework, cook a meal, or get dressed everyday. Usually, she ate food that didn't need much preparation. She went out of the house only when she absolutely had to. A "normal" person would be grossed out by the condition of her home—wouldn't want to sit on her furniture or eat or drink anything from her kitchen. She couldn't manage finances so that she had money for what she needed (food, gas, utilities). She would have "tantrums" in stores and other public places, and generally act childish.

Let me tell you something of my journey to come to this point of understanding and acceptance of my mother's sickness.

As a child, I didn't realize how my mother's thinking was distorted. I accepted her point of view as reality. When I was ten, I went to a sleep-over at a friend's house and had a great time. As I walked into my home, it was unusually clean and quiet. Then I noticed the kitchen window was smashed out. I asked my dad what had happened. He told me that he had broken the window, and that I could go talk to my mom. I found her alone in her bedroom. She said that she and my dad had gotten into a huge fight and told me all the details. Then she said, "You are no longer allowed to spend the night with your friends. When you're gone to your friend's house, *that* is when he drinks and does stuff like that." *It's my fault he drinks? Only when I go to my friend's house, he wrecks our home and beats up on my mom and brother?* I was stunned. This had never occurred to me before, and I could not understand how it could be true. But she was my mother, she would know. I had to accept what she told me as the truth. *If I would have stayed home, this would not have happened,* I thought. I was only ten.

I longed for my parents to act pleased with me. Desperately, I tried to anticipate what they wanted of me, but it was all in vain. My father's drinking continued, as did my mother's blaming and guilt-imposing voice. The efforts I spent in hope of fixing my dysfunctional family only served to frustrate and anger me. As a teenager, those emotions turned inward as I realized my situation was not going to get better any time soon. My jour-nal entry at age fifteen reflects my desperation:

*Diary: 15 years old, May*

> *I really wish that I would die or someone would be nice enough to kill me or something. I would've committed suicide a long time ago, but I know that I'm here on earth for a purpose and all. And if I killed myself then God would be mad at me. And then I wouldn't get into the celestial kingdom.*

I couldn't kill myself because I was afraid of God, yet I couldn't keep living because I was afraid of my mother. I couldn't live; I couldn't die. And so I was miserably unhappy. My only source of hope was the Church's teaching of a loving Father in Heaven. I longed for that unconditional love I had heard about, and the glimmer of it I felt at church kept my hope for happiness alive.

Nearly every day for over two years I got on my knees at my bedside, and, imagining my Father sitting on the edge of my bed, I prayed to him:

> *Oh, my Father who art in heaven. I don't think I can take it another day in this awful life. Father, please just send me one person who cares about me. Just one thing today to show me that someone cares, so that I can make it till tomorrow. Please.*

I prayed that prayer with all the emotion and tears you can imagine. And I believed he heard me, and I know he answered me: a letter, a smile, a phone call, a kind word, an invitation to something, a surprise visitor. Nearly every day.

During all of this, I looked forward to leaving home as soon as I graduated. I'd had a home teacher once tell me that I should go to BYU, and my mother agreed. As soon as I received the acceptance letter, my countdown to D-day began.

Moving into the dorms, I was thrilled to be in such a peaceful, happy place. But I was still haunted by my personal demons. During the second week at school, my mother called to tell me how much I did not love her. She carried on and on about how I did not care about my family. I sat silently as the tears dripped off my jawbone. My friends looked at me quizzically, "What's wrong, Madeleine?" I looked at the floor. They all grew up in good Mormon families. They would never understand what my mother was saying to me. "Nothing, I don't want to talk about it," I told them. But my heart ached, and I felt all alone. When their parents called, they asked how they were doing, if school was going well, and shared news and smiles. Why couldn't my mother treat me like that?

As the years went by, the calls continued. Shortly before my father's death, following one of her calls, I sat in the middle of the hallway and sobbed aloud for several minutes. *No one. No one is there. No one must know because they wouldn't understand. All they would do is feel sorry for me. I can't let these things get me down; I've got a lot of things that I have to do. I* stopped sobbing, got up, and took my shower so that I could get going with the day.

During my final year at BYU, I had finally gained enough spiritual strength to stand on my own. For the first time in my life, I was able to spiritually uplift others. Members of my ward family would make comments or write notes telling me what a strength my testimony was to them, how moved they were by my talk or lesson, and how much they appreciated being able to have me for their visiting teacher. I was always surprised at their comments. I even dismissed them at times because I could not understand how someone like me could possibly give a talk or teach a lesson that well. I still viewed myself through my mother's eyes, as a spiritual weakling incapable of doing good. But at the same time I was wearing myself out trying to be perfect.

The opportunity came for me to receive my endowment. I knew it was right, I could feel it was right through my whole being. My parents would not be able to accompany me: my father had passed away and my mother was not temple worthy. But I had a strong need for a continued source of spiritual strength, and the temple blessings were it. I was so excited. Knowing what an important step it was and thinking how proud my mother would be of me, I decided to call and tell her.

She was very upset and began to question me: "Are you going on a mission?" *No.* "Are you getting married?" *No.* "Then *why* are you going to the temple?!" I very briefly stated my reason. She then laid on the guilt: "You know I wanted to go to the temple with you. Why aren't you waiting to go with me?" I didn't dare say *because then I would never go.* "This isn't fair, Madeleine." She made it clear how unhappy she was with my decision. I hung up with tears in my eyes. This isn't the way it's supposed to be.

The big day arrived. My roommates had plastered my door with notes, letters, and a sign wishing me well, expressing their excitement and happiness for me. It really lifted my spirits. The sunshine burst forth over the mountains and spilled into the valley. It was a beautiful day to go to the temple. *I am doing the right thing.* My closest and most trusted friend, Ann, accompanied me to the temple. I was nervous and excited, and anticipated a great and wonderful experience. I was well rewarded.

The temple was beautiful inside and the spirit was strong. With each covenant I made, I felt the Spirit of God come through me even stronger than before. Moving from room to room in that temple enhanced the effect. By the time I sat down in the celestial room, I was filled with the Spirit and felt as if I were literally in the presence of my God.

I had never before felt such a complete sense of peace and love. I was totally at ease and comfortable. I knew then that I was a worthwhile person, loved and cared about beyond my wildest dreams. Looking around the room, I felt at home for the first time in my life. *This is what I have been waiting for my whole life. This is where I want to be forever.* I recognized the feelings as those I had been longing after for so long. It was as if I had finally reached my home. After the celestial room had emptied, the temple workers told us the temple would be closing soon. Ann said it was time for us to leave. *Me? Leave? I don't want to ever leave.*

I returned to the temple weekly and loved it. I have since realized that by doing this, I gained even more spiritual strength than I would have otherwise had. It was through this strength that I was able to get married in the temple. And I was so excited to get married!

However, I was afraid to tell my mom that I was getting married. I imagined her criticizing my choice of a spouse and criticizing me just for getting married. Her voice rang in my head, and I feared that it would be a reality.

After Steve and I called his family and broke the news (they were ecstatic to say the least), we called my mom. I don't remember the conversation or any of the words she spoke. I just remember that the words she spoke did not match her voice. She did not sound excited. She did not exclaim like Steve's mother. Her voice was just flat.

I remember when I was a teenager, my mother told me repeatedly that she would go to the temple with me when I got married. She also told me that she would take care of my reception. She talked at length of how perfect it would be. When I was in high school, a friend's mother told me she would help me with my wedding reception when the time came. My mother was offended that she had offered help. She told me that I didn't need to ask anyone else for help. I believed her promises. I believed she would be there for me and with me on the most important day of my life.

When the topic of her being at my wedding came up, she told me it was my fault she wouldn't be going, because I hadn't asked her earlier. I was shocked. Why did I have to *ask* my own mother to go to the temple with me? It never occurred to me to *ask* my mother to do something which I thought had been our mutual dream. But that's exactly what she told me. So, my ultimate dream and hope involving my mother was crushed by her.

I didn't know how to plan for a wedding. I was worried about having enough money. When I asked for some help with the wedding, my mother told me she could not spare any money and that she lived too far away to assist me. I was so frustrated and hurt. I trudged on. I bought the cheapest announcements, did not enclose a picture, and ended up having to borrow money from a friend to buy a dress. The church hall was not available for my reception. My mother insisted that we rent a conference room at the local hotel, rather than have an open house at our bishop's home. I did it only to please my mother, wondering all the while what "fairy godmother" would materialize to pay for the rest of the reception. So much for decorations—and flowers—and cake. I would have married Steve in the temple and not had a reception—but my dreams had been formulated and reinforced by my mother's promises, and the hurt came from continual broken promises, letdowns, and disappointments. She had always promised me that she would see to it that everything was perfect for my wedding day; somehow those promises came to symbolize in my mind the time when she would at last be the mother I dreamed of. Every disappointment surrounding my wedding reinforced the truth to me that my mother was never going to change.

The greatest disappointment came at the temple. As Steve and I were seated in the sealing room, the sealer asked an innocent question, "Is this all?" My heart ached as my eyes searched the room, wanting to say *No*, *there is another coming—my mother*. But I knew the true answer and quietly choked it out, "Yes, this is all."

When Steve and I exited the temple, I searched the crowded temple grounds looking for my mother to greet us. I had worried that she might have difficulty parking and finding me in the crowd. *That's it; she's having a hard time parking because there are so many people at the temple today.*

I forced a smile as our wedding party posed for the photographer on the temple steps. *She told me she would be here.* My mother wasn't there.

At last, over an hour after we came out, she arrived. I was glad I had gotten the photographer to wait. I am grateful for the two pictures I have with my mother on my wedding day.

At the reception, my relatives and new in-laws kept asking, "Where's your mom?" It was so devastating and awkward for me. At last, halfway through the reception, my mother did show up. But then she didn't mingle. She sat in a chair at the back of the room, visiting only when someone approached her.

I was used to my mother's critical and confusing voice. I was used to her blaming me and making demands. I was used to her anger and her loudness. I was used to her many broken promises. Nevertheless, I had believed my mom would come through for me on this one important day. When she didn't, I felt abandoned, hurt, frustrated, angry, devastated, and guilty.

After the reality of my wedding day sank in, one would have thought I could maybe have accepted the severity of my mother's emotional illness. Yet I still believed that she was capable of being a "normal" mom. And I did not recognize the fact that my mind had assimilated her voice, nor that it was continuing to have a powerful effect on me. This became very evident when I had my first child.

I went to the doctor because I was in so much pain and was nauseated. I was hoping I'd get some medicine to make it "all better." Instead, he told me, "You're just pregnant. Go home and rest; the pain and nausea will go away after a while." I cried. Not because I was happy, but because I didn't know how to deal with the way I was feeling.

❦

During a later doctor visit, I complained of emotional upheavals, explaining that I did not think it was normal. My doctor told me I just needed an "attitude adjustment"—implying that I could control what I was feeling. This frustrated me even more. But I did not know what to do about it.

Steve and I brought our newborn home, sat on the couch, and stared in awe at him. As I was holding the baby on my lap, I suddenly and clearly recognized that my Father in Heaven had answered my prayers from ten years earlier. I began crying. *So why don't I feel happy?* All Steve could do was hold me and tell me he loved me.

I was scared to death. I did not know how to be a mom. Whenever I tried to lovingly care for my newborn, I heard all Mom's critical, accusing voices in my head. I had to figure out how to put on a diaper so it wouldn't leak. I had to figure out how to take off his shirt without breaking his little stick arms. I was afraid to give him a bath for fear of dropping and killing him. I was afraid a small bump to his head would crack it. I fearfully imagined a police officer coming to my house and saying, "You are a child abuser." I had nightmares about standing in a courtroom in handcuffs and having my child taken away from me.

I needed help with my newborn because I was still sick, and my baby didn't sleep much. My mother really wanted to come and help me. I believed that she would be able to help me take care of the baby and the chores and cooking, too. After all, that's what moms did when they came to help with their new grandchild. But when my mom came, instead of being a welcome relief, she was more work. She questioned everything I did for the baby, but refused to change a diaper. The crying baby made her upset, so she would have to go lie down in a quiet room several times a day. I still had to do all the housework, including cleaning up after her. I was exhausted, and my emotions oscillated between extreme irritation and despair.

By the time of my six-week checkup I was feeling suicidal. I tried to reach out for help. The doctor asked me if I had any questions. Doing my best to maintain my composure, but still letting a tear escape, I managed to squeak out, "I'm so depressed." The doctor smiled, patted me on the back, and told me it was normal and would go away soon. I drove home in tears, wishing someone would put me out of my misery.

For nine months I waited for "it" to "go away." I was afraid to ask for help again. The doctor had rejected my one and only plea for help, and now I believed I had to endure my agony alone. Being ashamed of my condition, I continued turning inward, until I felt trapped, as if I were in a box. I could not think clearly. As hard as I tried, I couldn't see my life clearly. Once I wondered if my brain waves were simply out of sync with the dimension of time and space in which I lived.

Confused, frustrated, and lonely, I more diligently sought relief in prayer and the scriptures. I knew that my Father in Heaven was there, but I could not feel his Holy Spirit. It was as if I were being spiritually suffo-cated. The depression was a dark blanket blocking my spiritual passage-ways just as a real blanket can block one's air passages. No matter how hard I tried to "breathe," I just couldn't feel the Spirit enter.

And through this whole experience, I continued to hear Mom's voice in my head. "Madeleine, you can't do it right. Madeleine, you'll never get it right. Madeleine, it is your fault. Madeleine, everything is your fault." I believed I was an awful person, and the depression reinforced that false-hood. No manner of evidence to the contrary could break through my distorted reasoning.

But then a hospital television advertisement gave me a spark of hope. I changed doctors. My new doctor started me on Prozac. Within two weeks I felt like a new person. For the first time in my recent memory I was able to think clearly and interact socially. I could feel happy. It was at this point when I recognized my mother's voice was woven into my thoughts and dominating my own perceptions. I realized that my efforts had failed to exterminate her irrational words from my mind, so I sought an LDS therapist.

I have learned in therapy that I am normal, and my mother is not. This did not come to me easily. It took nearly a year before I accepted myself as a worthwhile person, capable of doing and saying the right things. I am finally believing in myself, learning to trust my own feelings and form my own opinions. The medication clarified my thinking, but therapy helped me to understand and reinterpret my experiences. Learning to recognize my mother's voice, and replace it with my own, has taken a great deal of effort.

It has taken a little longer for me to believe that other people view me in a positive light. I have believed my mother's voice for so long that it has colored much of my life. My perceptions, both of myself and others, have been rooted in her mentally ill thinking and not in reality. I am learning to recognize and accept reality as the truth.

Forgiving my mother is an essential part of my progression. It is not her fault that she has severe and incapacitating mental illnesses. When I am thinking clearly—spiritually—I can let go of the potency and poison of her voice. I can even feel sorry for her. I can ache for the tragedy of her life and the problems she has had. After more than two years of medica-tion and therapy, I am starting to feel compassion for my mother.

Now, I am able to hear the other voices in my life. My husband is so kind and patient. I have very dear friends who talk to me with loving, friendly voices. And I have the voice of the Savior: He says, "Come unto me . . . for my yoke is easy, and my burden is light . . . I will give you rest" (Matthew 11:28, 30). I am earnestly trying to listen to the right and good voices in my life.

A big part of my healing has been a spiritual journey. I see my life as a reflection of Lehi's vision of the tree of life. The depression acted as the exceedingly great mists of darkness. It was, at times, so dark that I did not know where I was or which way to go. The gospel of Jesus Christ gave me hope that happiness did exist. I wanted to get to it; I wanted to have it. So I clung to the iron rod, knowing that the tree of life existed, because I knew others who had reached it.

It was hard to hold onto the iron rod all the time. Sometimes I was so weak, all I could do was just sit next to it. Feeling as if I could not go on, I wondered if I could ever stand back up and grab hold of that rod. Each time I felt weak, someone on their journey to the tree would stop before passing me, help me up, and stay at my side until convinced I had a firm grasp on the rod. Often I think there was someone who left a comfortable spot near the beautiful tree, coming down to my side in the dank mists of my darkness to comfort and assist me so that I would not have to grope in the dark.

I got my first taste of the sweet fruit of the tree of life when I received my endowment. It was as Lehi described, most beautiful and desirable above all other things. Nothing else could compare, nothing else was worth the effort. I determined never to leave the safe haven, the shelter this beautiful tree provides me.

The love of God speaks peace to my soul. By his light I can at last look at my family pictures and believe what I see: A happy couple enjoying a wonderful life together. I am a good person, making good decisions, doing good things.

With the depression gone, I can finally savor the fruit my Father in Heaven has given me. The taste of it is so sweet, and the sweetness fills my entire being. The joy I can finally feel exceeds my dream of happiness for this life. It is, as the angel said, "most joyous to the soul" (1 Nephi 11:23). How grateful I am for a Father in Heaven who loves me, who has blessed me to be able to taste of his fruit and to now help you on your journey to the tree.

*This courageous woman has had to face neglect, abuse, abandonment, exploitation, and alcoholism. Her mother suffered from severely debilitating mental illnesses that became worse for lack of treatment. (These chronic and major mental illnesses are not to be confused with the very treatable episodes of major depression.)*

*Madeleine is a slim, pretty, very smart BYU graduate with a handsome, professional husband. They have absolutely adorable children. This sister's bishop called me several years ago and said, "I don't get it. Madeleine has everything, and she is one of the smartest women in the ward as well as one of the most devoted. She is serving in a presidency. But she tells me she needs to see a therapist, that she has no self-esteem. Betsy, you're going to have to help me understand this one—I just don't get it."*

*Upon meeting Madeleine the first time, I had to agree with the bishop. This young woman appeared to have and be everything. Yet she was miserably depressed. If any of you need to become believers in the power of "talk therapy," Madeleine's story is convincing. Therapy has helped her to develop the skills to quiet her mother's voice and believe in her own goodness.*

*One remarkable part of Madeleine's story is the strength and support she received from friends and ward members throughout her life. She recognizes with gratitude the way her prayers for help were answered through the loving service of others, especially through her teenage years. That care sustained her until she received the treatment she needed to silence the critical and demeaning voice which had dominated her thoughts.*

*Her therapeutic journey has concluded. She needed to hear, then to understand, then to accept that her mother is severely and chronically mentally ill. Only by accepting that truth could Madeleine ever be able to forgive her mother for a whole lifetime of neglect and emotional abuse. In her story, you have witnessed the miracle she received as she began writing because she wanted to help herself—and me—and you.*

# *Cold Christmas*

I'm a Hoosier: A conservative midwestern girl from a small midwestern town just outside of Indianapolis. The first time I went to Disneyland, "Main Street" reminded me of the hometown I grew up in. Our Main Street, called Center Street, was a hodgepodge of retail shops intermixed with 1930s bungalows where the poorer people lived.

We were the poorer people, but I didn't know that growing up. I grew up in an incredibly dysfunctional home. My divorced mother boarded my older brother and me out during the week to anyone she could, though we came home most weekends. In these places we learned of our nonexistent worth by the way we were treated differently from the other real members of the families. We ate different food than the rest of the families. We slept in cold, uncomfortable places. There were many other hard issues, but I always remember just wanting to "go home."

My mom married "Uncle Jim" when I was about four, and then my brother and I came home to live within the year. We were so excited to get to be with our own mom for the first time in our memory. At first our new dad tolerated us, but we soon learned that our "Mom" was "Uncle Jim's," and if we wanted to live to see the light of the next day, we would stay out of sight.

There were five of us: me, my mom, my stepfather, and two more kids—a sister and my brother. We lived in an apartment on top of Kratsky's Five and Dime. My mom worked downstairs and my stepfather worked for the railroad, but he didn't work very much. We as a family endured much fighting, drinking, crying, hiding, and beating. At one of my first remembered family gatherings, I watched in horror as my stepdad tried to kill my grandpa with a great big red lug wrench: my mom grabbed the wrench in the middle and was dragged all over the house and yard trying to stop them. Yes, I was home, but I still found myself pleading to "go home." It was very confusing. I didn't even know what I meant.

The best part about growing up in my town was the soda fountain/apothecary right next door. They played music all the time—happy music, which wafted up to our apartment. I used to go to bed listening to "Itsy Bitsy Teeny Weenie Yellow Polka Dot Bikini." I was seven and had just barely graduated from the itsy bitsy spider that went up the waterspout.

Our street was dry and dusty with just a few straggly trees that lost their leaves every fall. For some strange reason, the city fathers had planted forsythia bushes in clumps between the dime store and the soda fountain. Every June the ladybugs came. Trees, windshields, and flowers were covered with ladybugs. I guess that's why I liked the polka dot bikini song. I didn't know much about bikinis, but I knew lots about polka dots.

And before I ever knew the word *dysfunctional*, I knew something about my family wasn't right. When I was only thirteen and fourteen years old, I used to take the bus to downtown Indianapolis to the public library and read books and magazines about families. I wanted to understand all about families and what made good families.

When I was fifteen years old, we moved to Oregon. In my mind I was still a Hoosier. We bought another version of an Indiana bungalow on a small, scratchy patch of property. There was an old abandoned eight-foot trailer out back. It was one of those kinds with the rounded, humpback shells. I announced to my mother that I was going to sleep in the trailer. Nobody argued with me. The house only had two bedrooms. So the grownups got one room, my sister got the second bedroom, and my brother got the couch.

It was the first fall in Oregon that the kids at school were talking about ladybugs, and I realized I had started to hate them, but I didn't know why. I hadn't hated Hoosier ladybugs. One day, a kid at school was drawing a ladybug and talking about how cute they were with their humpback little red shiny bodies and their stubby little wings and big black polka dots.

I felt suddenly pukey. I felt myself shiver, and then I felt disgusted. I thought I could not bear to have one touch me. But I didn't know why.

Ladybugs. I hated ladybugs. I might have been happy to be a Hoosier; however, I was also weird. I was different from my friends in so many ways. I guess even saying "my friends" gives me a frog in my throat. I've always felt like an outsider, even when I was an honest-to-goodness Hoosier. Not only was I weird about ladybugs and other beetles, I hated Christmas.

When I was little and lived on top of Kratsky's Five and Dime, I used to hear the Christmas music playing on the jukebox from the soda fountain. I put my pillow over my head 'cause I didn't want to hear those Christmas songs. They made me shiver. And when they made us sing Christmas carols at school, I zoned out. At least, that's what I call it—zoning out. Who ever heard of a kid who hated Christmas? But I did. I could hardly wait to get back to school every January and escape the gloom that hovered around me while everybody else seemed so happy. I admit it. My brother called me the "nutcase." I didn't tell him, but I thought I was weird, too.

When my mother and stepfather planted us just outside Tigard, Oregon, I really felt like an outsider. The kids I hung out with were good kids, but I wondered what they saw in me.

Twelve years later, I was married and had five children, but in my heart I still was a simple, conservative Hoosier girl. I had always wanted to be a wife and a mother and live a good life in the Church, but there was an ever-present sadness in my heart.

In my life at that time I felt very wistful. I didn't know what I was missing. I just knew I had a sadness in my heart. It's like there were grave markers in my heart but what was buried was like the unknown soldier. I sensed that something big and maybe even terrible lay behind the gravestones in my heart, but I couldn't get to it.

As throughout my life, I had friends I loved and they were the best women, but I felt so far beneath them. I had one friend whose husband was the dean of students at our community college, and she was a theater instructor. I had another friend whose husband was one of the community's best-loved doctors; she was a quiet, unassuming woman. I had another friend who had just gone through a terrible divorce, but she had just graduated from nursing school with honors. And my very good friend and next-door neighbor, who was also the Relief Society president, was the director of nurses at the hospital.

Me? I cleaned houses. I cleaned for three of my closest friends and some pretty messy bachelors. They all said I did a good job, and they all paid me more than I asked. And I wondered, why do they like me? What do they see in me that I don't see?

I taught early morning seminary. I couldn't figure that out either. The bishop said I was doing a great job. I really loved the kids. (Well, three of them were my own, so of course I loved them.)

I admit that I studied about three hours a day and I read all the time to find stories to draw the kids into the scriptures, but I still just didn't feel worthy.

I guess that's because my marriage was so bad. Bix was a good man, honest and hardworking. He always tried to provide for our family. Neither of us had an education so we always lived from paycheck to paycheck.

I shouldn't complain though. I have the greatest kids in the world. Bix told me I'm too strict and my friends sometimes told me I'm too controlling. But I have to protect my children. I chose to be a mother and I chose to bring these children into the world. I have to protect them.

In many ways, Bix was like another child. The kids loved him because he played with them.

I couldn't sleep with him though. He slept in the bedroom and every night I slept on the living room couch. Bix got so mad at me about this. But I kept explaining to him that he had to work so hard, and he was so tired, and I snore, so I knew it was hard for him to get to sleep. So I went to the couch every night.

Bix was very hurt. And I don't blame him. We were so different when we met. I was sixteen and he was eighteen. At first, things were really good between us. He used to always tell me he "had to rescue me from that old trailer." I thought he was really sweet.

One summer, we took our little kids on a vacation to see my mom and stepdad. I always knew I hated my stepdad, but I can't describe how this made me feel. We were there at the beach. My stepdad was touching my kids. He hugged them and kissed them. And I knew I had to get them and me out of their house. So we left.

Maybe that's why my thinking wouldn't shut off. I had to think and think and think, and I couldn't shut it off. I started having nightmares. I added more houses to my cleaning route trying to wear myself out. At night I was so weary that I fell onto the couch and wrapped myself in a blanket. I became afraid to go to sleep.

> *Nightmares always start the same way. I hear a loud, oppressive humming that gets louder and louder and louder and then the beetles are clanging into each other and crawling in armies all over my body. I am flailing helplessly against them and fighting as they cover my eyes and ears and mouth. I cannot breathe and yet I feel—am aware of— panting.*
>
> *I wake up in terror.*
>
> *And again and again I have this dream of beetles devouring my "self." And the next night and the next until I feel a stranger has crept into my body and some alien presence lives within me.*
>
> *I become angry. I sob uncontrollably. I am so mad at my husband. And he didn't do anything. I am getting up every night and curling up on the couch. I keep repeating, "I told you that I snore too loudly, and you have to work so hard." He is saying words to me. I can see his lips moving but I can't understand him. He looks angry, too, but I feel pro- pelled into some dimension where I can see what's around me but I can't hear or understand. I think I'm going crazy.*
>
> *I look up to see that Bix has brought Sally, my next-door neighbor who is the nurse, over to see me. Sally is talking to me; like Bix, I can see her lips move but I can't hear her, and I can't figure out why she is at my house in the middle of the night. I hear ambulance sirens in the distance.*
>
> *I am in the hospital. Dr. Dawson is standing over my hospital bed. He tells me that I've have had a depressive break. I do feel broken. I also feel detached from myself and my life as I have known it. I still*

don't know why I am in the hospital. It is Christmas and I should be at home with my children.

The piped-in Christmas music is playing softly through the intercom when suddenly I am aware that "Silent Night" has just begun.

I swallow my first scream. And then a disembodied wail courses through my vocal cords as "Silent Night" unleashes a memory that had finally broken through the veil in my conscious mind.

I come out of my body. I see a little girl, about seven in a white eyelet hand-me-down Christmas nightgown. I hover over the child, then drift and float through the frosted windowpane to watch the Christmas carolers stroll the street below. They are in front of the five and dime singing "Silent Night." Whoosh. Back into the body of the little girl.

There is sour breath harshly expelling, panting. Heavy body pressing my smallness into the bed. Thrust of pain so bad. Familiar voice panting in my ear, "Baby, baby, I love you so. All daddies love their little Christmas angels. This won't hurt long. You're daddy's big girl."

"Silent Night, Holy Night. All is calm. All is bright." Cold Christmas. Cold, cold Christmas.

I always feel numb and cold at Christmas. Christmas carols make me shiver. I feel raw and exposed when I hear them. Cold, cold Christmas. Now I know. I am not weird. Dr. Dawson speaks so gently and says he will give me something so I can sleep tonight. He says I won't have nightmares tonight.

The next morning I want to talk. I can't talk fast enough. I tell Dr. Dawson about my phobia about ladybugs and beetles. He gives me a sentence completion test. I instinctively know this item is not on the test, but as he reads me the beginning sentence fragments, he slips in "Ladybugs."

Out of my mouth pops "trailer."

Immediately, I see what my mind had hidden from me for almost twenty years. The trailer where I had fled when I was fifteen years old had not been the refuge I had sought.

❧

Memories I did not want to remember crashed into me. I puked. Dry heaves and rupturing wails of suffering escaped with my memories. And in the belly of the trailer where I had sought my teenage freedom I was once again imprisoned under monstrous weight. My mind escaped the confines of the trailer and hovered over it. With my child's eye, the hulk of the eight-foot rounded trailer looked just like the hard impenetrable shell of a beetle.

The large and shifting pieces of the puzzle of my life flew together. I was not weird. I was not a nutcase. Beetles. Trailers. "Silent Night." Christmas. Cold Christmas. What my stepfather had done. The pieces flew into bright shards of color that pierced me with vengeance and then shattered into my mind, exploding.

Dr. Dawson said I became psychotic. He said that for about seventy-two hours I lost touch with reality. He kindly told me that if he had to relive the memories that crashed in on me he might have become psychotic, too. That was strangely comforting. I liked Dr. Dawson.

He did not try to be so professional. He really tried to be kind. I was in the hospital for three weeks. It was so very hard. I cried. I was tormented. There were days I was not sure I'd ever get out of the hospital. I felt ashamed to see my friends and family. I did not want to go to the groups. I did not want to talk. I did not want to set goals. I did not want to understand. I just wanted the pain to stop.

It did not stop. But it did begin to become bearable. I don't know all the medications they gave me, but I left on Elavil.

I didn't have good luck with medications, but I did find a very good therapist whom I liked and trusted. I can remember a time when I was washing dishes. I thought to myself it was going to be impossible to go on; then I realized that ten years had gone by since I had gone into the hospital. Life *had* gone on.

Sometimes, the shadow of my past steals into my mind unbidden. And I've named the unknown dead that resided with their markers in my mind. As just a little girl, I buried innocence, and I buried trust, and I buried intimacy. Bix and I are now divorced. I still love him but the skeletons in the graveyard of my mind were too hard for him. Though I miss him and wish he were back, I cannot blame him. How can I be angry with him when the grave markers were so hard for me, too?

I am still teaching early morning seminary. I sense an urgency to share the Savior with these teenagers. Perhaps it's because of the illumination I have experienced about the Savior. Years ago, right after I joined the Church, I was asked to substitute-teach in a Primary class, giving a lesson on "Why we need a Savior." I was so concerned with getting this very important message across to the children, who (for the most part), lived in dysfunctional households and would probably not ever hear this message outside of the Primary setting. I wanted to make it simple so they would remember and use this information in times of need during their lives. The one-line simplified concept I used was—*We need a Savior to help us do the things we can't do for ourselves.* I don't remember how the lesson was received by the Primary class, but I do know this one sentence will help me throughout the rest of my life.

What do my personal story and my substitute Primary class experience have to do with the Atonement?

The Lord tells us, "And if men come unto me I will show unto them their weakness. I give unto men weakness that they may be humble; and my grace is sufficient for all men who humble themselves before me; for if they humble themselves before me, and have faith in me, then will I make weak things become strong unto them" (Ether 12:27). When I read this scripture for the first time, I literally shouted for joy because I knew I was *filled* with many weaknesses I had learned as a child. I thought to myself, "Boy, am I going to be strong!" I also knew this was the real way home—and to the real home, the home I had longed for as a child, the haven of our Heavenly Father.

When you grow up in a dysfunctional home, you feel a sense of achievement just getting out alive. Unfortunately, when we leave that house, most of us believe all the bad times are behind us. However, we still need to learn the lessons we were supposed to learn in childhood—

like how to listen, to share, to give, to trust, and to learn other things besides survival techniques.

As a young mother with my first small baby, I did not have a clue as to what to do. I had not learned how to nurture: I had learned how to survive.

I was terrified that I was going to hurt my baby so I constantly read magazines, books, and newspaper articles that helped me know the best things to do for my family. The baby would cry sometimes, and I would get so frustrated, even angry. And I was so afraid I might repeat my past. One day I vividly remember praying what to do with this crying baby and a thought came to my mind to lay her down, cover her up, and walk out of the room. She cried for a short while and then fell asleep.

This was not always the answer, but the Lord knew I didn't know what to do and he helped me. He helped me move past the hurts of my past and those gravestones in my brain and find the way—his way.

The *Atonement* is a big word with infinite meanings; using it in small, everyday ways, as I did with my baby, may often be overlooked by people. When there is something you cannot do for yourself, *this is when you need a Savior.*

I'm still a Hoosier, but I am far more complex than my girlhood in Indiana. I am a Mormon and a Christian. And most importantly of all, I am a striving disciple of Christ who daily tries to call on the blessings of the Atonement.

When I was called to teach early morning seminary, it was something I had longed to do for years. Many hours were spent each day pouring over my scriptures, making charts, listening to music, making posters, learning new games, and learning about my seminary students. Being totally immersed in the scriptures was heaven to me. And that's where I was when I learned about hell.

My husband of almost thirty years left the family. It totally devastated all five of the children and me. It was like the atomic bomb had dropped on our house. We couldn't eat, drink, or sleep. All we could do was cry— sometimes we couldn't do that. My children could hardly go to school and make it through the day because they were so upset. Sometimes, they didn't make it and would come home. We were so frantic all the time looking for answers that weren't there. We were in a deep abyss trying to climb out.

Realizing I was without financial support, my friends rallied to quickly locate a job for me in a nearby city. It was a good job because a devout LDS family owned the company, and my stake president also worked there. I didn't make a lot of money but it allowed me to meet my children's needs, and they also allowed me to come in a little late because I taught seminary.

During this time of greatest stress and heartache, I still taught seminary. In fact, it was seminary that enabled me to go on with my life. I worked all day, helped my children at night, and with whatever time I had left, I prepared for seminary. It was the constant immersion in the scriptures that *literally* kept me alive. And this immersion in the scriptures, combined with pleading with the Lord for help to prepare his lesson, was what allowed me to present lessons every day.

The course of study was the New Testament. I watched the Savior teach his disciples who he was and why they would need him. One of the things I noticed most was his constant communication to his Father in Heaven through prayer. Secondly, I could feel the great love he had for his disciples because he always tried to prepare them for what was to come. And then, as he knew he was leaving them, he let them know they would not be "comfortless."

I desperately needed to know the Savior and depend upon him on a daily, sometimes hourly, basis while I was trying to survive my Gethsemane. The good parts of my life were produced by constantly relying on the Atonement to get me through each day.

I cannot say my life has been easy. But I can say I have learned to give meaning to my suffering. I have come to know the Savior. I have experienced the healing joy of his atonement. I have experienced the darkest abuse, but "Nevertheless . . . [I] knowest the greatness of God; and [that] he shall consecrate thine afflictions for thy gain" (2 Nephi 2:2).

Sometimes my life feels so full of things that need to change that I do not feel up to the challenge. But the scriptures are helpful in overcoming "self" and moving forward. For me, knowing that the Savior can help us overcome our past, and overcome ourselves, is joy.

*A book about depression cannot be written without including a story of sexual abuse. Statistics show that one out of every four women has experienced some form of sexual abuse, ranging from sexual harassment to fondling to rape to incest to pedophilia. Victims of sexual abuse commonly experience depression as a result of these violations.*

*In this story, we come to understand vividly the horror of early sexual abuse. Several themes expressed by the author are common to sexual abuse victims: not remembering the sexual abuse until a later event triggers or begins to trigger the memory—in this case, witnessing her stepfather touching her own children; an awareness of a profound underlying sadness, but without an understanding of what the sadness means; "shutting down" sexually—in this case to the extent that she was unable even to share her bed with her husband. (In other cases, rather than "shutting down" a sexual abuse victim may "act out" sexually, becoming promiscuous.) Other common themes in these cases are a sense of powerlessness, guilt, and feelings of unworthiness.*

*Despite such traumatic sexual abuse, this woman has found a way to heal. Though I was her therapist for a number of years, I can truthfully claim that she was my teacher. She remains, after all her trials, one of the most purehearted, utterly giving women I know. The centerpiece of her story is her tenacious struggle to make the Savior a defining part of her life. She has found healing through bringing together the interventions of man (talk therapy and medication) and the interventions of God. The ultimate healing comes through embracing the Atonement and letting Christ carry our burdens and make us whole.*

# A Gift of Love

. . . I did walk a path of darkness of my own. I know what it is like to feel that you are a nobody, unworthy of being loved or even liked by anyone. I know what it is to try to believe that drinking will cure the problem, that death would be oh, so welcome. I know what it is like to fear human touch because it leaves you feeling so dirty, or brings physical pain and hatred. I also know what it's like to crave love from someone, anyone. But at an early age, while I struggled with those feelings, somewhere deep inside of me, I wanted to believe that I was different, that I was of worth. So although there was much despair, there were also strong moments of hope that I recognized and clung to.

Somewhere along the way I also realized that the neglect and abuse that I lived through were just possibly not my fault. Then the anger took over and the anger gave me more strength, not only to fight, but also to look for good things in other sources. When I joined the Church, felt the hands on my head in priesthood blessing, I knew, really knew for the first time, that there was a Heavenly Father who truly loved me in the way that I felt my earthly parents could not. I could also recognize how much he had loved and protected me, and note the earthly angels that he had sent along my way, who always seemed to be at the crossroads when I needed them. . . . There was no great earth-shaking moment; it was just a strong affirmation of something I already knew deep down within myself.

The Atonement in my life gave me a different kind of strength, the strength that comes with learning how to love: love others, love Christ, and most importantly, love myself. I have slowly learned to replace the anger with the love. Although I was strong in some ways, it has taken me many years to reach the point where I can put that scared, lonely little girl to rest. I will carry the scars of my childhood for the rest of my life, just as I carry the scar on my knee from a bike fall. Through the gift of Christ's Atonement, though, for every sorrow, I have a much bigger joy. Maybe there is a part of me that holds on a little to those sad things because they help me to see all the joy and beauty there is in this life, help me to know what a truly blessed being I am.

The Atonement, the gift of life given to me by a loving Brother, daily brings to me the reminder that I really am of infinite worth, that Christ died so that I could have a clear path back to my Heavenly Father. Learning of the Atonement seemed to answer some question that I didn't have words for, but that my soul had been trying to tell me all along. I'd had moments throughout my life when I'd felt something whispering to me that would leave me longing for a home I couldn't remember. Many times I'd falter, but always the earthly angels were there, at different stages throughout my life. A teacher, an aunt, my parents, brothers and sisters. The look of love in my husband's eyes, the touch of his hands, the love we share. My children, nursing them, their hugs and kisses, their light and joy. There were two times in my life though, when this gift seemed to open me up in a new way to the light of Christ. First was meeting my husband. Among the many things he brought to me was his sure knowledge of the gift of the Atonement, his personal relationship with the Savior. He had a belief so strong that it led his whole life, defined who he was, showed him what to be. From him I learned the beginning of the meaning of infinite love, and how to live it.

The next time was some years later, when I looked into the eyes of a woman who looked back at me with a beautiful healing smile, and in her eyes was a bond of sisterhood that spoke beyond words into my soul. Through her, with her, I learned the meaning of true friendship, how to open myself up to reaching for the celestial friendships that we can have with each other. Because of her I have learned to love more deeply, and I am able to be a much better friend to others and see the beauty of their souls, including my own. Even still, I am healing, and the spirit speaks to me showing me what the Atonement really has brought to me, that the angels are still there and will always be there. I am still growing and learning. With each new growth comes a re-enforcement of the Atonement in my life, and new angels who join the circle of love that I am so much a part of. And every day I am relearning the true meaning of the Atonement in my life.

. . . I did start to write of the challenges of my childhood, but writing of the hard things just made me feel bad. As strongly as I feel the need to write, those sad things just shrivel something up inside of me, not because I haven't dealt with them, because I have, but I think because that is not what my writing is supposed to be about. One of the things that I know is that the strongest gift I have is the gift of love. My writing is to help me to strengthen that gift, exemplify it if I can. It is through the writing that I see things so clearly, it is my way of whistling in the dark, hearing the voices of angels and the whisperings of the songs my earthly ears can't hear, but that my soul can. It helps me to see the beauty in each person, keep the heavenly love coursing through my veins. I do not need to write of sadness but of joy, to help myself and others remember how precious we truly are. The sad things will always be a part of me, but they are not all of me.

My relationship with my parents is also different; it is much, much better. We can come to each other without the chains of guilt and anger. It took me a long time to forgive myself, and to forgive my parents for the things they did not see. We enjoy loving one another, and it is truly a wonderful thing and took me a long, long time to reach.

For every sad memory, I have learned to replace it with a happy one. Now I have far more happy than sad. I have also learned to re-see the triggers that bring the scary ones so that they no longer haunt me. I can take them out, acknowledge them, then move on. I am telling you this only because I believe that we can, with the grace of God and people who truly love us, be healed.

*At the beginning of this project, I contacted a dear friend of mine to ask her write her story for us. She tried. Then, uncharacteristically, she turned me down. She felt she had moved beyond the pains of the past and is now looking forward, into the future. When I received her letter explaining this, I was awed by the healing power the Atonement has brought to her life. I asked her if,*

*instead of the story I had originally suggested, she would allow me to use her letter of refusal.*

*What you have just read are excerpts from that letter. It is a compelling testimony of the joy and beauty that come to a person's life as the Atonement of the Savior lifts heavy burdens from bowed shoulders.*

CHAPTER ELEVEN

# Life's Burdens: Personal Accounts

In this chapter we illustrate some of life's burdens which can lead to depression. While elements of sin may be a part of the adversity, many of these trials are simply the result of living a mortal life where bad things happen to good people.

Willa Cather wrote: "There are only two or three great human stories and they go on repeating themselves as fiercely as if they had never happened before."[1] This quotation captures the essence of the human drama we call life. It also captures the essence of why most of us are able to feel either sympathy or empathy for others. While our "events" may be diverse and dissimilar, our suffering weighs in on the same scales.

Most major emotional catastrophes involve a loss of some type: loss of a loved one to death, loss of a marriage in divorce, loss of a relationship, loss of health, loss of a job, etc. The most frequent losses I have witnessed in therapy sessions are losses that have come about as a result of living in a mortal world. Many of these trials are not a result of the person's choices; however, sometimes the trials are the result of sinning by or sins against the client.

If we examine the kinds of life burdens which may lead to depression, we could list misfortune, accident, disease, hereditary problems, congenital problems, natural calamities, distressing relationships, general afflictions of mortality, and the tribulation of "opposition in all things."

As we contemplated the stories we wanted to include as examples in our book, we came up with thirty-eight different trials people often face, and that was just a simple list created with no great effort on our part. We realized there could be hundreds of trials, and we could not illustrate each one individually. Then I remembered the Willa Cather quote, which I have always loved, because what she said is undeniably true. While we may not have included your exact trial in this chapter, the essence of your struggle will probably be similar to one we did include. Often, the trigger (or psychological precipitant) to your trial will be a loss due to adversity over which you had little or no control.

In any event, our message is the same: We hope to crystallize the drama of depression. Further, and most important, we wish to inspire you to believe in the truth that depression is treatable. It is *very* treatable, and the best statistics we have indicate that the vast majority of people can find relief from their despair.

One final note: Though each of these authors writes of hope and healing, these brief autobiographies are not happy accounts. They are true, and truth can be hard. But these are not, in the end, sad stories. They are stories of mortality, where there has been suffering, but also where the light of the gospel and God's tender mercies have brought peace and understanding.

---

1. Willa Cather, O, *Pioneers!* (Boston, New York: Houghton Mifflin), 1913, part II, chapter 4.

# Unequally Yoked

I knew we couldn't afford it. He was a recent college graduate. We were young marrieds with a two-year old, a new pregnancy, school loans, and a new low-paying job.

But it was exquisite. "It" was a Tiffany table lamp. The entire lamp base was a leaded mosaic of tiny, hexagon-shaped autumn-colored glass. The hues of the glass ranged from green to bright orange to gold to amber. The shimmery colors caught the light and cast them onto the nearest wall. This wonderful lamp was capped with a soft, creamy, accordion-pleated shade, which offset the vivid glass colors.

*How could a lamp be so splendid?* we wondered. But, of course, we agreed it was splendid because we were so alike. We both had such good taste—the same, of course. Together, we were not very practical. Well, I had always been practical before, but his way was so much more fun. And I wanted to please him.

So, though we had few other worldly possessions after four years of marriage, we bought the lamp we could not afford. We continued eating picnic-style on the floor; we had a Tiffany lamp, but no kitchen table.

It was strange to me. I had always been so practical and sensible and never cared much for "things." Now I was enjoying choosing and buying things we could not afford. I admit it: it was fun to be extravagant. And I wanted to make him happy. I had made a commitment for eternity, and I was committed to being the best wife any man ever had. After all, I had gotten an "A" in my "Achieving a Successful Marriage" class at BYU. Armed with all my hard-won knowledge, I felt certain of success because I cared passionately about my marriage.

We bought many other things we could not afford, and I became more and more uncomfortable about this. But I have to admit, I loved the Tiffany lamp as much as he did. We bought the lamp shortly after our fourth anniversary. It was a type of reconciliation present for both of us. We were trying to mend from some of his hurtful flirtations with other women as we prepared for the birth of our second child. His mother had explained to me that I needed to realize that it was not his fault that girls flirted with him. "He's so attractive and smart," she said. "You have to understand it's not his fault these other girls pursue him."

It was bewildering to me. When we first met, I thought we were twins, but of the opposite sex. We both loved the gospel. I admired how knowledgeable he was about the scriptures. We both loved art and painted as a hobby. I thought he could do anything.

We enjoyed drama, and we had both acted in local plays and road shows. We both liked to write and had written ward road shows. We both wrote poetry. I thought he was the smartest guy I had ever dated. Shortly after we were married, he took the Air Force entrance exam and scored 100% on all four parts. Unfortunately, he flunked the physical because of health problems.

I thought he was the smartest, most talented, and most gospel-centered man in the world. He was also so cute. I didn't think I was very good-looking, and I wondered why he had chosen me.

All in all, I had expected it to be a great marriage.

Two weeks after we were married in the Salt Lake Temple, he began school at a university in the state where his parents lived. It was far from my home, but I was the only member in my family, so I looked forward to being a part of his large Mormon family. On our first Sunday as young marrieds I jumped out of bed to get ready for Church, but he stayed in bed. At first, I was worried that he was sick, so I asked, "Aren't you going to go to church today?"

"No," he replied, "I don't know how to be married—I've never been married before." I thought he was teasing me, so I replied, "I don't know how to be married either!" But his further response was "You just go." Then he turned over to go back to sleep.

I felt hurt and rejected—and alone. But on the very first Sunday of our married life, I went off to our student ward by myself.

It was to be like that for the two years we stayed at the state college. I went to church every Sunday, usually by myself. He just didn't want to go. Since he had recently returned from serving a mission before we were married, I didn't understand his attitude, but I tried to be cheerful. I tried to believe if I could be a good example, eventually he'd want to come with me.

Another blow awaited me when we both got our first paychecks. I was sitting at the table figuring out how much tithing we owed when he announced, "I'm not going to pay tithing. I got out of the habit when I was on my mission. You can pay it on your check if you want to; but I think Heavenly Father knows we're students—we'll do it later."

This was so confusing to me. I was the one who was the fairly recent convert. He was the lifetime member from the good family.

I really tried to figure out what was wrong with our marriage. This wasn't like the movies. This wasn't like my teachers described in Mutual. This wasn't what I read about in my college marriage text. It wasn't like my dreams. I felt like I had to walk on eggshells about everything I cared about—church, tithing, being kind, trying to get along. I certainly wasn't the bride I'd dreamed of becoming. Still, my friends had always called me "Pollyanna," and I really tried to be that cheerful, unfailingly optimistic girl.

I praised him and encouraged him. I helped him study. I did everything I knew how to do. He wanted his dinner on the table at five o'clock, and I made sure it was. He wanted to drive the five hours to his family's home every weekend. As tired as I sometimes was because I worked six days every week, I went along cheerfully. He wanted to stay up and play Hearts with his family until three in the morning. That was difficult for me because I'm not a night owl. I didn't do very well at this. But what was harder was that he seemed to relish sarcasm. It frightened me.

This was supposed to be a joyous time of my life, but it was not. One night we were lying in bed talking together and all of a sudden he said, "You know, I ought to be able to have two wives. You are very organized and very smart, but you aren't very fun or very domestic. I think you should learn to sew like my mother and sisters."

I was devastated. I had tried so hard to please him in every way. It was true that I didn't know how to sew, but I could cook and bake circles around his family. I tried to be a fun person—his family loved to water ski together and to go fishing and swimming, they played board games till the wee hours of the morning, and they all loved to play Hearts. I wasn't good at any of those things, but I tried to do them. I guess I wasn't very successful. Here was my new husband telling me I wasn't domestic because I couldn't sew, and I wasn't very fun. Here was my new husband telling me he wanted a second wife. I was devastated.

Another night came when I was lying in bed, exhausted from work and alone. Our student apartment was tiny and only had two rooms: a bedroom and a living room with kitchen appliances in a row along the far wall.

He came in late that night with a friend. He didn't even bother to come tell me he was home. I guess he assumed I was asleep, because he had come to know that I wasn't a night person. He was studying with a friend who was a graduate student. Because my husband was so smart and tested so highly, the university had permitted him to enroll in a graduate experimental psychology class. That night as I lay in my bed trying to fall asleep, I heard my husband of two months contrive a plan with his fellow student.

I could not believe what I heard. My mind recoiled with horror at the plan these two students were hatching! They were enrolled in a class which required spending a semester logging experimental trials with mice and their performance in mazes. Following weekly labs, they were to turn in that week's results into the box on the professor's door. Their credit would follow the completion of sixteen weekly trials over the course of the semester. I heard them plan that every week one of them would "steal" a lab report from the teacher's box, copy the results, and then change enough of the data that it would not be an exact replica of another student's actual trial test. Then they would sneak back up to the lab and return both the stolen original and their fabricated copy.

I was stunned. I tried to make sense of what I had heard. Could I have misunderstood? Tears coursed silently down my cheeks as the harsh truth sunk in.

I didn't understand. He was so smart. He got 100% on the Air Force entrance exam. The university let him take a graduate course while he was only a junior. Why would he do this? I considered telling him what I had overheard. But I was too afraid. Why was I afraid? I didn't know. He had yelled at me and sworn at me. He had been sarcastic and had compared me to his family many times. But I had a fear of something more. I had only been married two months.

When grades came in that semester, even with the cheating in lab, my very "smart" husband got below a "D" average. How did he do that? I got up and went to work every day to pay our bills, so I wasn't aware of how or where he spent his day. How could the man who had gotten a 3.81 GPA the semester before let his grades drop so far? It was a double hurt to me because I loved school and excelled in it, but I was willingly foregoing my own education to support him in his.

The grade issue got worse when the day after he got his grade report in the mail, he taunted me, "This wouldn't have happened if I had married my old girl friend."

Sometimes I got up and went to work feeling like a hollow person. I don't know how I smiled and greeted the customers at my job in the student bookstore.

I thought I had married a spiritual, smart, talented, competent, and handsome man. What I really married was a *huge* potential and a very small reality. He was like a demanding child. But I still hoped for the best. After all, I reasoned, "People can grow up." I held on to the belief that if I prayed hard enough, fasted faithfully enough, and was patient long enough, Heavenly Father would answer the righteous prayer of my heart and everything would be just fine. After all, we had eternity, and I was so sure that I had approached this marriage with the right attitude and the right commitment. I had prayed, and I had fasted. So had he. I still clung to the hope that things would improve.

I carefully wrote in my daily plan book, "Matthew 3:7." I believed with all my heart that if I just looked at my own "beams," and not his "motes," things would get better.

I think that, for me, my heart broke the day of my twenty-seventh birthday. We had a good friend who worked at the studio where the

Osmonds filmed their television variety program. She knew that my husband and I both loved drama, so she had gotten passes on the day of my birthday for us to spend the day watching the filming. I was so excited, and I honestly thought he would be too. But when I told him of our plans, he was kind of surly and said, "You go. I don't want to go. I'll keep the baby."

I asked a girlfriend to go with me. I was determined to have a happy birthday, even though my husband apparently didn't want to spend it with me. So I left early in the morning to drive to the studio. It was a happy, exciting, fun-filled birthday for me watching a television program being filmed, although I still couldn't help wondering why he didn't want to spend the day with me. My friend and I returned home at about five o'clock. As we turned down the street to my apartment, we drove past my husband and a woman I did not know walking together, hand-in-hand, laughing and talking and pushing our stroller with my little daughter in it.

My friend was so embarrassed she couldn't say a thing to me when she drove in front of the apartment to let me off. I was numb as the two of them realized who had just come home. The girl looked away as he introduced us. I can't remember what I said or how I acted.

I do vividly remember that night in bed when he said, "You know, the Church is apostate. I should be able to have two wives. You can be the organized one. But I deserve to have a fun one, too. I deserve to have a wife who makes me laugh and is domestic, too." The coldness of his voice matched the coldness of my fear and the coldness of my heartache. I did not know what to do or what to say. Later he blamed me, saying, "You should have fought for me when I said that to you."

Shortly after that event, he graduated, and we moved to accept a job in another city. Although I didn't know it at the time, she followed us in our move.

His angry words became aggression. He would grab my shoulders and shake me. Then he would hit me on the arm, leaving bruises, but he'd always say, "I was just kidding." One night—the only night in our marriage I did not have dinner on the table promptly at five o'clock—he came home and became enraged. He opened a can of pork and beans, threw them in a pan, and broke the dinner plate on the stove as he ranted about his dinner not being ready. I was scared to death. By this time, I was pregnant with our third child. When I had discovered at my six week check-up that I was pregnant, he raged at me, "How could you do this to me? We can't afford this!"

By this time, he had left the girlfriend that had followed us. Now he was always talking about his secretary. For her twenty-first birthday, he insisted on making her a homemade German chocolate cake, and he bought her a pair of 24-carat gold earrings. Off he went to work bearing cake, earrings, card, and balloons. "It's her twenty-first birthday," he said to me. "It ought to be special."

Four months later, I got nothing for my birthday—not even a card.

He was rarely home. When he was, he was in the darkroom he had created in our bathtub, developing the photographs that he and his sec-retary had taken on one of their expeditions.

I was afraid to talk to him because he just got mad. I was afraid to confront him about the secretary, because I didn't want to accuse him. But how do you hurt someone you love? I didn't know. I could still see all the potential, abilities, and talents. I was still waiting for him to grow up.

My closest friend told me she thought I was depressed. Although I had kept my private shame a secret, even from her, she told me she felt I was "hiding my light under a bushel." I didn't think I had any light any-more. Is that what depression is? No light? If that was it, I *was* depressed. I lost any confidence I had once enjoyed in my talents and abilities.

I guess he had long since forgotten that I had any talents or abilities. I had pretty much forgotten myself. I clung to the Church. My husband told me I was a fanatic. I tried to be a good mom. I tried to be a good Primary teacher and a good spiritual living teacher (I had both callings at the same time). I tried to be a good neighbor. I tried to do a good job in my daughter's preschool co-op. I tried to look nice in hand-me down maternity clothes from my sister-in-law. He said I was a slob. He told me I was fat and ugly and smelled. He told me, "No man would ever want you."

And then, one night in our bedroom, he became especially enraged with me. He picked up our Tiffany lamp, the one we had chosen and cherished together, the one with the glass mosaic tiles. He hurled it across the room at me. I ducked. It hit the wall behind me and shattered into thousands of colored shards.

I collapsed in a pool of splintered glass. Shattered, like the lamp we had both cherished. I guess I felt like the lamp. In an instant of pure madness, a lamp was shattered. A person was shattered.

How do you break something beautiful? How do you break something you have loved? How do you break someone you have loved? I did not know.

I was broken and depressed and sad. To my neighbors and ward members and friends, I kept up appearances. I had never told my family what was going on. Fortunately for my deception, they lived three thousand miles away, so I could write newsy letters about the kids.

But on Palm Sunday, everything changed. Because I had been raised in another denomination, I was very conscious of Palm Sunday, the Sunday before Easter. I had gone to Church with my children, who were all little at the time. We had been challenged in sacrament meeting to increase our temple attendance. Although I kept a current temple recommend, he had not had one for eight years. And so I went home with new enthusiasm of a new intensity, but the absolute naiveté of an inexperienced young woman.

After putting the kids down for a nap, I went into the living room. I thought I was being forthright and sincere as I entreated him to become worthy to receive a temple recommend. I told him I needed for him to come home, to stop his relationship with his secretary, to stop swearing at me, and to stop drinking. I thought I was being very calm and rational and making reasonable requests.

He struck me across the face. He grabbed me, picked me up, and threw me into the wall. He was screaming at me, "I'll kill you, you b——!" Over and over he threw me into the walls and yelled that he was going to kill me. He was maniacal.

I thought I was going to die, if not from violence, then from fear. I finally escaped and fled through the back door to my neighbor's. She went over to my house to get the children. He barricaded her in the house. She never told me what happened. She said I don't need to know. He finally bolted out of the house, got in our car, and roared out of the driveway. Later we discovered that he had driven the eight hundred miles to his parents' home.

But it was over. I was devastated, but my four little children were there. I needed to function.

How had this happened? Where were my dreams? How did things go so terribly wrong? What had happened to my temple marriage? I did not understand. I still don't.

The hardest concept I've had to accept in my life is the principle of agency. No matter how hard one person tries, she cannot overcome another person's freedom to make his own choices. But it is hard to understand agency when what you want so badly is righteous. I knew it was righteous to want my marriage to work. But I couldn't make it work.

Which leads me to the other hard principle I had to grapple with. I could only do my part of the process. For so long he had accused me of trying to be his conscience. I am guilty. I did try to be his conscience. I thought he was a righteous person who just hadn't quite grown up yet. I thought of him as "Peter Pan," and I believed that if I were patient he would grow up. So I tried to be his conscience until he could get his own. A day came when I realized he was not going to get one.

I went into mourning. It was horrible enough to face the prospect of a divorce. It is agonizing to go through one, even ones that are necessary.

I was so sad. No, I was worse. I was crushed. He left with a master's degree, his secretary-mistress, and both of our cars. I was left with a broken heart, no education, and a broken-down furnace in the middle of winter. I cried daily. I functioned on autopilot. I took care of my children's basic needs, but I would not have won "the fun mom contest." In seven years, we saw one movie. We made every cheap tuna and macaroni and cheese casserole known to the most frugal of mothers. My kitchen sink had to be turned on with a pair of vice grips. My good friend continued to remind me that "my light was hidden under a bushel."

I thought she was mistaken about my light being hidden. It was extinguished.

About a year after the divorce, another friend in my ward lined me up with a man who worked with her husband. I'm sure he was a very nice man and he was a gentleman, but I came home from that first post-divorce date and was sick all night long.

Life was not good. I felt self-loathing. My former husband had spent ten years criticizing me, belittling me, and controlling my life. When it was over, he had won. I believed his words.

It was a slow, struggling journey back to the confidence of the young woman who had married with stars in her eyes and dreams in her heart. My stars had faded into the lusterless look of depression and my dreams were dashed. I felt like a colossal failure. On top of failure, I wrapped myself in guilt. My bishop and stake president said nice things to me. Sometimes my mind heard them, but my heart couldn't hear them. Yet the words were sustaining.

In my lifetime, I have witnessed miracles related to other people. Then I had one myself. It was through this miracle that I was able to finally gain an understanding of what I was living through. Up until that time, my husband kept telling me that I was confused, or that I hadn't understood, or that I had misinterpreted what he had said. He felt that he was never wrong, and therefore he never had to be sorry. I, on the other hand, was always wrong and ought to be grateful to him for putting up with me. He frequently told me the only reason that he stayed was for the children. I had no problem believing that.

The day of my miracle was a spring day shortly before Easter. I hadn't had any new clothes for years. One of my friends told me she had some extra material, and she'd like to make an Easter dress for me. I was grateful and happy, so I went over to her house for a fitting. As I walked into her family room where she had set up her sewing machine, I stepped on a sheaf of papers.

I bent down, picked them up, and set them on her table saying, "Linda, I found these papers on your floor."

She picked them up, and then with a puzzled look on her face said, "I can't imagine how these papers got here. These have been filed for years in my bedroom file. I haven't looked at them or thought about them for ages." She began to tell me that approximately seven years before, her youngest brother had gotten into repeated trouble with the law. He had been violent to members of the family. He accepted no responsibility for his behaviors. In fact, he blamed everyone around him for his shortcomings. He lied even about things that were silly to lie about. He appeared to have no conscience and no empathy for how his actions were affecting the rest of the family. Finally, the parents made an appointment with a therapist to see how to help their son, who was by now locked up in a juvenile detention facility.

This paper was what Linda and her family had been given seven years before, to help them understand her brother. It had been in her file, undisturbed all those years.

Until now, when it landed three rooms away, on the floor in her family room.

As I read this paper called "The Sociopathic Personality," my mind and heart were opened to a truth I had not ever before known. It described individuals who function without a conscience. It described my husband.

It was *not* me who was confused or wrong.

For ten years I had lived believing something was very wrong with me. Through a miracle just for me, the truth was revealed. I read it. I felt it. I got it!

In my college English classes, I had learned of the point of enlightenment. Finding this five-page article was my point of enlightenment. I could start to crawl out from under the heavy bushel of despair. My patriarchal blessing told me I was to be a "light." I had believed that my blessing no longer pertained to me because I was a divorced female in a

❧

church which celebrates marriage and family. But I discovered there are victims in some marriages.

This was also a new revelation, because I had believed "it takes two to tango" and "it takes two to fight" and "it takes two to wreck a marriage." It was a happy day for me when I could believe that those three stereotypes are not always true.

Another pivotal occurrence for me came in an interview with my bishop. I will love him and his position forever for this gift. I had been the spiritual living teacher in Relief Society for a number of years. I made an appointment with the bishop to tell him I understood that he needed to release me because, after all, no ward could have a spiritual living teacher who was going through a divorce.

He said, with the most kind and gentle voice, "Why would I release you? You haven't done anything wrong."

His words, his kindness, and his gentleness sustained me through the rough times and tormenting days and harrowing weeks and years that seemed to last for eternity—but not the good kind of eternity.

As I write this today, twenty years later, I still wish that I had never had to go through a divorce. I still wince when an occasion comes up where I have to report this. I hate that in my permanent papers file, there is a divorce decree. I hate that this has to be on my family group sheet. I feel so sorrowful for the burdens this has given—and continues to give—my children. I do not like that my former husband despises me today. I grieve over the ongoing mean-spiritedness he exhibits to my children. It makes forgiveness the new challenge of my mortal life. I would give almost anything to be able to rewrite my history, and I would erase this divorce.

But I do not want to erase all the lessons I have learned, all the compassion I have gained, and the confidence I have now, born of continuing in the face of what appeared to me, at the time, to be insurmountable obstacles. So, while I would never have wished for this, I suppose my *self* is a product of the suffering I have experienced.

Suffering. Depression. Who needs them?

In the end, I did. Depression became the loathsome companion who walked me to the fiery furnace, dragging me further into the heat when I thought I could only be silver. I told my bishop, "I can only reach 'silver,' I can't do 'gold.'" Yet the Lord revealed to me that I had it in me to achieve gold.

And depression—my loathsome companion who walked me to the edge of despair and to the chasm of hopelessness—that loathsome companion also fanned the golden spark of divinity that was within me all the time. Depression was the catalyst that propelled me to summon the faith and courage to "keep on keeping on" in my reach towards my fledgling immortality.

*Though Debbie doesn't understand why her marriage evolved so differently than she had expected, she has been able to recover from her shattered illusions and create a happy, productive life for herself. When she served as a Relief Society president years ago, she was able to bring a degree of wisdom, born from her singular experiences, to help the divorced sisters in her ward. They, too, were facing the destruction of their dreams and wondered about their place in the Church. In Debbie, they found an example to inspire them, comfort them, and give them hope.*

*The young couple in this story shared the same religion, race, and socio-economic status; however, their value choices about truth, honesty, church attendance, tithing, and many other subjects created serious marital problems. Perhaps the initial value conflicts could have been bridged through repentance, spiritual counsel, and marriage therapy. However, the descent into unrepentant sin, violence, and abuse resulted in the destruction of their marriage.*

*Far more common than this example is the unequal yoking of a couple with differing faiths, cultures, ethnicity, race, education levels, or social class. Any of these differences are potential conflicts. These conflicts can be resolved and frequently are; frequently they are not. The critical point is for the couple to realize that these differences may be flash points of conflict if they are not addressed.*

*It is a sad truth to learn that "love is not enough" to make a marriage work. Commitment to shared values is essential to an enduring marriage.*

# I Am the Wretched One

*O wretched man that I am! who shall deliver me*
*from the body of this death?*
*Romans 7:24*

I can't tell you when it started but I can tell you when it hit full force: Friday at work. I wanted to cry all the time. I felt as if I were "the wretched one"—the awful one the Lord "hated." I know the Lord doesn't hate, but I was sure it was me who would teach him to hate. I was sure I was "off my gourd."

I remember saying good-bye to one of my co-workers. I hugged her and started to sob. She said, "Go home this weekend and do something fun, get your mind off work." She thought work had pushed me over. I guess in part it had.

\* \* \*

Loneliness gave me a shove, too. It's hard being thirtyish and single—in or out of the Church. It seems as if everyone I know is married with kids. I feel abnormal.

*At least I'm fat,* I think to myself, *and people can see the obvious reason why nobody wants me.* How's that for self-esteem? Then I started noticing that fat people are married. Well . . . they probably were skinny at first, and then they gained weight. People say, "You have a pretty face." Yeah, I know. Wow, if people only had a clue how bad that makes me feel about the rest of me.

The worst is feeling that I'm letting the Lord down. *Maybe I am doing something that is preventing me from getting married,* I think. *Well, then, all hope is gone.*

In our doctrine, it states something like if I'm worthy, and I don't get married in this life, I will receive all the blessings in the next life. *What if it's me and I'm not worthy?* That's so scary. I've even thought about eternal life below the celestial kingdom and does that stress me out! I only want the celestial kingdom, but I can't get there alone. That is so scary.

I've gone to Young Single Adult dances and activities for eleven years, and not once have I been asked out or asked to dance (unless you count friends asking for *pity* dances). It's hard. I thought men who know the truth would act differently, but I guess they're human.

This marriage issue is one of the reasons I've been suffering this depression. I know the Church is true, and I am not saying it's the Church's fault. I absolutely love the doctrine, and I would love to be married, but it isn't happening, and that is "depressing." It is devastating when I feel my salvation is on the line.

*Can't any man find my heart? I think I am funny and cute. I would be a great wife and mother.*

These are deep down feelings that I'm sharing. Usually I keep them locked up tight.

Guess what? The depression actually helped me accept life the way it comes. I'm trusting in the Lord, and if I am to be married, it will happen. If not, there are a lot of advantages, too. Oh, my. See I feel guilty even saying that. I feel as if I have to put the disclaimer, "Of course, I'd rather be married."

Seems like any way I turn, it's bleak. I always feel my family thinks I'm a failure because I'm not married. I dread Christmas and family gatherings. My cousin, who is ten years my junior, always brings her beau. I always feel like I've failed.

* * *

That night after work, I went to the scriptures. Usually just reading makes me feel better, but not this time. I wrote scriptures on cards to keep in my pockets—nothing helped. I read them over and over. *Why is it not helping?* I asked myself. *My thoughts must be true. I'm awful, and the Lord no longer can help me.*

Saturday I went to go shopping with my mom. I tried to speak to her. I felt like a freak. "What are you talking about?" she'd say. She didn't have a clue to the agony I felt. At the end of the day I left in tears. I had a social engagement—a dinner at a friend's. My cousin would be there and it was at my neighbor's house, so there was no way out. I felt as if they all could see right through me, as if I had "the wretched one" marked on my forehead. I knew I was in hell.

\* \* \*

I really knew something was off with me because I was obsessively worrying about my teeth. My back molar was hurting. I went to the dentist, and he said, "You need a cap."

What?! *I'm going to lose all my teeth! It's bad enough no one wants to love me, but without teeth it will be impossible.* Logical thinking, right? I started asking everyone I knew, even strangers, "How many caps do you have?" I talked and worried so much about my teeth that my co-worker dreamed she had lost all her teeth.

Three weeks of pure hell! *Help me get a grip! I really am going off my gourd. What's wrong with me?*

I couldn't focus. All I did was worry and cry. Despair caused so much fear and endless bellyaches. Soon I started having all sorts of worries. I was out of control worrying. I was driving the people around me nuts. Oh, yeah, I never liked to use the word *nuts*. I even told my co-workers not to use that word, or any words like it, because I was sure I was nuts.

\* \* \*

When Sunday came, I lay in bed telling myself, "Get it together. This will pass—*Tell no one.*" I cried through the sacrament song. Then I pulled my Relief Society president, who I knew was a therapist, into a Sunday School room and through tear-drenched eyes and with a voice of pure desperation I begged: "You have to help me."

She said, "With what?"

I explained all that had happened. She told me three things I needed to do:

1. Get a blessing
2. Call a doctor and be evaluated for medication
3. See a therapist

OK, one and three I could do, but medication, no way. My Relief Society president was firm: medication was a must. After about three times of hearing that, I agreed. Boy, was I scared. I was afraid that I finally went nuts. I received a blessing, but still felt no comfort. What was happening to me? In all my life I had never experienced a time when I wasn't comforted by the scriptures, church, or at least a blessing. *God must hate me*, I thought. *I know he's punishing me for all the gossiping I'm doing, or for judging others—oh, that's it for sure.* I just couldn't figure it out.

The next day I went to see the doctor. A good friend made me promise that I would do *everything* my doctor and therapist said. I am careful to take the medication exactly as prescribed, and it has made me feel better. It has helped me gain the edge I need so that I can concentrate on therapy and make some lifestyle changes that will really heal me.

I also started seeing a therapist, and she educated me on what was happening to me.

"Am I having a nervous breakdown?" I asked.

"No," she explained, "nerves can't break. You're having a major depressive break."

*Oh, great!* I thought. The two sounded the same to me, but what wasn't the same was what I thought and what she taught me. She gave me knowledge. She helped me to see what was really happening to me and suggested ways to deal with my depression. A great therapist is the greatest tool to battle depression. Somehow just knowing what it was made me feel better.

* * *

For me, the first medication I was on made me feel worse. The second kind really helped, but it did take five weeks to make a difference. Also, the doctor had to work with my dosage. It takes time. It's hard to wait, but trust me, it will help. My therapist told me that if I hadn't gone to my doctor to get medicine, she would have admitted me to the hospital. (If I were telling you this, the word *hospital* would have been whispered.) Please don't just depend on your medication, however. You need to follow your doctor's and your therapist's suggestions to help yourself heal. Healing involves all aspects of your life, not just medication. Medicine can only give you the lift you need to be able to implement other changes or behaviors into your life that can truly heal you.

I still had a long road, and today reading the scriptures is hard. I'm still recovering from the depression. I guess the hardest part of depression is how it makes you feel distant from Heavenly Father. How it makes you feel like you're being punished.

There is hope. I can write that only because today is a good day. You see, hope comes in patches. First it is an itty-bitty patch. As you hang on to that, you learn how to help the patches of hope grow. The secret is to completely enjoy the *good* moments. I remember thinking to myself, "Wow, I felt normal for a second." Oh, how I enjoyed that second. The next time the second was longer.

I believe that's the secret. Also, knowing that this was only a trial, like all the other trials I've been through. That helped me to focus my view on eternity and not just the miserable moments that passed so slowly.

"Hope Springs Eternal." Sheryl Crow sings that in one of her songs. It does spring eternal and it is a gift from God. Pray for it. I remember just praying for a desire to have hope. It will come. I promise. Just hold on.

*Singleness, loneliness, body image issues. These issues—being single, feeling lonely and/or isolated, and feeling too fat, too thin, or too flabby—may be separate or intertwined, but they are all frequent issues within the therapy process. Also, each of these worries may be found in combination with other emotional concerns. What is particularly moving and illustrative in this story is that it highlights the complexity of human beings. In the midst of extreme suffering—to the point of feeling suicidal—this young woman maintained a high level of performance in her career and in her church responsibility. Although not everyone is able to do this, many can. This sister held herself together in public and then went into total "meltdown" at home every night and every weekend. While her social situation has not changed a great deal, her feelings about herself and life have changed dramatically for the better.*

## My Daughter with Jello-Blue Hair

She wears all black clothes, fire-engine red fingernail polish, silver snake bracelets, and a skull ring on her middle finger. She says she has her own style. I am perplexed by how black-on-black-on-black can be style.

More than anything she loves her cat, Urchin. I have often wondered at the cosmic humor that led her to name her Siamese mix such a prescient name.

She has just gotten out of a year-long residential treatment program. So far, her 145 IQ has only empowered her to get in more trouble in four years than her four siblings have gotten into all their years put together.

She is my daughter. Her name is Haney (this is my mother's maiden name). Where do I start to explain Haney?

Birth. She was one of those babies who arched her back away from cuddling. She never slept. She was allergic to milk. Before she could stand or walk, she could knock her sister over. She had a twenty-four word vocabulary at nine months old. When she was two-and-a-half, she went to a grocery store with my mother. While perched in the child seat of the shopping cart in the check-out lane, she leaned over to the candy display. She began pulling suckers out of the display rack and counted thirty-seven lollipops to the amazement of the checker and my mother.

About that same time I took her shopping with me. As I pushed my cart down an aisle, there was a display of miniature, two-toned stuffed bears. She grabbed a honey color and beige little bear about six inches high and announced to me, "This bear's name is Juliana." (She pronounced the name Juliana as "Joo lah nah" as though this was a basic ordinary sort of a name one hears every day. I've never heard the name before or since.) She hugged that bear as if Juliana were her lifeline. Obviously, I bought Juliana. At that precise moment in the department store, it appeared I had two choices: buy Juliana or leave Haney at the store. Juliana came home.

And that was Haney. Our family called her Sugar Bear. One minute she could be as cute as a cub, then she could switch in an instant to the Momma Bear from Hell. She is now twenty-three years old and the only material possession to which she has maintained a long-term attachment is Juliana.

Preschool. Haney was precocious. That's the nice word. Frequently she was reckless. One day her Sunbeam teacher, who was a longtime elementary school teacher in our Utah town, told me Haney was the single most creative child she had ever taught. While the other Sunbeams were coloring pictures of animals of the earth for a creation lesson, Haney was dismantling the tape dispenser and making Scotch tape animal sculptures.

Age Three. Haney already had a mind of her own. One day she and her dearest friend Tamber (a like-minded child) decided to hide in a backyard shed. Tamber's mom and I became worried when neither little girl would come when we called. Pretty soon our whole neighborhood was searching for the two little girls. We even called the police. Three hours later, they came out of the shed, hand-in-hand, smiling and laughing.

We were not smiling and laughing. Years later, Haney admitted to me that she and Tamber had heard everyone calling for them the whole time, but they thought it was funny.

A study in contrasts. That's what Haney was. A child who fearlessly tackled a boy twice her size. A child who terrorized her older siblings with her inventive meanness. She thought Candyland was boring, but locking her siblings in the bathroom was great fun. And yet, this same child, at age three, announced, "I'm going to be a vet, but I am only going to be a bear vet. I am going to make house calls in my bear van to give the bears shots." She always thought dolls were stupid. The Christmas right before her fourth birthday she asked Santa for a "bear with bear clothes."

First Grade. Haney's first grade teacher told me this story at teacher conference. "The office aide had brought the children's class pictures to the classroom for distribution right before the Christmas holidays. When the stack of pictures was delivered, Haney's picture happened to be on the top. Craig, one of Haney's first grade classmates, saw the picture and exclaimed, 'Teacher, teacher, come look at this picture of Haney. She looks like an angel, but she ain't. She's mean as an alligator!'"

Sixth Grade. Haney's sixth grade teacher was our stake president. He had been teaching for forty years. This was his last year before he retired. He expelled her. Not suspended, expelled. He was crushed. He told me he had never expelled a girl student in his career. He began to have nightmares about it. Haney, who thought it was "no big deal," became a sixth-grade folk hero. I was mortified. I didn't even want to go to stake conference anymore.

Eighth Grade. 2:00 A.M. I am awakened by a loud, persistent knock on the door. My husband and I go to the door to find two police officers who ask, "What kind of car do you drive?"

"A two-door red Subaru."

"Do you know where it is?"

"Yes, sir, in the garage."

"I don't think so, folks. Sorry to tell you but we just picked up two fourteen-year-old boys and two thirteen-year-old girls driving your car, in the dark. We caught them because none of them knew how to turn on the headlights. You'll have to go to the police station and pick up your daughter. She'll have a referral to juvenile court for 'joyriding.'" I had never heard of joyriding, but I wasn't feeling very much joy. I cried the rest of the night.

We began the juvenile court appearances. Haney didn't appear to be affected by them. She wore her most offensive black T-shirts to court. The one that horrified me the most was "Jane's Addiction." If you've never heard of them, say a prayer of thanks. The T-shirt picture was worse than their music. I used to pray she'd lose that shirt. She lost so many things or had them stolen, but that one somehow stayed. It was her favorite, probably because she knew I loathed the repulsive silk-screened picture on the front.

She had five winter coats lost or stolen that year. She traded so many T-shirts I saw new grotesque silk-screened punk and heavy metal slogans all the time. But that shirt kept making frequent appearances. I used to tell my husband that I thought "Jane's Addiction" multiplied in her closet like some rat family.

It was her favorite shirt to wear to court. I had read somewhere to always wear pink to court. I did. But I found myself crying frequently. I was grieving for the daughter who defied me and verbally assaulted me on a daily basis.

Every time—all twenty-six of them—that I had to go to that court I felt physically ill. One time I was throwing up because I was so ashamed. My husband had to go without me. Every time we went, I felt hollow. My heart was clenched in a vise and every court appearance turned the crank of my heart-vise another notch into the pain of depression. In that court-room I could not breathe. My lungs and heart together burst with anguish. I wanted to move from the community. I was the director of a large program that served handicapped children. I was visible in the community. Suddenly I prayed to be invisible. I cried silently in court, and I cried noisily to myself at night.

The police knew her well. She had been picked up for curfew violation (she sneaked out her window). She was picked up for truancy. I drove her to the front door of the school (she went through the back door). She had been picked up for "doing Scotchguard" (sniffing an inhalant) in Denny's—at the next booth over from four police officers. It seemed to me she was on a self-destruct course at warp speed. I could not relate to this daughter in any way. I had been such a fearful child I had never thought to do a rebellious thing. I did not have high "freedom needs." She lived for what she called "freedom." She constantly said, "No one can control me when I'm eighteen." I hadn't observed that anyone could control her at thirteen.

The first time she was sent to juvenile detention, I went to see her. Juvenile detention was in a cold, musty basement with small barren rooms. Only a cot and a stainless steel toilet with no cover were in the room. I truly thought I might die right in that place. The image of that dank place where our society puts throw-away children turned my stomach. I felt sick. I was sick. I was powerless. I wanted to grab her and hold her and make this insanity end.

She was cold and dispassionate and snarled at me, "The next time you come, bring my cat."

She was locked up in juvenile detention. And she wanted to see her cat. I thought it was totally positive that this tough-talking, rules-defying teen wanted a passive little blue-eyed Siamese cat with a white triangle marking on his nose and four white paws. I got in trouble for bringing Urchin. I now know that cats cannot visit jail, even kiddie jail. I think that is very sad. I would have become an activist for pet visitors to jail, but I had no energy for even normal routine things like brushing my teeth. Most of my energy I had to save to stop the tears. By this time, I had cried so much, I felt numb. I no longer had any joy in life. It was all effort and duty and despair.

This was the year that my daughter snarled her life philosophy to me in a moment of pure rage. She had come in late one night wearing a black leather jacket which smelled like three cartons of smoked cigarettes. I was furious, and I'm not a furious-type person. But this night I grabbed the offending jacket while my daughter was in the bathroom and hurled it through the garage door. My daughter, who would not have noticed an elephant sitting in our living room at that point in her life, noticed immediately that the jacket was gone.

In abject rage, she screamed at me, "Mom, why don't you just accept that I'm one of those people who has to learn everything the hard way?"

My personality is such that I would have made a great Pharisee who had to count the steps on Sunday. I am so rules-based I make myself frustrated. And I have a child who daily assaults my value system and my conservative ways. I am the Gospel Doctrine teacher, and she is a charter member of the local police department's "Most Wanted" juvenile delinquents.

There seemed to be no focal point for her rage. She spewed it all over me, her dad, and her teachers. Her personality, which had always been high-spirited anyway, became more and more intense, aggressive, and violent. The only thing she continued to love passionately was her cat. I began to love Urchin as passionately as she did. I held on to the idea that if she could love a Siamese cat that much, she couldn't be all bad.

One night her father came home from work, and she had spray-painted black graffiti all over the inside of our garage: "Die, Dad, Die."

It was then we discovered the drugs. I was truly shocked. Maybe I shouldn't have been, but I was. Although she had continued her smoking in spite of all the Reader's Digest articles I made her read (I paid her to read them—$10 a page—a mother gets desperate!), I had never believed she would do drugs. She had always been such a "control freak"—she wanted to control everything and she was always talking about "control." I honestly thought we were safe from that one.

How wrong I was. Her juvenile probation officer (he and I were on a first-name basis after all her arrests) told me that he, too, was shocked by the level and intensity of her drug usage. He said, "I have been doing my job for eighteen years, and I don't miss much with kids. I've seen it all, but I didn't suspect Haney was doing drugs, either."

Haney did them all. Pot. Acid. Amphetamines. Crystal Meth. PCP. You can tell you're the mom of a kid doing drugs when you know all the street names. I remember my good old days when a "Mary Jane" was a black shoe with a thick strap over the arch. Now a "Mary Jane" is another name for marijuana. It's also called "weed," "roach," "grass," "bud." I gained a drug vocabulary.

But the worst was still to come. One day, Haney's older sister and the sister's best friend were laughing and talking in our den. I overheard the friend say to my daughter, "All the kids at school are talking about Haney. They call her a 'druggie slut.'"

A "druggie slut." I had never heard those words before either. I had buckled under disgust at "Jane's Addiction." I had gone to visit her in kiddie jail—many times. I had confronted polysubstance abuse. By this time, the smoking seemed the small stuff.

But "druggie slut?" My tears were dry. But my heart was broken. I felt something in me die when I heard those awful words. The unthinkable descended upon my naïve mind like the shovels of dirt to cover a coffin. It was too heavy. I was shut into my own cold vault.

The words "druggie slut" had punched me in the stomach. But the punch that knocked me out was the day my daughter screamed at me, "I'm going to kill you—you deserve to die!" I sank from depression and despair straight into agony.

I learned a lot about juvenile court. I got to go twenty-six times. I was humiliated. The judge was furious. The last time we went, he gave her a lecture about her "God-given IQ" that she was "wasting." He then shook his finger at us, the parents, and blamed us. Couldn't he see I was dying right before his eyes? Didn't he know we had done everything we could think of? Didn't he see the reams of police reports that showed all the therapy, psychological evaluations, counseling, and outdoor wilderness experiences we had paid for to try and interrupt her self destruction? Didn't he see the mother, sitting in one more pink suit, whose eyes were puffy and red from hours of tears? Didn't he see the two people who got up and went to work every day and did their church jobs faithfully? That day, the judge put me on trial. When he shook his finger at me and directed his red-faced rage towards me, I descended into the final level of a depression that would consume me. I was already on the brink. That day, January 4, I went right over the edge.

He ordered Haney away to residential treatment.

For the second time in my forty-year life, I knew I needed help. I found a therapist who specialized in helping parents of a "Haney" kind of kid. By this time, professionals had given her eleven different psychiatric diagnoses.

I could not cope. The only problem was the specialist was 324 miles from my home—one way. But I was so desperate to understand that I drove the distance twice a month.

While I went to treatment over 300 miles away, Haney was sent 90 miles away to the first treatment center—she lasted only eleven days.

The director there wanted to send her to a state hospital. I went to visit the adolescent unit. I saw a group of pale, zombie-looking kids. I couldn't let them send my daughter there. So the judge sent her to another residential treatment program. One of the worst days of my life was when I read my daughter's psychological report. A psychologist wrote,

"Haney has homicidal ideation [thoughts] and she could likely be a Charles Whitman and go up into a control tower and shoot eight people."

He might as well have shot me. Reading that sentence put me over the brink of over the brink. I had been sad, frustrated, and confused by the behavior of this child of my own flesh. I frequently thought we were as different as any two people could possibly be. I had been intimidated by her amazing intelligence. I had been the victim of her uncanny ability to pick up on people's most vulnerable parts and then punish them by exposing their weakness. She was a master manipulator. But, murderer?

Reading this cold black-and-white report calling my daughter homicidal, I began to unravel. I began to withdraw from my friends. I began a major withdrawal from my husband. He was struggling himself. After all, it was he who had been the brunt of the black spray paint: "Die, Dad, Die."

Was her rage the drugs? Was her rage her? Was her rage something I had done? Was her rage something we had done? I had thousands of questions and not one answer.

My heart was broken. I didn't think I could ever teach another Gospel Doctrine class. I didn't want to be looked at. I felt like I was wearing a scarlet letter. It was not an "A." It was a scarlet "F" for Failure. I had utterly, completely, undisputedly failed as a parent. Anytime a church speaker began a theme like "No success in life can compensate for failure in the home," I felt condemned.

Age Sixteen. Haney came home from Valley Treatment Center days before her sixteenth birthday. We were excited because we thought she was doing better. The first week back she brought her new friend "Turtle" home to meet us. We didn't know if this was to shock us or to share a friend. It did both. "Turtle," who was neither small nor benign-looking like a real turtle, had a bright orange Mohawk, a pierced eyebrow, a pierced nose, a lip ring, and dozens of studs and chains on his black leather jacket. He also had brass knuckles on his fingers. Haney shared her new friend who sat in our den and carried on a conversation that went something like "duh . . . and like . . . and man . . . and you know."

I was scared of "Turtle." Later my 6'4" not-too-skinny husband admitted he was, too. I guess we both perceived the message of the Holy Ghost exactly right because later that night, my husband discovered that the Swiss Army Utility knife another daughter had given him for Christmas was gone. Many months later, Haney told us "Turtle" was a Heroin addict.

I thought "Turtle" was bad. Turtle looked like a Howdy-Doody compared to her next friend, "Rodent." (I'm not making these names up—street kids all had monikers and they were not pretty.) "Rodent" came to our door one night looking for Haney. He had on white face makeup, black eyeliner, purple lipstick, a long flowing black trench coat, and a rat sitting on his shoulder. Not a mouse. A rat. A live rat. I had heard about "Rodent" but I had never expected to find him on my front porch. I was scared out of my mind.

One rare night, Haney actually talked to me. She seemed like a nice normal teen for about ten minutes. She was in a reflective mood. She said, "You know, Mom, I'm only sixteen years old and I have nine friends who have committed suicide." (I had only known about one—a boy who had been her closest friend at Valley Treatment Center had gone up in the canyon and put a shotgun to his head the day he was released from the facility.) While I struggled hard against nausea, she continued, " . . . and one skinhead friend from North Las Vegas who got murdered."

Who is this alien creature I call my daughter?

I cried so hard that night. I felt so helpless. I prayed and prayed and begged Heavenly Father to tell me what to do to help her. By this time she had been in twenty-four different mental-health treatment programs, and we had spent thousands of dollars to help her. The residential treatment program cost $70,000. I had to fight our insurance. They ended up paying a lot of it, but our share was beyond our financial abilities.

I prayed and cried. And cried and prayed. One night I had a dream. It was so vivid I woke my husband and told him. He said it was an answer to my prayers. In my dream, I heard a voice tell me, "All you can do is love her."

But I want to do more. I am compelled to do more. I make myself miserable. I make myself sick. I unravel more. I feel like I am coming apart and am powerless to stop. I stop praying; I stop crying. I function, barely.

Age Seventeen. My daughter lives in a storage shed in Provo, Utah. It is actually a long skeletal warehouse with twenty empty rooms that bands can rent to practice. Because it was never intended for habitation, there is one small toilet and sink, but no other amenities.

On her birthday, we send money. That is the only gift that has any meaning in her life right now. My married daughter, a student at BYU, picks up Haney from the shed and takes her to the store. Elizabeth tells Haney she can spend $25.00. Elizabeth calls me to report. "Haney bought *The Shining* (a Stephen King novel) and two large bottles of Gatorade. It cost $7.50 so I told her she could spend the other $18.00. Haney told me, 'A present isn't how much you spend, it's getting something you want, and I just got what I wanted.'" Go figure. My seventeen year old is living in a warehouse in one room with six other kids, including "Raven," "Roach," "Tiger Stripe," another girl named "Seven," and two names I can't remember. And for her birthday, she is happy with a Stephen King novel and two bottles of Gatorade. Soon after this birthday, Haney moves to Las Vegas.

Age Nineteen. "Hi, Mom, don't get upset." (I am amused to think after all we've been through she still thinks there is something that could upset me. I think on the yardstick of raw human emotion "upset" was a long time ago. Devastation seems more like it now. Or dread.)

"Mom, I've dyed my hair jello-blue."

"Oh, gee, Haney, is that all? I thought it was something serious." I have come a long ways. Jello-blue hair seems painless to me now. I have had to change my expectations for Haney. And I have had to realize she is a daughter of God. I am sure he loves her, jello-blue hair and all.

Age Nineteen and a half. "Hi, Mom." (I haven't heard from Haney for six months.) "Mom, I got a job and it pays good money. I dispatch tow trucks. I work the night shifts and they gave me a beeper." I ask (optimistically), "Haney, did the tow truck company let you keep your jello-blue hair?" "Oh, sure, Mom. They don't care. I work at night so no one sees me anyway."

Somehow, I never read in Mormonism 101 that a "good Mormon mother" raises a daughter who dispatches a tow truck and has jello-blue hair.

Age Nineteen and three-quarters. "Hi, Mom. Don't freak out. Please be happy for me. I'm going to Mexico this weekend and, Mom, I'm getting married!"

"Tell me about him, Haney."

"Well, Mom, he's awesome. I met him playing chess. He's a master chess player and I haven't played for years. After three nights I can beat him." (This is my daughter with the genius IQ who has no sense. She can play chess, but her ability to make sound judgments has been checkmated.)

I have learned a few investigative skills over the years. I discover that "Mr. Awesome" is twenty-six years older than Haney and unemployed and this is the good news. He has one son who has been missing for three and a half years and one son who is in prison. How do I tell my jello-blue-haired daughter who dispatches tow trucks that her "beloved" is probably a sociopath?

While I'm reeling from her announcement and striving to act happy for my daughter who is so obviously elated, she pauses, then rushes forth with a flurry of words.

"Mom, I'm making an adult decision to get married right now, and I want to have everything on the up-and-up with us. So I need to tell you. The part about my jello-blue hair is true. And the part about my having a beeper and working a night shift is true. But, Mom, don't freak out, I don't dispatch tow trucks. I dispatch 'strippers.'"

Some black hole swallows me. I can't breathe, but I have to breathe. She can still surprise me, this daughter of mine. I have to love my daughter. I have to be "present" for her. She is going to Mexico to get married tomorrow. I never knew strippers were "dispatched." Well, of course, I never knew anything about strippers.

With every ounce of strength I can gather, I hold on to a positive voice, and I wish her well. I tell her I am happy for her. I know as this lie crosses my lips that it is a kind lie. I have a sinking and prophetic feeling that Haney will someday regret this decision. I feel it is the Holy Ghost whispering to me. When she crashes, I don't want critical judgments and harsh warnings from me to be in her memory. I want her to remember a Mom who wished her well.

But, it was almost harder than I could bear. The next Sunday at church we sang, "Love at Home." I choked. But that was better than vomiting, which I almost did. I sure didn't tell all my friends about this wedding. It was not an occasion to celebrate.

Haney didn't call much after that. And I began to obsess about my fears for her. I began to shut down. It was harder and harder to go to work. And then one November I told my husband, "I can't keep going. I think I have one more month in me. That's all."

I crashed. I had to take a leave of absence from work. I could not even put one foot in front of another without a supreme effort. I could not direct my program anymore. There was no "straw that broke the camel's back." There was no clear trigger to identify. It was the accumulation of heartache and worry and shame and embarrassment and hopelessness and powerlessness that finally just became a mountain of depression, bigger than me.

Age Twenty-Three. "Mom." (Haney is sobbing hysterically and Haney does not cry.) "Mom, I'm so sorry. I am so embarrassed. Please don't freak out. I tried to kill myself this morning. If I had a gun, I would be dead because when I did this, I really wanted to be dead at that moment. But now I don't want to be dead. I sliced my arm with a knife from the inside of my elbow to my wrist. The doctor who stitched me up told me I needed some serious therapy. I'm calling you from the hospital, but Mom, I'm coming home."

"Haney, where's your husband?"

"Mom, he's not here. Oh, Mom, he's a jerk. He told me I had to leave. He told me I'm a nothing."

"Haney, why is he not with you?"

"Mom, I think he has a girlfriend. And Mom, it's his nephew's twenty-three year old wife. Mom, I think he used me. I am so stupid. He is one of those people who is drawn to easy pleasures." (I was amazed at this insight from my usually insight-free daughter. While she too had been drawn to a lot of easy pleasures, perhaps the difference was she still had a conscience.)

"Mom, I have Juliana." (Oh, my strange, child-woman of a daughter that is such a "mess" of contradictions.)

Haney goes to sacrament meeting for the first time since she was fifteen years old. I want to hug the bishop. He spends Sunday School talking with her. Haney tells me, "Mom, the bishop was so nice to me. He didn't judge me or anything. He filled out a form so I could get free counseling. He really listened to me."

The hair is no longer jello-blue. The job is no longer dispatcher of strippers. The husband really was a sociopath. The road back will be long. Her path may not be mine. But the prodigal has returned.

I had come unraveled. I had walked, through my daughter, into an ugly world I did not know, understand, or like. In fact, I was frightened by it. But Heavenly Father had told me all those years before that "All you can do is love her." Sometimes that was excruciatingly hard. I fell into a deep depression for a number of years because Haney's choices forced me to confront my own self, and I found myself emptied. I had poured so much of myself, my energy, and my time into Haney that my well was dry. There were times I was unable to extricate myself from the tangles of Haney's life. I had read and studied and tried to research the best ways to parent a "Haney." I never did find that book! And so I judged myself harshly. I blamed myself for her omissions and her commissions. I was long on justice and short on mercy. Another unfortunate thing from my Pharisee personality.

I felt like a failure. I felt embarrassed. I felt that if "No success can compensate for failure in the home" then I had gotten a big, fat "F" in life.

But I loved Haney fiercely. Another of my daughters told me once I was kind of like one of those Momma Bears from Hell when her cubs are threatened. That made me feel happy. At least someone thought I did something right. My husband, too, was very supportive of both Haney and me.

In one of those instances that appears to be coincidental, but probably is inspired, I happened upon a magazine advertisement for a Christian book that had just been published about prodigal children. I never bought the book because it was not LDS and I did not want to wade through doctrine that was not ours. I did, however, keep (and still have in my files) the one-page advertisement that quoted two scriptures. The author makes the point that parents do not cause their children to become prodigals. That was a novel thought to me. I was struggling to think he might be right. He wrote that many parents condemn themselves with the proverb "The fathers eat sour grapes, and the children's teeth are set on edge."

I felt déjà vue. One of my favorite classes at BYU had used that proverb to talk about parents' failures. I had impaled myself on the sharpness of that proverb for almost ten years with my very own prodigal daughter. But in this book review, the author contrasted the "sour grapes" mentality with the scripture "The soul who sins is the one who will die. The son will not share the guilt of the father, nor will the father share the guilt of the son" (Ezekiel 18:20).

This scripture in an advertisement was as powerful for me as the scripture that drove the young fourteen-year-old Joseph Smith to the Sacred Grove. God does move in mysterious ways. Reading an advertisement for a book was the beginning of my hope, for myself, as the mother of a prodigal. And in a way, it was the beginning of my hope for my daughter. I had held in my mind and in my heart a picture of a young woman deeply flawed and incapable. Until I shifted my picture of Haney to be a daughter of God, it had been almost impossible for me to relate to her with sensitivity, patience, and unconditional love.

She is not the daughter of my dreams. But she is much better than the daughter of my illusions. How could I ever have dreamed of the richness and fire of my refining furnace and hers? How many times did she protest, "You are not fair! Life is not fair!" And I would argue, "No, Haney, life is not fair." I wish I could have been wiser and said, "Haney, tell me about what you *think* when you say life is not fair." (I could not have asked her what she *felt* because she thought feelings were stupid.) But I could have asked her open-ended questions. However, my rigid and "morally right" Pharisee of the counting steps personality frequently led me to deliver sermons when I ought.to have been listening. I wish instead of telling her "Life is not fair" that I could have been infinitely wiser and taught her the larger truth that "Eternal life is fair."

I am reminded of a powerful insight I had gained four years earlier when I returned from the leave of absence I had taken because my depression had stopped me in my tracks. (My Board had kept my position as director of services for handicapped children open for me.)

The very first morning of my return I was in a meeting with the program director from across the hall. She ran the program for developmentally delayed adults. She was so excited. Alvey had learned to tie his shoelaces that day. Alvey was a thirty-seven-year-old Downs Syndrome man.

We have a saying in my field that I really like. "Retarded people are not stupid. They are just slow learners. They learn like everyone else, but they learn more slowly." Alvey learned to tie his shoelaces after thirty-seven years. And he was just as excited at his accomplishment as any proud four-year-old who has just learned to tie his shoelaces.

Haney is not retarded like Alvey. But I know that something misfires in Haney's brain. Haney was blessed with large intelligence but small "sense."

I think about Haney. For me, here is another lesson about eternity. Haney is a daughter of God, and he has a loving timetable for her. I have been so worried about justice and truth and laws and rules and right and wrong. But he has been loving and patient and long-suffering for her. Most of all, he has mercy for Haney, plenty of mercy. Maybe I have been the one with large intelligence, but small "sense." My prodigal is my teacher. I, too, have many "spiritual shoe laces" left to tie before eternity.

❧

*Sue struggled—still struggles—with the pain of watching a daughter suffer the effects of mental illness and poor choices. Sue is not alone in her sorrow. Many parents feel the hurt of a child's rejection of their teachings, even their affection. The scriptures, too, are filled with stories of these parents whose children choose a self-destructive path—including our Heavenly Father and a third part of his children.*

*While we most commonly associate a prodigal with a son or daughter, a prodigal may be any other family member who has fallen into a reckless, wasteful lifestyle. Whoever the prodigal may be, remaining family members frequently feel bewildered, hurt, angry, heartbroken, and guilty.*

*The truth is that good parents do not always turn out good children, and the worst of parents do not always produce bad kids.*

*In Ezekiel 18:20, we read, "The soul that sinneth [is the one who] shall die [spiritually]. The son shall not bear the iniquity of the father, neither shall the father bear the iniquity of the son."*

*To those of you who are experiencing this heartache, the crucial gospel messages are to never give up and to know that the gospel is the most powerful force in the world. It is the time to kneel in mighty prayer asking God to give you all those attributes of love as described in the Thirteenth Article of Faith. You may have perfected the long-suffering, even the patience and kindness. It is now time to perfect the trusting in the Lord. You are not in charge of your prodigal's timetable. You are in charge of your own commitment to trust in the Lord.*

❧

# To Feel Life Again

Secret hurts and secret sorrows created pain and anger in my life. I got through life by hiding behind several things: anger, perfectionism, denial, and attempts to control my whole environment, when in fact the only thing I managed to successfully control was my weight. I'm not anorexic, but I have managed to keep my weight well below normal for my height and structure. If I even gained more than two pounds I felt like I just lost control of my entire world. That's where the perfectionism came into play. I was measuring my self-worth in all the wrong areas; I thought if I could keep the perfect home, the perfect kids, and perfectly maintain a part-time job that all those things would bring me happiness, self-esteem, self-worth, and confidence. That's where the distortion came into play (although I didn't know it at the time).

My perfectionism didn't do any of the good things for me I thought it would; in fact it only managed to bring about more problems, headaches, heartaches, stress, and deeper depression. I have made my own life miserable, by always racing against myself. I feel like a prisoner in my own world from which there is no escape. My entire family (which at that time consisted of my husband, and me, and our three girls) couldn't figure out what they kept doing wrong and wondered: "Why can't we live up to Mom's standards?"

As a mom, wife, and Mormon, you can imagine the guilt I imposed upon myself for "allowing" myself to be so severely depressed. With the knowledge we have about the premortal existence, mortality, and eternal life, how in the world could I let all these earthly experiences cloud my thinking, take away my faith, destroy my ability to love unconditionally, and instill in me a strong desire to throw it all away? My thinking was so distorted I actually thought that I might have slipped through heaven's veil at the wrong time. That I wasn't even supposed to be here. Where was my faith during all of this?

*Depression* wasn't a word I associated with my life. The years filled with severe mood swings were just written off as typical bad days. When the bad days became part of my everyday life, I knew there had to be more to it.

I finally realized I could no longer carry the ball on my own. I had learned all I could about myself and done all I could to help myself. It was now time for outside intervention. It wasn't an easy step, but I was grabbing at my last straw. I was one of the lucky ones, for I found an LDS therapist whom I liked and trusted right from the start. It felt right: I'm not saying comfortable, but I knew and felt I was doing the right thing.

Before too long into therapy, my therapist suggested that I be evaluated for medication, because she said: "You have a biological depression." I thought it was just her polite way of having me admit to being a failure. Of course I stubbornly resisted until she said: "I can maintain my partnership in all of this, but you will need to meet me half way." So I tried medication. It's not easy to pick which adverse side effects you would like to live with, seeing that all the medication all seemed to come with one or another. I didn't like any of the side effects so therefore, I didn't take my medication as directed, and because I didn't, talk therapy wasn't as effective as it should have been. I still was not meeting my therapist half way. My thinking became distorted once again; depression was setting in heavy. I felt hopeless, worthless, and like a big failure. Happiness was meant for everyone else, but not me. I wanted to die. So I went on a mini-starvation diet for about four days. I also was driving down the highway doing about 110 M.P.H., aggravated that no one took me out on the way home.

When depression entangles you in its evil coils and has stolen all your reasons to live, and you find yourself alone backed into your own isolated corner, left with nothing but deep despair—you know, you need to make the biggest decision you've ever made. Do I want to live, or do I want to die? So where and how does a person find a solitary reason to live? These are questions I found myself asking.

One particular evening, my therapist noticed something in me that wasn't quite right. I tried to deny anything was out of the ordinary, but she wouldn't fall for it. If it were visible to the human eye, you probably would have been able to see those evil coils of depression entangled all around me, with the scent of suicide right in the middle. She sensed that depression, and within seconds of my departure, she telephoned my husband to tell him of her concerns for me. When I arrived at home, my husband and I had a long discussion. He then told me of my therapist's wishes for me. She suggested that I check myself into a mental facility. I was filled with mixed emotions, but decided to go because I did feel emotionally unstable, and at that time I didn't care what happened to me.

Upon entry of this facility, I felt like it was happening to someone else. I had no emotions at the time. I took it lightly until night set in, and I found myself alone. It was almost unbearable, and my emotions could no longer be held back. I called my husband begging him to come get me. Being the calm person that he is, he gently helped me gain back the much-needed control over my emotions. It was then I decided to keep a journal, as they suggested we do. It helped out a lot, for it kept me focused.

The next day came with a bit of relief, because I accepted the reality of where I was. I actually enjoyed the first class of the day, which was called cognitive therapy. We all had the opportunity to share our thoughts, feelings, and experiences with each other, if we chose. This kind of therapy brought me out of myself, because it was then that I realized I wasn't the only one who had been afflicted by depression. It gave me a sense of connection to some of the people. I knew how they were feeling, because I'd been there. That gave me the strength I needed to believe that someday I would be healed of my own depression.

While I was in the hospital I had some very inspiring thoughts that have changed my life—I hope forever. The following are from my journal:

*Recap of Thursday Night 12–10–98*

Feelings that surfaced . . . overwhelmed, real depressed, abandoned, alone and lost. I feel like I am just imprisoned, and what the heck did I get myself into. Really starting to miss my freedom. Some anger starting to creep in, but only on a low intensity. Besides feeling embarrassed, I feel even more like a failure.

"So what did I learn?"

Even though things weren't better by circumstances they definitely felt better emotionally, because I realized it wasn't as bad as
I perceived it to be on the outside.

*Friday Morning 12–11–98*

Starting to gain back some control over my emotions, which
feels good. Starting to feel a little stronger, like I can get through
this. Starting to relax a little, feeling ok in my surroundings just a
little. I am also starting to realize that my burdens aren't as near
what they could be. I feel like a small portion of this program can
and may help me. I like the class called cognitive therapy the best
because I am able to see how other people process, how their
abuses are affecting their lives. This also helps me to not feel
alone, or unique with my own situation.

*Friday Night 12–11–98*

It was nice to have from 3:00 p.m. on, off to do nothing. I was
able to relax a little more, to read and write. I'm more focused.
It's giving me plenty of time to accept and make possible goals for
when I get back home. This is definitely more attention than I
wanted. At 7:30 p.m. I had the wisest thought that I've had in
the last two days. I would much rather exchange the attention
I'm receiving here, for a college course, for it would be much
more exciting and rewarding. This is the hardest thing I've ever
done. I believe this experience will definitely encourage me to go
try new things since I know they will never measure up to this
level of difficulty. Meeting some of the others, well, I'm just
thankful for my own unique problems. I no longer feel alone.
*Heavenly Father I thank thee.*

*Saturday Morning 12–12–98*

At 2:00 a.m. it finally came to me why I'm more emotionally
stable than the rest. It's because of my testimony of The Church

of Jesus Christ of Latter-day Saints! All these years I knew the Church was true, but now I have that affirmation. I'm finally being able to feel its realness, and I feel it a revelation to know that Heavenly Father has and is really watching over me; what a great new insight for me! I know that beyond a shadow of a doubt that there is a next life filled with eternal happiness that awaits me. That seems to be one of people's problems here; they think life ends at death. Wow! I'd probably be as bad off as them, if I believed that. This will definitely help me to stop feeling sorry for myself and move on. This was definitely worth missing sleep for.

*Saturday 3:00 A.M. 12–12–98*

In my Patriarchal Blessing it says, "You are a choice daughter born of goodly parents." That always confused me until now. Even though they made their mistakes along the way, they did the best they could, because of the limited resources they had. The greatest blessing of all is, at this moment I strongly feel that Heavenly Father spoke directly through the missionaries to my dad just for me. Heavenly Father knew that the Church was going to be my solid base for living, which has made it possible for me to have the insight I now have. I'm beginning to see how strength is connected directly to adversity.

*Sunday 3:00 A.M. 12–13–98*

First time to really connect with feelings since I've been here. Woke up crying, was feeling emotionally lost, alone, and scared. I'm even afraid to find out who the real me is; I feel like I need to get rid of the poison inside myself. I'm also afraid to let other people see the real side of me, the side that's not in control. I now know the meaning of the comment that my family physician made to me, when she said: "Your wall is so tall, even you can't knock it down." I'm afraid to let feeling in, I'm afraid I won't be able to break through my own barriers. I know I tell myself I want help, so now I want to feel the need for help. I'm ready, or want to be ready, to trade in the old me for a new me. I'm tired of hating myself. I'm afraid of me, because I don't know who I am. I'm afraid I won't like her. I want to stop pretending that everything is all right and that it has to be perfect all the time. Making a mistake doesn't mean the end of the world for me, and I don't need to control everyone and everything around me to be happy. I resist change because it's scary and it also forces me out of my comfort zone . . . could mean failure.

*Sunday 9:45 P.M. 12–13–98*

Today left me with some confidence, a little peaceful, on a little high, and I actually felt good about myself. It was the first in a long time. I think it all started when a therapist here said to me: "Good job today." That little phrase stayed with me all day, but I'm not quite sure how I'm suppose to feel; it's hard for me to feel that I deserve help. I'm finally getting what I longed for, for so long now, the insight and wisdom to turn this great experience into a positive stepping-stone. I admit some anger towards my therapist, because I failed to understand, " What am I suppose to get?" Four days later I got it. She did me a favor by getting me to come here, to get in touch with my feelings just a little quicker, so that we could speed up that process we call healing.

*Monday 12–14–98*

I know people who have been abused are actually pretty wise people: why? Because they have survived, for one thing. I feel I may know one girl's reason for not wanting to leave here. It's because she feels safety, comfort, friends, and she feels loved. She has already connected to it here, and she's afraid of losing that connection when she's gone. I have noticed one more thing I have going for myself, it's the fact that I have a great support group back home waiting for me. The one thing that I will take with me through the rest of my life is the intellectual knowledge I have gained here.

*Monday Group Therapy 11:30 A.M.*

I have a feeling a lot of people here still have that same lost hopeless feeling when they leave here; partly it could be that they haven't got a support group waiting for them. They definitely need The Church of Jesus Christ of Latter Day Saints in their lives. I also believe that it's because they don't have that eternal perspective that we do. Deep down inside, their lives are meaningless to them. I truly feel for these people, so I did what Sister Okazaki suggests, and that's to pray for people all over the world, no matter what their circumstances are. I can't help but wonder how Heavenly Father processes all this, because I'm having a hard time with it myself. I had asked a staff member, "What are your emotions and answers to the people who leave this facility, not being too many steps ahead of their depression than they were to begin with?" Her reply: "We just do what we can."

*Monday 12–14–98*

I know why people zone out. It didn't come to me until I zoned out today. For me, it meant that I didn't want to feel, or even know what to feel at the time, so I chose not to feel at all. Maybe that's what I did as a child, so maybe that's why I don't connect any feelings with it.

*Monday 12–14–98*

While showering, of all places, it dawned on me that maybe I don't retain as much of my memory because I forget to feel it before I store it; and because of that it doesn't know how to be stored. These people who come here without the gospel in their lives may have some new positive tools to take out with them, but not enough to make a difference in their lives, because they believe that deep down inside they are still worthless and no good. I know it won't happen to me, because even though I'm in a facility right now, I know that God loves me and will help me through this. So after that realization I said a prayer for them. People around here are starting to tease me with my journal in hand, and saying: "What are we doing, writing a book?" And I say: "You never know." I've noticed something else around here. There are people who try to pretend they're interested, but their facial expressions say otherwise. There are those who still walk around with their heads down; I feel that they are going to leave with their heads down as well. Now there are people like me, who want to know, who want to change, want to understand, want to feel and who want to get through this. It's funny, attitude is everything. People here mope in the halls; the whole attitude of this place says gloom and depression. It's not the floors, walls, or tables, it's the people and their projection of their own attitude. I've been feeling kind of out of place here, because I smile at people until they smile back, I say good morning and greet everyone I meet. These people act like they are purposely trying to keep themselves down and out: like they're waiting for someone to wave the magic wand and make it all better. I'm feeling pretty good, because I want to get better, and I'm going to take pride in getting better.

To think the hospital said many years ago that I was in fact a failure-to-thrive baby. Huh, if they could only see me now! So jump into life, and live it! I've functioned on only three and a half hours of sleep today, and I'm still wide-awake. That's OK, because I wouldn't have wanted to miss this wonderful insight from my Heavenly Father. I'm not going to insinuate that this program isn't educational, because it is. If I could let it help me, anybody can. The program was designed for everyone to succeed, and it's up to the individual to have that strong desire to succeed. The psychiatrist said to me this morning: "It's so wonderful to see you so enthused with the program." I got the feeling that doesn't happen too often.

Today in psychodrama, it was almost too highly intense for me to deal with, because it was about a girl's sexual abuse. I broke down and just cried. I wanted to run and almost did, until a gentleman stopped me. I felt pretty saddened for the rest of the day.

I know why I like music, sad music, thinking music, and feeling music, it's because I didn't realize I'd forgotten how to feel, due to bad coping mechanisms. Music helped me connect with feelings again, even if it did leave me feeling more down.

I came up with an exercise for myself to help me learn to feel again on a daily basis. It involves grabbing your thought, holding onto to your thought long enough to feel it, then storing it in a safe, retrievable place. So that you can go back into your memory, and retrieve it whenever you want. And for me, it's also helped me gain a better memory. My oldest sister is coming to visit today. I want to feel her love for me. So at 5:00 A.M., I put my exercise to the test. I had faith it would work. Two hours later the tears came. I felt my sister's love; it worked. I plan on applying this exercise every chance I get. So hopefully it will become automatic like it was suppose to be in the first place. I trust now, I'll be able to finally have my day when I can feel my Savior's love . . .

*Tuesday 12–15–98*

I think I learned something new, or just realized it. A young girl here has been spending everyday trying to figure out how to bring love and hate together. When I first heard that here I didn't process that, either, until now: love + hate = feelings. When my husband and my therapist came to visit, I didn't realize that I had spent the whole day trying not to feel their visit, but that's exactly what I did. I didn't want to cry. If I could do it over, I would process it differently. I know I totally skipped feeling, because it felt too hard.

*Tuesday 12–15–98*

So now how do I change that? First I think I need to recognize that it's OK to feel, and then keep steady reminders throughout any given day, that's its OK to feel. Then as long as I store it in a safe retrievable place, it will get easier to remember and feel.

*Therapist's Big Question 12–15–98*

"So what's changed for you?" Well, first off I kept forgetting to feel my blessings at home, in life and with myself. I am a good person, and I know that; I've just always denied it, because I didn't feel like a good person. Now I want to try to feel and love me, as I am. I didn't connect with my true feelings—it's called cognitive distortion—I was so cut off from my feelings that I didn't feel my family, friends, or even the gospel in my life. I didn't feel the Spirit. I made myself cold to that. How sorry I am now for missing out on all those years. But if it took that to get to where I'm at today, it feels worth it! I am on my way to healing, and I can feel it. I'm really going to work on not holding myself back anymore. I just needed to feel love just long enough for me to gain the strength to go out and reach for the stars!

I love the Lord, and I'm thankful for the special challenges he's put before me, while here in mortality, to help me become the person he knows and sees me to be. I'm thankful for family, and the family of friends I currently have, for without any of them, my life would be lacking a significant meaning. All my life I've just wanted to be heard, validated, and loved. Getting married and starting a family helped fill that gap, but it was only the beginning. It wasn't until I started therapy and medication that I realized that I did have the insight and courage to go back to school and capture my dream of becoming a therapist myself.

It's weird you know, before I was in therapy or on medications, I felt cold and dead on the inside. I was just waiting for my physical body to catch up to it. Now one year into therapy and four months on medications, my physical body is warm and alive, trying to do all those right things to lift myself out of the darkness also. Now I'm just waiting for the inside to catch up with the outside. I will not remain a prisoner to depression anymore!

I still have my work cut out for me. I know I have a long way to go yet, but because I'm not going it alone anymore; I know I'll be able to make it.

*This story was written by a woman who was suffering profoundly with a major depressive episode when we first met. She came to me by way of physician referral because she was reporting active suicidal thoughts and plans. Her issues are complex and intertwined. It was a risk for me to invite her to share her thoughts with you because her suffering remains present-tense. However, following her hospitalization for a serious suicide attempt she began journaling. As she shared her compelling thoughts with me, I knew that her own words pave the path that will eventually lead to her healing. I believe that there will be those among you who have "walked her walk" and may be moved forward in your own healing as you ponder the insights she has gained.*

## No Lamb in the Thicket

I remember the phone call as an indelible, hot branding explosion to my mind.

My daughter was gone.

I felt an explosion, a blinding horror. I was gasping to breathe, but could not breathe. I was sliding down to the floor, losing sense, losing time, losing self, losing reality.

My daughter was gone.

No longer would I enjoy our daily closeness; no longer would I relish our fierce family loyalty. Gone were the ever-present soft sugar cookies we loved to decorate and the miracle brownies and the millions of pounds of homemade French fries. Gone forever were her inimitable blessings on the food that blessed everything from the food, to the butterflies, to the clouds. Gone were our intimate, philosophical conversations about life. Gone were the nights huddled over the wobbly kitchen table making candy bar posters or designing our latest ingenious and intricate invitation to invite John to a dance.

My daughter, my soul friend. My daughter, my light, my touchstone— gone. One phone call, punctuating my life with an inconsolable exclamation of grief.

The phone call was my daughter calling from 800 miles away to tell me she was not going to come home. She made a choice. She chose her father.

*  *  *

My soul's breath is crushed from me.

I am losing time. Time stands still. Time flies. Time careens out of control. Time is lost in freeze frames and warp speeds. Memories are fragmentary. Memories are unreliable. I used to have an amazing memory. Now I have a patchwork memory. Friends try to console me. I am inconsolable.

Questions rage within me. What did I ever do to deserve this? I joined the Church and was despised by my parents. I endured a personal harm that has invaded my brain with nightmares. I lived through a marriage of hell and a divorce of even worse. In all this I never "blamed God nor charged him foolishly."

How could a merciful God allow me to lose my daughter?

As I mourned, I began to doubt that our love had been the wondrous thing I had felt. I began to doubt my feelings. I began to doubt my thoughts. I began to doubt myself. I began to doubt her. Grief is an anesthetic, steel cocoon. I cannot escape it. I metamorphose backwards.

I am in slow motion. My thinking slurs. My other two children need me, and I am only an automaton. I am a mother shell. The creature that once inhabited the shell has left.

My daughter is gone. I am emotionally, physically, socially, spiritually bereft. My brain, which has always been my ally, becomes my tormentor.

I cannot breathe; I cannot sit still; I cannot escape this pain. I cannot draw comfort; I cannot pray; I cannot believe. I cannot hope. I want to be dead. I want to be gone, too. I cannot live. I cannot die.

I think I must be bad. I must have done something awful, but I don't know what it is. Maybe it was in the preexistence. Someone help me. I feel my self slipping away. I am sliding out of reality. I'm absolutely going crazy.

But there are other people. I have two more children. I have a husband. I have friends. I have a "big" Church calling. I have a job. I fix a smile on my face, comb my hair, wear sunglasses, and move on automatic pilot. Life goes on, but I do not.

\* \* \*

It seems like some sick joke. I am a therapist. I'm supposed to help people. Now, I am an impaired person. I am an impaired mother and wife. I am an impaired therapist. Actually, though I am definitely an impaired person, I think I am a better therapist because I now know the secret code of despair. No words. I wear the cipher on my soul: Hidden Sorrow— Beware.

On quite another level, I am detached. I think my clients do not know this. I find an uncanny ability to be there for them. But I am gone.

Temporarily, permanently . . . I do not know. I fear it is permanent. I am gone.

I withdraw from all my friends. I make lots of excuses. I withdraw from my husband. He neither understands nor accepts my emotional death spiral. It is not his daughter. I descend into a world where I am untouchable, inconsolable, unlovable.

I do know that what I am feeling is the very essence of *physical*. Because I am a trained therapist, I know the name is *depression*. The word seems sterile. What I feel is barren.

My soul is harrowed up. Pain wracks me physically in the madness that leads me to contemplate suicide. I am bludgeoned, crushed, slashed by the melancholia we name depression.

My child is gone. I yearn to be gone, too.

* * *

I become obsessed with the story of the Prophet Abraham being asked to sacrifice his beloved son, Isaac. Abraham is provided a ram stuck in the thicket by his horns. Where was my lamb? I have empty arms.

And empty heart and empty thoughts and empty soul. Where, O, God, was *my* lamb?

"I am a therapist," I tell myself. I know what to do about this. "He that hath himself for a physician hath a fool for a doctor." I am a fool.

I do not talk to anyone. I deliberately, but dispassionately, cloister myself from everyone familiar and warm. My life becomes "sectors" which I control. Work. Church. Cook. Clean. Say appropriate things so no one knows my death wish.

All the advice and counsel I have given in my years of being a thera-pist, I do not take. It is not arrogance that makes me think I'm different. It is shame. I am so unworthy. If Heavenly Father would take from me my greatest light, I must be lacking. I envy Abraham. He got a lamb in the thicket. I have empty arms.

* * *

🌾

There are, in my opinion, some deaths which are more cruel than other deaths.

Sometimes we even pray that, with God willing, a loved one can experience the peace and relief of death. Other times, even a tragic death can be experienced as the person going to a better place. Some profoundly moving experiences occur even with the kind of death that results from an act of terrorism, an act of war, an act of violence, an act of nature, a terrible accident.

But what about a death of a different kind? What about the choice one person makes to lay down a relationship? What about the death to a mother who is forced through divorce to surrender her child—emotionally, socially, physically, geographically—to the adversarial parent? What way does a mother have to tell the children the truth when the truth would hurt them further?

After fifteen, almost sixteen years of a remarkably close relationship with my oldest daughter, she had made a choice which I knew forever threatened the cherished mutuality of our wonderful mother/daughter relationship.

* * *

And so the final, sometimes inexorable sacrifice the mother makes is the giving up of the very last vestige of her dreams, her hopes, her vision for the future. To me it is a death worse than physical death. Physical death is forced separation and loss. This other death is made by choice. She chose the offending father over the victim mother. She utterly rejected, excluded, and abandoned her mother. The break was chosen. The wound was mortal.

* * *

After all our little family had been through together since she was seven years old, and with all the loyalty and honor she had shown to me, after all the amazing bonding experiences we had shared, with her friends and my friends expressing envy at our closeness, she left. She did not look back. For reasons still not understood, she was unable to stay in touch with me. Perhaps it was too painful for her. That is the kindest motivation I can ascribe to her.

On one occasion, Mother's Day came and went, and I did not hear from her. The next night, two of her dearest friends showed up on my doorstep. They told me she had called them to ask them to go buy me a card and deliver it. These two great young men handed me a card, saying, "We are sorry we couldn't find a Mother's Day card—they were all sold out." Then they gave me a card that said "Happy Father's Day." They had scribbled over the bright cheery "Father" and in black magic marker written "Mother." That was me. It was the perfect symbol. I was crossed out and scribbled over in my daughter's life. Though the boys were well-intentioned and my mind knew this, that card put me over the precipice and back down into the black hole of depression. I had just barely peeked over the edge, and the irony of that greeting card reminded me of being replaced and "scratched out." The original wound was viciously ripped open.

I met with the psychiatrist who worked at my agency. He prescribed a sedating antidepressant for me, which he instructed me to take at night. I became agitated. I was hyper and couldn't sleep. I couldn't sit still. My thoughts were flying. I paced around my house all night. Next, he tried one of the newer antidepressants. I developed diarrhea; it was two months before I realized it was from the medication. He tried another. Again, I was slammed with horrible stomach cramps and gastric distress. It appeared I was one of those people who did not have a good response to the medications available at that time. Maybe I didn't give them enough of a chance.

But I did find a therapist, Dr. Donald Christopher. He told me to call him "Don." I told him, "I don't want a Don. I need a Dr. Christopher." He helped me to be able to work and go through the motions of life.

My thoughts were obsessive, and I ruminated about my daughter. I felt detached from my life as I had known it. Loss, fear, and guilt were all entangled. My therapist let me cry and rage and agonize. While I could not let go of the rejection and guilt, and the loss was incomprehensible, he helped me compartmentalize the pain in a way that I again was able to take control of my life. It was autopilot, but I could function. His warmth and empathy made me feel valued and secure for at least one hour every week.

Dr. Christopher added another "benign" sounding word to my vocabulary in the wake of my daughter's move and her continuance to exclude me from her life: post-traumatic stress disorder, or PTSD. In a nutshell, PTSD can occur when a person has experienced a horrific event, outside the range of *normal* experience. Common examples are men in war, victims of rape or incest, or people experiencing other catastrophic events.

In PTSD, the brain experiences a profound wounding. Normal memories are encoded in the brain through neural pathways. In PTSD, the memory is encoded, but the neural pathway is more like a super highway. It is deeper and stronger and harder. That is why the person afflicted with PTSD is so vulnerable to exposure to events which trigger the memory of the original trauma. And, unfortunately, when the memory of the event is triggered, the memory slams into the consciousness with the same energy, or nearly the same, as the original trauma.

When I received the card with the scratched out salutation, that "crossing out" was symbolic of how I felt my daughter had "crossed me out" of her life. The original loss was my devastation at her choice to move.

I had truly likened my sacrifice to Abraham's sacrifice, but in my mind, Abraham did get the lamb in the thicket. But, not only did Abraham find the ram in the thicket and the Lord did *not* provide a lamb for me, my brain also added the twin curse of "It is your fault—you were not worthy as was Abraham."

A rational mind would recognize this distortion of thinking. PTSD is not rational. It is a reliving of the original horror—in Technicolor with stereophonic sound.

A person who suffers from PTSD relives the same torment over and over and over. The treatment of choice for PTSD is to be able to "talk" about the event. The irony is that the usual PTSD victim is compelled to secrecy by the "shame" of the event.

As a therapist, I knew all this intellectually. But I did not trust my own mind. I believed I was different, that other people "truly" had PTSD—I was just an inferior, weak woman who was so horribly awful that her own daughter had to leave her. I thought I must have been really stupid because I didn't see it coming. I thought she had loved me as life itself—as I had loved her.

During this horrible time, the second greatest assault to my soul was my confusion about prayer. I had prayed and begged, and begged and prayed for Heavenly Father to tell my daughter "to come right back home to her mother"—to where I knew she belonged. She did not listen. Heavenly Father did not listen. I felt forced to conclude I was unrighteous. And so my descent into depression and PTSD added another spiral into my total collapse. I couldn't even trust my prayers. I thought with every molecule of motherly devotion that my prayers were "right," but obviously my daughter and I had gotten different answers.

How was I to understand this dichotomy?

* * *

I never saw my daughter cheer at a game.
I never saw my daughter dressed up for a prom.
I never cheered as my daughter was crowned a homecoming princess.
I never got to go to Young Women's events.
I never got to hear her sing in sacrament meeting.
I never watched my daughter sing in Madrigals.
I never saw her teachers or her projects.
I never met her friends.
I never got to assess her boyfriends.
I never saw her get tapped into the National Honor Society.
I did not see her receive notice of her scholarship from BYU.
I did not watch proudly as my firstborn graduated from high school.

* * *

I could not afford to attend her high school graduation. The one thing I did get to see was her perform the lead in *Oklahoma*. I flew the 800 miles with her two sisters and my husband. We stayed four days. I went to see her sing every night.

\* \* \*

One month before my daughter's marriage, I was "uninvited" to attend her temple sealing. Her father said "he" could not be in the temple with me. I, who had had my recommend for twenty-six years. He, who had had a recommend for one month.

I considered calling his stake president. It might have changed the decision, but what a price tag for my daughter. I did not want her to pay a price on her wedding day. So I paid it. I was not noble. I was vanquished.

I scheduled eleven hours straight of clients that day. 7:00 A.M. to 7:00 P.M. Go, go, go. Work, work, work. Force your brain to think of others. Force, force, force. Do not eat. Do not stop. Run, run, run. Think your life depends on it. It does.

It was the only way I could conceive of living through that exclusion. I forced myself to see those eleven clients in therapy that day; I took every emergency client. I was an emergency client; but no one but me knew that. I willed myself to compartmentalize my pain because I knew it would swallow me.

It did. And that night, once again and for the hundredth time, I spiraled into the death abyss where life was sucked out of me, and I fought the beckoning of suicide. I could not do that to the date of my daughter's marriage. I still had some glimmer of hope that she might care.

\* \* \*

Virginia Satir is a renowned marriage and family therapist who has written, "Life is not the way it's supposed to be. Life is the way it is."

In many ways I have been a hollow person since my tragedy. My daughter has never looked back. She has never apologized, nor probably even realized what her choice did to her mother. We are cordial now. We express love, and we talk frequently. We can talk comfortably about everything but us.

But, for me, my relationship with my daughter has not been

resurrected. I live daily with her choice that became as a mushroom cloud following an atomic blast, spewing wreckage far beyond an intended target. On a fragile, intellectual level, I believe she did not mean to do this "to" me. On an emotional and spiritual level, her choice was a silent killer of my soul. I paid the ultimate price for a divorce. I do not know why.

It's not the way it was supposed to be. It is the way it is. With the "death" of my daughter, there was no funeral. She lived on in new circumstances. The death was to my world, my hopes, my dreams, my life. We live in parallel universes. I strive to press forward with "that perfect brightness of hope," and everyone I know would attest I am "anxiously engaged." But I have had to accept that the healing for which I long may not happen in this lifetime.

I feel a real kinship with the Apostle Paul because I keep a rather large size "thorn in my flesh."

\* \* \*

Today, once again I am reporting in to my journal. I most want to figure out the mother "issue."

I wanted to be a mother. I chose to be a mother. I was twenty-five years old and it was my dream. I wanted it to be my most important job, my most important goal, the most important thing I would ever do.

I had never believed I would be a statistic. I was twenty-three when I married a returned missionary in the temple. That did not sound like a divorce in the making to me.

I guess I had never really understood the principle of agency until I was confronted with someone—a husband—who knew better and didn't do better. I became a single mom with three small children. I had to work three jobs to sustain us, and eventually re-enrolled in school to finish my degree.

Maybe part of my anguish really is that I cannot forgive myself for how much time I was away. But, there was no other choice. I blame myself for not making a choice I did not have.

I wonder if my children resented me. I asked them. All of them either protected me—or told a kind lie.

What can I do if they do resent me—or if they did? Hopefully, none of them will ever have to walk in my shoes. They are hard, unyielding shoes; they are painful shoes.

But, I can't change any of this. Take the worst-case scenario. Say I *failed!* What would failure look like? To me, the worst failure would be if they were mean, bad people. They are not. Another failure would be if they were criminals. They are not. I guess the failure I feel is that I don't feel any of them really love *me*.

It is so sad. I feel like, passively, they all like me okay. But it is not that deep, abiding love which I have for them. They do not have the relationship with me as their mother I dreamed of, thought of, wished for, hoped for.

And with my eldest, I have agony over her choice to choose her father over me. Her choice at age fifteen continues today. The evidence is overwhelming.

So what can I do? Actually, *nothing*. I cannot change her feelings. Nothing I can say or do will ever change her as long as she chooses denial and avoidance over facing the complexity of both her parents. Until and unless she is willing to face a different and harsher version of her past it will never change, for me. I think my hurt is too profound for her; she does not understand she holds some ability to soothe it.

So, it reverts back to my inability to change any of the three of them. "It's not the way it was supposed to be; it's the way it is." All I can do is what I can do. I can call, send cards, remember birthdays, send Christmas presents, pray for them. That's it. The rest of the time, I need to get on with life. I think it would be easier if I had ever truly felt I had "belonged" to, or with, anyone for a sustained time. I know this is *my* thorn in the flesh. But I do not like it.

Intellectually, I accept that the only lasting way of feeling special is to develop a relationship with Christ. Perhaps, that is why we all get a thorn in the flesh to remind us. I also understand I have way too much negative energy around this. I have wanted my whole life to feel loved by someone—first and best. Mothers get to enjoy that wonderful attach-ment—I had to give it up too soon.

So, I can't change it because it involves other people. I am so exhausted from the ache of it. So I need, want, choose to accept that I don't get this thorn removed in my lifetime. I must focus on what I can do and what I have.

I need a word. I search for a word. The word eludes me.

So, what's the word I need?

It's not *stop*. I can't stop being their mother.

It's not *fire*. I can't fire myself as their mother because I don't want to; and anyway I am still their mother.

It's not *resign* or *retire*.

What is the word?

It's not *hibernate* or *repose*.

What is the word? What is the word? What is the *word*? If I can find the language, maybe I can accept the concept.

I have longed for a personal discernment. I have pled for an eternal point of view. And this day, the Savior gives me a word in my heart and in my mind.

*Wait.* The word is *wait*. It's what God does.

He stands at the door and waits.

He remains a loving parent, but he rarely comes to us except through the Holy Ghost in a still, small voice.

He waits patiently for us to come to him.

Just as he has waited patiently for me to humble myself and talk to him about this hole in my heart, so it is my job to *wait, wait, wait* patiently and lovingly for my children as he has waited patiently and lovingly for me.

This is very hard, but I know it is right and true.

For the first time in twelve years, I feel my heart has lightened. I feel the thorn in my side is gone. This is a miracle. My new understanding has released me into the "peace which passeth all understanding," and I felt the power of the Savior's love for me as he took my pain. He did not remove it entirely. He shared the burden. He gave me insight into how he stands at the door to our hearts. I am a new person.

* * *

The thorn is back today. I did not know it would be such hard work to be happy. Happiness is a skill and I am much better at other skills. My heart is "tugged" again.

The thorn is not as deep. It's not hurting as long; the interval between the jab of its sharpness has stretched out.

*Intensity. Duration. Interval.* These are the words of my profession. I understand them.

*Intensity:* My thorn is less sharp.

*Duration:* My thorn's pain lasts less time.

*Interval:* There is longer time between the pricks of the thorn.

My thorn is back. But I can embrace it now, for I have finally learned its lesson. I cannot always hold that lesson securely and faithfully in my heart. But since I have learned it once, I can find it again.

*A death of a loved one under any circumstances is a most profound loss. Death can be a trigger to a major depressive episode.*

*I have spent many therapy hours with those who have experienced death. Those deaths have ranged from tragic to blessed. They have ranged from murder, to suicide, to fatal accident, to devastating illness, to lingering illness, to natural death at an unnatural time, to the death that comes to the elderly with grace, but still as a tremendous loss.*

*These deaths, to some degree, have a protocol. That is, there is a memorial or a funeral. Most often, there are some happy memories. Most often, there is the assurance or hope of seeing the loved one in the hereafter. Although there is grief—profound grief—there is also hope.*

*There are also deaths of a different kind. There are deaths of relationships. These deaths are a rejection, an abandonment, a betrayal. The sufferers who are left behind in these kinds of "deaths" will live out similar pronounced grief, but without a sense of hope. There is no protocol. There is no funeral, no* memorial. It feels very final, but there is no finality. This kind of "death" is more frequent than you might suppose.

A common relationship-death with which I have worked as a therapist is the loss of a child through divorce, as described in this story.

# Hell and Back

*I really don't feel much like writing today. In fact, I'd much rather lie down and take a nap, but I feel I must do something more than lie around and feel sorry for myself.*

*Today's topic is depression. What is depression? For me it's an overwhelming feeling that my life is beyond my control. It is terrifying; no it's beyond terrifying: it is madness and insanity. Why is it happening to me? Despite my intense reading and research, which says depression is caused by a chemical imbalance, I can't help but believe that depression is brought on by the natural consequences of sin. I am being punished for my lack of faith, not by God, but by my own conscience that tells me I am a bad person, that I am not living up to the covenants and promises I made when I joined the Church.*

I wrote that one day while trying to get my act together. I had been diagnosed with depression in May of 1994. After reading everything I could get my hands on about the subject, I decided I had to do something to stay sane. So I tried to write about it sometimes.

In November 1991, after I spent sixteen years as an army wife, my husband retired from twenty years of active duty. Along with our six children, we moved back to his hometown. I wasn't happy about moving here, but here is where he wanted to be. We ended up living in a small two-bedroom apartment for four and a half years. I had been a stay-at-home mom since my first child was born, but after seventeen years of staying home, my husband decided I should work outside of the home. I found a job at a plant that did hospital laundry and worked there for a year and a half. Although I liked the job I was bitterly unhappy. I hated being out of the home.

One day during the summer, I was working at my table folding laundry when I started feeling a bit strange. A few minutes later was lunch break. I went upstairs to the break room and sat at a table to eat. Suddenly my head started swimming, and my stomach felt upset. I was overwhelmed with fear for no apparent reason. I could not go back downstairs to work when the break was over. I didn't know what was wrong; then other people started getting sick. Three people passed out, and another one had to be sent home. It was the heat. The building had no air conditioning and little ventilation, so I figured my problem was the heat, and I recovered enough to return to my job. The following weeks I kept feeling bad, lightheaded, dizzy, pounding heart, nervousness, vomiting— you name it, I had it. I still thought it was a result of the heat.

One day was particularly bad. I was at my table when all of a sudden I started to feel like I was going to pass out. I could feel it coming. My legs turned to jelly, heat filled my body as the jelly-like feeling climbed from my feet to my head. I had a heavy crushing sensation in my chest. My supervisor thought I might be having a heart attack. I was taken home where I collapsed on the bed and couldn't move.

Later that evening, my husband decided to take me to the emergency room. After the usual questions and the pre-exam, I was led to an exam room and told to get on the table. A few minutes later, a doctor came in. Without even looking at me, he told me I had an inner ear "thing." *An inner ear "thing?"* I thought, *What kind of terminology is that? Couldn't he have said an infection or something?* He said he would get me a shot, and then I would be okay. He came back sometime later and insisted that I was feeling better now, wrote me a prescription for some pills, and then sent me home. I was not feeling better.

Unhappy with that diagnosis, my husband found a doctor in the phone book who would see me the next day. I did not tell him I was there for a second opinion. He walked in the room, checked my heart rate, and told me that all I had was anxiety. He never looked in my ears. He told me he could give me some pills, but that he doubted I would want to take them, so I just left. I continued to feel bad. The crushing sensation in my chest got worse. After a year and a half in the work force, with much relief, I had to quit my job. I wasn't getting any better.

Within hours of quitting that job, my husband was after me to get another one. Three days later I was working at a childcare center. I loved the children but hated the job! My symptoms came and went, getting worse each time. My employer kept after me to see a doctor and finally made an appointment for me with a doctor she knew. He told me I had a hiatal hernia and gave me some pills. I took them for three days but didn't like the side affects, so I quit taking them. I felt worse all the time.

I started sleeping all day. I'd get up to go to work, put in my eight hours, then come home and sleep until it was time to go to work again. I dragged through each day.

After four years in the little apartment, we were ready to buy a house. I was ecstatic! I had waited twenty years to have my own home, a place where we could finally settle down and stay put for a while. The day we went to finalize the paper work was the worst day of my life, or so it seemed. It should have been the happiest day, but for some reason I felt like I was coming unglued. It was supposed to take up to five hours to go through all the red tape and sign the papers. Thank goodness the whole thing only lasted forty-five minutes. I sat at the conference table with my husband and the other participants just trying to concentrate on putting my signature on each of the dozens of papers that were placed before me. I felt I was going to crack up any second if this thing didn't hurry up and get over.

Finally we were finished and we were the proud owners of our very own home. I didn't care; I just had to get out of there. Somehow I made it back to the car. Somehow I made it to the house . . . and I completely broke down. I started screaming, crying, and shaking so bad that I couldn't control it. My husband held me and tried to reassure me that it was just menopause. I wanted to believe him, but I felt I was much too young to be going through menopause. I was only thirty-nine.

We didn't have a family doctor, but I had found one that gave my son a sports physical for school, so I called and made an appointment for myself. In the exam room, the nurse took my information and left. A few minutes later, a hand with a clipboard reached around the door. I was told to fill out the attached papers and the doctor would be in later. I looked at the paper and became angry. *What is this?* I said to myself. *I come in here with stomach problems, and they're giving me the crazy quiz.* (By now my symptoms seemed to be coming from my stomach, so I thought this was where the problem was). However, before coming to this appointment, my husband had told me to behave myself and to keep my mouth shut. So I took the test, but I didn't answer the questions truthfully. I was afraid that if I did, I would have to be committed.

When the doctor came in, he looked at my answers, totaled my score, then explained that a high score was bad, and a lower score was good. I had scored in the middle. I realized that if I had answered all the questions truthfully, I would have gotten the highest score possible. I kept my mouth shut.

He told me that I had depression. He said I should not be ashamed because at least eighty percent of his patients were being treated for the same illness. I was furious! I didn't care what eighty percent of his other patients had; I was not depressed! I did not have depression! Good members of the Church don't get depression! But I kept my mouth shut and behaved myself even though I wanted to slug him and walk out.

He explained to me that it was a chemical imbalance in the brain and drew me a diagram. Finally he gave me some pills and explained that it would take four to six weeks before I began to notice a change. I didn't want to believe him, but by now I was calm enough to listen. I decided I had nothing to lose. I went home, having decided to try the pills.

I didn't want my husband to know what was happening. I wasn't going to tell him because I knew he would be angry and would not understand, but the next morning he asked me what the doctor said. I was right; as soon as I told him he blew up in my face. Then he tried to calm down and be understanding. It didn't work. I took one of the pills and almost immediately I felt like I was off the wall and suffering all the side effects listed on the label—in the extreme. I got into a really bad argument with my husband, which ended up with him walking out. I thought he was gone for good. He came back late that night and wouldn't speak to me. The next day he was okay and encouraging me to take the pill again. I didn't want to after the hell I had experienced the day before, but he pleaded with me to take them so I did, with the same consequences and worse. He called the doctor to tell him what was happening, but the doctor said to continue with the pills and the side effects would go away.

In the midst of all this we were packing and getting ready to move into our new home. I wanted to help and be a part of it, but I could do nothing. I felt bad and guilty at making my family, especially my husband, do all the work. The day we finally moved, I was no help whatsoever. It was my third day on the pills and my husband had to beg, plead, and cry to get me to finally take one. I spent all day in bed while the work of moving went on around me. Later that same day I was able to get to the new house. I found myself a place in the corner to lie down out of the way, and stayed there in my misery all night. In the morning there was absolutely no way I was going to take another pill. My husband agreed and called the doctor again and my prescription was changed.

I took a week's leave of absence from my job to get adjusted to my medication. During that week, it was a living hell. I felt like I was losing my mind and never going to get it back again. I felt like my brain was being beamed into outer space into a million, billion little particles never to come together again. My husband tried but just couldn't understand. Whenever I needed him the most he'd walk out on me. He couldn't handle it, and I couldn't understand why, so I stayed angry with him. My children tried to help but this was all new to them.

The following week I returned to work. I was still miserable and unhappy. At church I didn't tell anyone what was going on. I was so ashamed, embarrassed, and humiliated. I thought I was the only one. I thought that this could get me excommunicated, and I didn't want to lose my membership in the Church, so I kept silent while I put my family through hell.

Suddenly, one day out of the blue, I realized that I was feeling better than I ever had in my whole life. I could think clearly. Everything around me was in focus. I was elated: life was good!

Over the next two years I continued to have my ups and downs, my good days and bad. Some days were fine and dandy. Some days I could deal with nothing, and every little molehill became a mountain. My husband still had trouble accepting this thing. He tried hard to understand and be supportive but sometimes he just couldn't take it either. But through my reading, I learned this was the normal way for a man to deal with things, and I became more understanding of him.

Finally I became too overwhelmed by my job. I dreaded going to work every day and started sleeping a lot again. So after three years of it, I quit to stay home again. Immediately I started feeling better and everything was wonderful for about six months, then I felt myself going downhill again.

One day, in the middle of it, I had an interview with my bishop for a temple recommend. I certainly didn't feel worthy. During the interview, though, everything came out. "Surely," I thought, "this is it. I'm going to be kicked out of the Church." But the bishop was a wonderful and very understanding man. When he signed my temple recommend, he said it would make me feel better. He was right!

Later that year, I went on a temple trip with the Relief Society. Before the car even pulled out of the church parking lot to leave for Washington, D.C., my nerves started acting up, but I said nothing. After we had been on the road a short time, I was so bad I thought I'd have to ask the driver to turn around and take me home, but I was determined not to let the adversary beat me, so I hung in there.

Being in the temple again after many years brought me great peace, comfort, and a new perspective on life. I didn't want to go home.

Going to the temple is different from going to church. When we go to the temple we leave the world outside. When we go to church we take it with us. I don't know if I can adequately describe with words what this temple experience was like for me. It was feelings and thoughts: quietude—gratitude, solitude, reverence, peace, love—quietude. There is a poem called "Desiderata." One line from that poem says, "Avoid loud and aggressive persons, they are vexations to the spirit." In the temple I realized that many things are vexations to the spirit and that my spirit needed this quietude and peace that can only come from being in the temple. This was a turning point in my life. I had thought of my affliction as a curse or a punishment. Here I realized it was a blessing. Not one I would have asked for, and maybe *blessing* is not the word I want to use. What I want to say is that I received many blessings from this experience. Doctrine and Covenants 24:8 was a scripture that took on new meaning for me: "Be patient in afflictions, for thou shalt have many; but endure them, for, lo, I am with thee, even unto the end of thy days." I knew my Heavenly Father loved me and I knew that Christ had taken upon him my afflictions. Other people did not understand what I was going through, but *he* did. I realized that in the words of another "stuff doesn't matter." I don't know how to explain it any better than that.

My heart was filled with gratitude for all that my Father had given me. I learned to be more understanding of others. I learned to slow down, not to run faster than I had strength.

I left the temple with the longing to make my home a temple. A place of love, quietude, and sanctuary from the world. It's a slow process—line upon line—and may take a lifetime to accomplish, but with gratitude for each small blessing things are changing.

For example, last year after Thanksgiving I removed the television set from the house. It was not a popular move with my family, and they turned to the radio for entertainment. Now, several months later, I notice the radio is on less and less. The kids read more. We talk to each other more. We have become closer and do more things together. I have recently come back from another temple trip, and I am more determined to invite the Spirit back into my life and my home.

Today I still have my bad days when every little thing becomes a monumental task, or I feel so overwhelmed I think I can't stand it anymore, or I can't deal with anything. On these days I just want to pull the covers over my head and wait for it to pass, but these days are coming fewer and farther between and are much less intense. But I am so much better. I have a positive attitude . . . well, most of the time. I've begun to turn my life around and try not to take things so seriously. Even though I can't always see the light at the end of the tunnel, I know He's there, and that no matter what happens everything will be okay in the end.

Many of Marie's experiences will be familiar to others. Some of the feelings she describes are common to people suffering from anxiety as well as depression. In addition, Marie was later diagnosed with severely low thyroid levels. Depression is also one of the symptoms of this disorder. Marie's frustration at trying to arrive at the correct diagnosis is not uncommon, though as more is known of the nature of depression, stories like these will hopefully become rare.

Some people also experience side effects to medication, especially during the first couple of weeks (though usually not as extreme as hers—slight nausea or a headache is probably more common). You should notify the doctor if you are having side effects, especially if they are disruptive to your life. He or she may switch you to another medication that will be more acceptable. It's important to give the medication a chance; it may take a few weeks until the side effects disappear and the medication becomes effective in controlling your depression.

Marie lived in my ward in Ohio for a couple of years before I ever heard her say a word. She usually sat quietly, eyes on the floor, avoiding contact with others. Her story is one of a person bowed down by the stresses and disappointments of life.

I was surprised when she showed up at our first writer's group meeting, though we had made a general announcement and invitation to all the sisters at church. I didn't know Marie was interested in writing—but then, I didn't know anything else about Marie, either. We took turns telling why we were interested in a writer's group. When it was Marie's turn, gazing at the floor she quietly said, in response to our questions, that she enjoyed composition in high school and dreamed of writing and illustrating a children's story someday.

As time went on, Marie changed from being silent to being the life of the party. Her humorous poems left us in hysterics, especially when they were accompanied by funny little dances. She was the first one of our group to have a piece accepted for publication, and we all rejoiced with her. As her confidence increased, she became involved in Young Women's camp and other activities, and she is now a teacher in Relief Society. She came out of hiding and onto a stage.

I don't know how all this coincides with Marie's personal journey out of depression. I do know that for many of us in our writer's group, the "Buckeye Bards," our writing was very therapeutic. Writing about our lives helped us to understand them better. In fact, that little writer's group was where this book was born. Many of the women who have given us their stories have commented on the healing they experienced as they wrote of their lives. It was not enjoyable writing, but it was worth it. For some, it brought a peace they had not expected to feel. Others were able to look at their lives from a more objective perspective. At times, it helps just to let the pain spill out onto a page.

CHAPTER TWELVE

*Bipolar Illness:
Personal Account*

Although the focus of this book is major depression, or what is commonly referred to as clinical depression, it is important to mention the other clearly biological brain illness which is now coded in the *Diagnostic and Statistical Manual of Mental Disorder—4th edition* (*DSM-IV*) as bipolar disorder (formerly named manic-depression).

Currently in the *DSM-IV* there are two categories of bipolar disorder: bipolar I and bipolar II. While the differences are important to the treating physician or clinician, the essential characteristic of both is an alternation between a depressive episode and a manic episode. The characteristics of the depressive cycle are the same as a major depressive episode.

However, the other mood experienced by a person who is afflicted with bipolar illness is the mania, which is defined as "a distinct period during which there is an abnormally and persistently elevated, expansive, or irritable mood. This period of abnormal mood must last at least one week (or less if hospitalization is required). The mood disturbance must be accompanied by at least three additional symptoms from a list that includes inflated self-esteem or grandiosity, decreased need for sleep, pressure of speech, flight of ideas, distractibility, increased involvement in goal-oriented activity, or psychomotor agitation, and excessive involvement in pleasurable activities with a high potential for painful consequences. If the mood is irritable (rather than elevated or expansive), at least four of the above symptoms must be present."[1]

People who suffer from this disorder frequently refuse to accept their illness when they are in its manic stage and they rebuff efforts to assist them in treatment. Unlike depression, which appears to be more prevalent for women, bipolar I is approximately equally common in men and women. The lifetime prevalence of bipolar I ranges from 0.4% to 1.6% of the population. Twin and adoption studies indicate a strong genetic influence for bipolar I. Current studies of first-degree biological relatives of people diagnosed with bipolar illness show elevated rates of the illness.

Karen has struggled with bipolar illness for much of her life. The following story tells of her mood swings and her struggle to find a balance between the swings in her life. This is a transcript of a recording she made over the period of a few weeks. We have used punctuation to give the reader a feeling of her speaking voice. The ellipses do not indicate material has been left out, rather, they give a feel for the slow pauses and searching for words that characterized her speech during depressive periods. During the manic phases her speech was rapid and without hesitation.

## Living with Bipolar Illness

It's hard to talk about depression when I am in the midst of it, because it's hard to see the hope, it's hard to see the light, but I know that it's there, and that's what gets me through. . . . I didn't want to be awake today, I wanted to sleep all day, and I pretty much did. I slept until two o'clock this afternoon actually. I got up and took my medication and went right back to sleep. . . . Now I just took my nighttime medication so I'll be going to sleep again. . . . It's painful to be awake. I feel anguish and anxiety. Those are two emotions I'm very familiar with lately . . . I don't like them. I'd just as soon be drugged and not feel anything as feel those things constantly.

I had an appointment today . . . to go see . . . a woman at the mental health department about getting into a partial hospitalization program and I canceled it. I changed it until tomorrow so I can go at the same time I go to see my regular counselor . . . um . . . I just wasn't up to dealing with it today. I wasn't up to . . . taking a shower and . . . getting dressed to go and . . . the pain was too excruciating. The anguish, pain . . . at that time. What brought me out of it was talking to Janet. She has family members that suffer from depression so she's familiar with it and she knows how hard it can be . . . and she gave me a little pep talk, not the "Oh, everything's going to be all right tomorrow" kind of a pep talk, but the more realistic kind of talk where . . . she told me I would be better able to handle it . . . umm . . . it will ease up. I will have my ups and downs but that it will ease up. And I told her I'm going to see Dr. Arnold, Meghan's doctor . . . next week, which I'm really excited about, the cognitive behavioral therapist, I have great hopes for that. I feel more hopeful about that than I felt about anything for a long time. Umm . . . I got a note from Meghan today and she said she was glad I'm going too . . . that she's convinced the principles behind it are true . . . so that's a good note, coming from Meghan that means a lot, and I know it did her a lot of good so . . . hopefully it will me too . . . if I'm willing to work at it which I am. Definitely anything's better than this.

Yesterday I went to see my counselor and my husband went with me. He sat in with me during the session and we discussed some issues. Some of the things that maybe he doesn't understand.

Yesterday was something of a loss—I mean today was something of a loss. I started my period last night and . . . had the cramps and . . . didn't sleep well it . . . carried over until this morning. I was supposed to go and see . . . to have my first session of the partial hospitalization program this morning at nine o'clock but I didn't make it so I'll have to go Monday at noon and we'll see how that goes, at least it'll give me something to do during the day and . . . I'm convinced it's gonna do me some good. Today I just feel really suspended, in and out of reality at the same time, not really here, not really there . . . suspended . . . it's so nice to see the people around me wanting to help and trying to help. Just that helps. Just the fact that they want to help and they try to help . . . helps. I appreciate it. I appreciate their love and their concern. I don't like it when somebody tries to push me into doing something I don't want to do or tries to stop me from doing something that I do want to do. I don't deal with that very well. My husband is very supportive. He's quiet, doesn't make much noise, plays . . . on the computer and watches television, but he is very supportive. He loves me and I know it. He's not perfect, he makes mistakes, but he cares.

Write this day off as . . . a non-day. I didn't feel good. I didn't feel good physically, I didn't feel good mentally . . . not sharp, I'm dull today; mentally dull that's the best way to describe it. I've just been . . . like a knife . . . that hasn't been sharpened in years and years and years and you try to cut a tomato with it and . . . you don't have any . . . luck at all. That's my mind today, and tonight.

Sometimes I really enjoy going to bed at night. I get in my night gown . . . turn the lights down in the room, just the reading light by my bed . . . listen to the scriptures on tape . . . listen to maybe another book on tape . . . kind of snuggle up under the covers, be comfortable, and let my mind drift. This is a positive time. Sometimes it's very painful to go to bed because I can't sleep and I want more than anything to sleep because I'm in pain. Tonight I'm not. Tonight . . . tonight I feel good in my room. Our puppy's sleeping by the bed. I'm not depressed tonight.

Sometimes when I'm depressed, I pretend I'm in the hospital. I'll lay in my bed at night, and I just pretend that I'm laying in my hospital room on my bed there. I'll feel so safe and secure and so snuggled . . . and I'll try to . . . imagine what I'm going to have for breakfast . . . in the morning

. . . and how I don't have to worry about it, it'll just be brought to me . . . whatever I ordered the day before . . . it just kind of gives me a warm cozy feeling when I do that . . . don't have to worry about anything . . . everything's taken care of.

* * *

Being bipolar can be such a drag. All that stuff I recorded earlier about being down in the dumps, and now I'm up and now I wanna talk—carry on a lively conversation with someone and there's no one to talk to except my dog. When I'm really up, when I'm really manic, this is when I make those long distance phone calls out West 'cause it's late here but it's not late there!

* * *

Yesterday was Friday the nineteenth and it was one of those quiet days that . . . that doesn't have anything outstanding at all. I've been having a lot of those lately . . . non-descript . . . I can really have them and I seem to and be pretty comfortable with that and um, I get tense, I get nervous . . . I want to do something but I don't know what to do. I feel frozen up, I can't really do anything. . . . I just kind of wander around . . . and sit . . . and watch television and sit at the kitchen table and . . . think about stuff . . . call people on the telephone, talk to them . . . maybe go visit my mother . . . kind of fumble through the day. I have a real terrible depression. It's kind of an overall dysthymia. Dysthymia is an interesting . . . interesting thing. It's a low-grade depression, it's not a full-blown depression, just enough to make your life . . . dull, uninteresting, and miserable . . . umm, and that's still where I am dull . . . not really miserable, but uninteresting.

* * *

This is Saturday the twentieth of February. I got up at five o'clock in the morning and I thought maybe I'd go to Institute, but my mother doesn't feel well so she didn't go. I didn't go and that was really fine with me because I didn't feel like getting in the shower and getting ready to go anyway. Things are happening in the world, Kosovo, India, Pakistan, eruptions in the last days, and it's very exciting to me, there's so much going on in the world! I have a nervous feeling; could be the caffeine I had this morning, I need to stop buying caffeine pop, just buy no caffeine.

* * *

It's Saturday, whatever the date is I'm not sure . . . day after yesterday, I think the twentieth. I feel better today, in some ways. In some ways I feel a lot better. My mother said I look better. There's a skit at church tonight. Our writers group is putting it on, at the talent show, but I'm not up to going. I've got the cramps. If I didn't have the cramps I could probably go, but I'm so sensitive to outside influences now that . . . that's enough to . . . make me miserable, and I don't want to go somewhere and sit there and be miserable, Can't handle it yet. I know it seems silly and my mother doesn't understand, but I just can't handle it.

My friend from the hospital, Tom, called. Another woman that he met at the hospital after I left called him and was threatening suicide. She's taking Valium, I guess just popping them like candy and he wanted my advice as to what to do. . . . She didn't want the police involved or anything but, you know, he said he was going to have her call crisis hot line, if she would, and I said if not call the squad. He was afraid she'd get mad at him. I said it's better to have her alive and mad at him than dead and not so even if they just knocked on her door and talked to her that might scare her back into reality a little bit. I know how she feels . . . I know exactly how she feels . . . she's going through a bad time.

* * *

February 22, 1999. I got lost for a couple of days there. . . . Today was my first session in group at partial hospitalization. . . . It went pretty well . . . I guess. . . . One of the counselors . . . accused me of sitting around and feeling sorry for myself all the time instead of getting up and doing something about my problems . . . instead of doing anything about the things that bother me, like my messy house, which really isn't that bad when you really look at it. Maybe she was trying to test me . . . I should have been a little more assertive with her than I was. I told her she was right though, I probably am sitting around feeling sorry for myself. I was too quick to agree . . . I don't know, we'll see how it goes. I think I'm starting to get better adjusted to the . . . medications I'm taking . . . and the high . . . dosage . . . I'm taking . . . I'm still dizzy . . . still unsteady on my feet . . . and my husband still nags me about it . . . I feel tired . . . I feel when already depressed I get depressed about being depressed . . . maybe feel like I'm coming out of it some . . . I don't know, maybe it's the medication, maybe it's the group, maybe a combination of the two, we'll have to wait and see.

\* \* \*

This is Tuesday. Group went good today, and I feel pretty good. I'm not having so many dizzy spells—don't feel so much like I'm going to fall over. I actually smiled and laughed today. My visiting teachers came over, and I visited with them. That was rather pleasant. I didn't have any anxiety attacks—ummm—I didn't have that horrible feeling inside that I get sometimes.

\* \* \*

Wednesday. The emphasis today was on the fact that I have a mental illness . . . that I might have all my life, not just the fact that I'm depressed, that I have a full blown mental-illness . . . and I'm not going to just be able to take antidepressants for awhile and then quit taking them when I get better. . . . That there's a delicate balance between . . . the manic and the depressed. When I'm manic, I'm the life of the party, I'm a lot of fun, I just . . . everybody loves me . . . I'm sharp as a tack, I get ten things done at once . . . I take on all sorts of things, it used to be that I would run out and get me a full-time job . . . umm . . . do wonderful at it, get promoted real quick . . . then when I start coming out of the manic phase into the depressed phase, I'd start failing at work and . . . I'd start drinking to cover it up and . . . everything would fall apart . . . I wish . . . I want to have the manic without the depressed. I want the hypomania, I love it, it's fun, and it's wonderful. I meet people, and I think "Oh, they're manic, hypomanic" and think "I wish I could be like that all the time like they are and just never have the depressive side," but I don't . . . I can't have the hypo-mania because of the depression that follows it inevitably . . . so I'm learning how to walk that delicate balance like walking in a canoe . . . between the mania and the depression . . . and stay on the medications, find the right balance of the medication, sometimes it takes years to find the right balance. I've got the right medication, now I just have to find the right balance. The Luvox is taking care of my obsessive-compulsive disorder. I don't have any desire to count anymore like I used to . . . I'm not stuck on that.

School—I started going back to school when I was manic once, and I did great and the teachers loved me, and I got good grades. I studied and studied. I was working on getting a paralegal degree, but boy, when the . . . depression was triggered . . . by having financial problems with my husband and the . . . depression was triggered I just . . . tumbled down . . . so fast.

\* \* \*

It's Thursday again. I'm feeling a lot better these days and I'm sure it's because of partial hospitalization. I don't lie around and feel sorry for myself all day long, I get out and I'm around people—people who have the same problems, who understand each other. We know how to talk to each other, and that makes a big difference.

We talk about things that cloud our vision of life. Things that get in the way of enjoying life—like anger control. We talked about that today—I'm very passive-aggressive.

\* \* \*

This is Friday, the twenty-sixth, and I went to see Dr. Arnold today. . . . It was very interesting. We got there . . . oh, about forty-five minutes early, and it's a good thing because I had a pile of forms to fill out, and I still didn't even get them all filled out. He said I could mail them back to him so that's what I did, and he went down the checklist where it talked about . . . checked out the things that . . . concerned me. At the bottom of this form I have to pick one that most concerned me. Of course I picked depression. I changed it to confusion then I changed it back to depression. . . . When I asked him what he thought I said, "Am I a hopeless case?" . . . and he didn't come back all of a sudden with a "no, no, no" . . . he hesitated, then he said "no, you're not hopeless . . . but . . . you're a complicated case. . . . It's not gonna be . . . three or four sessions and you're out of here . . . it's going to take some time and it's gonna take a lot of work . . . But if you're willing to do it, I feel we can accomplish a lot." . . . I feel confident in him, I really do. . . . A book he made me aware of, called *A Brilliant Sky*, it's Danielle Steel's book about her son who committed suicide . . . He was bipolar . . . The doctor asked me to read this book. He wants me to educate myself as much as I can about my illness . . . and he stressed that I need to stay on my medication, keep balance in my life . . . avoid things . . . that shut me off . . . what the stresses are and avoid those situations that are going to get me into trouble . . . so . . . that'll be good . . . just to know those.

While I was fixing dinner tonight I cried. I was talking to Margot on the phone . . . at the same time . . . I remembered that . . . on Friday nights . . . when I had my kids and they were small . . . we used to have hot dogs with . . . baked beans and . . . that's what we were having for dinner tonight . . . it's Friday night and it was always Friday nights then, and it was a special thing that we did, and I felt so sad but it felt good to cry . . . I have so many things like that locked up inside of me, so many things I need to get out, and that's what this therapy can do for me is help me get these things out so I can look at them and see them, so they don't eat me up inside . . . so they won't keep me from living and laughing . . . thinking and feeling.

Well, this hasn't been very much and this hasn't been very good . . . but my intelligence is so blunted by the medications that I'm taking that I just can't seem to come up with anything . . . meaningful.

For those of us that are bipolar there is no such thing as going without medication any more than a diabetic can go without insulin . . . The chemical imbalance we are born with and we will die with . . . If I didn't take my medications I would end up in an institution, and I know that. I don't want any more hospitalizations and I don't want any more shock treatments . . . I know that my intelligence is blunted, I know that . . . but that's the price I have to pay, I have a choice . . . I can be sharp . . . sharp-witted, sharp-minded . . . clever . . . hypomanic, being able to take on through medicine lots of responsibility, being able get everything done . . . be super woman . . . and I can be that for a while and then the bottom falls out and it's the inevitable question of depression that follows, and it isn't worth it . . . to me . . . to go through that . . . the highs are not worth the lows . . . it's too much of a price to pay. . . . It's a progressive illness. It gets worse as we get older and mine has gotten worse . . . and the worse it gets and the higher dosages of medication I have to take the more blunted my intelligence becomes . . . I used to be able to write poetry, beautiful poetry . . . and things . . . I can't do it anymore . . . not at this point anyway, perhaps it's in my future. I don't know, but at this point I can't . . . I couldn't even fill out the forms at the doctor's office. I couldn't write. . . . I could write my name and that's about it. I couldn't fill in the names of my drugs that I'm taking . . . I couldn't write words without making mistakes on the letters . . . how discouraging it all is . . . but . . . I can do the best that I can and I can live within my limitations and I can have as good a life as I can within those limitations . . . I have to be aware of them . . . I have to know what the red flags are. I have to know what to watch for . . . signs that . . . that I'm . . . going off in the wrong direction. . . . I do believe that Dr. Arnold can help me . . . to deal with my feelings . . . I pray that he can . . . I feel hopeful.

I'm gonna give this to you Margot . . . with this little bit of recording that I did. I'm sorry I didn't do more, I'm sorry I didn't do better . . . I just can't. I hope you understand, I hope Meghan understands. . . . I love you both and I wish I could give you more . . . I truly do love you.

\* \* \*

I wasn't depressed. I don't know where I was but I obviously wasn't depressed because I came out of it too quick. Either that or I was triggered into a manic stage but, two days ago on Sunday, the seventh, my first surviving grandchild was born, born to my firstborn son, my firstborn child! I can't tell you how elated and happy I am! I went to the super-market with my husband, and I was telling people in the line at the checkout counter, and the checkout girl, that I was a grandma now and all about the baby and her name, Lynn, and how big she was, and is, and I'm so excited about life, the renewal of life, brand new beginnings. I think it's like when I'm so depressed everything seems so old and worn and used and dirtied and stained. Something about the birth of a new born baby—so clean and fresh and sweet and untouched, brilliant, the brilliance of a newborn spirit. And the greatest news is, the greatest news of all is, I get to go out West to see her and my son, who I haven't seen in four years, and my daughter, who I haven't seen in four years. It's all falling together so perfectly. The first thing that happened was a miracle and my husband and I were able to get a regular mortgage on the house. We were on a land contract. We were able to get a regular mortgage, drop the percentage rate about three and a half points, drop the monthly payments, etc., etc., dropped our insurance rate. Through paying a lot less over time for the house, less monthly than we were, plus it gave us a little bit of cash to help out! Well, that little bit of cash turned out to be enough for me to fly out to Utah, but then it was going to cut into my sessions with Dr. Arnold if I used it for that, so Brother S—— and Sister S——, who in the midst of this—I'm sure they have their calling and election made sure—called and said they had an extra ticket that I can use for the trip out there, and Brother S—— made all the arrangements for me to use the ticket and he is going to Columbus tomorrow to sign the papers for it. Just—had to be such beautiful people who live on the face of the earth that they do—and you'll find it in the LDS Church more than likely. I'm probably not making any sense I'm so excited and I'm probably up so— but this is what it's like when I'm not depressed, this is how happy I can be when I'm not depressed. It's the opposite of the depression. The depres-sion runs so deep and the horrible chasm of depression, the depth of it and the, the, uh, swallowed-up feeling of it and this is the height of the other side, this is the height of the hypomanic—the elation. I was up all night last night, practically. I didn't wanna sleep. I was on the go constantly. I didn't stop doing things until it was very, very late, but then I slept in this morning until late, so that's a good sign. But that's how it was with me, back and forth, back and forth, between one or the other, up or down, very rarely am I in the middle. That's what we're searching for is that middle ground; meanwhile I'm off to Utah here on Monday and this is Tuesday of the week before. Monday I'll be off to Salt Lake City to see my granddaughter and my children, and my daughter-in-law. I'm so excited and so grateful to my Heavenly Father, and I'm so thrilled that I'm not depressed because if I were really depressed I wouldn't be able to enjoy this. I've been depressed like that before so I know it's real.

*When I talked to Karen to let her know the publisher had accepted this book, she was thrilled to know her experiences might help others to know they are not alone. Not much has changed for her; life is still up and down. Bipolar illness takes a special brand of courage: to face every day and draw out of it what measure of happiness you can, while trudging on, trying to do the best you can. Bipolar illness is a heavy burden, and those who carry on beneath its weight are heroes among us.*

---

1. *DSM-IV*, (1994), 328.

# Joy Cometh in the Morning

Weeping may endure for the night—in fact, for many, many nights—but joy *will* come in the morning. And there will be morning for you, though now you may feel plunged into deepest night. You have read the stories of several women, all witnesses that the night will pass and the sun will shine again. They have been there. They know the desolation and anguish of depression, and they have found hope. You can share in their hope while you seek for your own.

Most people have had experiences coping with physical pain or illness. In a childbirth class, I was told that it was important for me to know what was happening to my body, so I would have a greater sense of understanding and control. Depression is emotional pain. We may feel only agony, with no end in sight, and no ability to remember or imagine life without anguish. Understanding what is happening in our brains, and how to cope with it or change it, gives us a sense of control.

In the deep despair of a major depressive episode, it may seem that no hope exists, or ever will exist. Yet some small measure of optimism may be found in understanding three facts about depression:

1. Depression is a brain illness.

2. Depression may remit by itself, though it could take years; medication and/or talk therapy will almost certainly be effective in speeding recovery.

3. The sense of spiritual loss accompanying depression is due to a biologically depressed ability to feel joyous emotions, not to unworthiness.

Depression is a brain illness: it is physical in nature. Past experiences, such as a painful loss or abuse, may affect our brain function in such a way that depression results. Some people may be genetically predisposed to depression, and a life event might trigger its appearance. But depression is not weakness, a character flaw, laziness, or self-pity. As Betsy has pointed out, one must be tremendously strong to face each day in the grip of depression.

It is sometimes necessary and sensible to consider medication. Medication is frequently needed to combat clinical depression, just as it is needed for strep throat, diabetes, or high blood pressure. Antidepressants and/or mood stabilizers are prescribed to combat specific chemical imbalances in the brain. They are not a cause for shame or self-condemnation. The antidepressants of today are not the "nerve pills" or tranquilizers of yesterday.

Medication, by itself, can be inadequate. The way we think affects the way our brain functions, and taking medication without examining our thought processes can be like applying the brake and the gas simultaneously in a car. We're doing something, it's true, but we're not getting anywhere. Therapy is often the long-term solution which medication doesn't provide.

Here are a few guidelines to heed. If you choose to consider medication, there are two good ways to be evaluated to assess whether or not you might benefit from medication:

• You may have a family practice doctor or internist with whom you have a trusting relationship. Frequently this medical professional will work to help you find a medication that is right for you.

• If you do not have an ongoing professional relationship with a physician, or if you feel more comfortable with a specialist, you will need to select a psychiatrist—a medical doctor specifically trained to evaluate and prescribe psychotropic medications (medications which regulate and enhance mood).

If you go to a doctor and you don't feel helped, talk to another doctor.

One of the best ways to find a good doctor or a good therapist is through personal recommendations from someone you know and respect. A critical part to selecting a good doctor or therapist is to know the licensing laws in your state. *Never put yourself at risk* by utilizing someone who is not licensed in his or her respective field (I could tell you horror stories of people who have subjected themselves at fragile times to "quacks"— but that's another book).

Trust your instincts. With either physician or therapist, if you don't feel safe, valued, and respected, listen to those feelings and exit the relationship. Note, I did not say you ought to feel "comfortable." There are times that a good therapist must challenge your irrational and distorted thinking. But a skilled therapist is able to confront faulty thinking without devaluing you, disrespecting you, or making you feel unsafe.

One concrete thing you can do before you see a therapist is to try to list the ways you are experiencing your depression. What was different in your life before you felt so much despair? If you are already seeing a therapist, but are now considering finding a psychiatrist, ask your therapist to help you make a list of symptoms and characteristics of your emotional distress. This will assist the physician to more easily understand the particular type of depression you may be suffering.

Nightgowns, sweatshirts, and mittens may be "one size fits all." Therapists are not. Ask a prospective therapist what specialties he or she has. Therapists practice many different approaches and philosophies. Research suggests that the most important aspect of therapy is the "therapeutic alliance": a fancy way of saying how well you relate to and trust the therapist. Listen to your thoughts and feelings. You have a good fit when you feel secure with the therapist, both intellectually and emotionally.

One final caution. There are therapists who practice "confrontational" models. I personally believe that most of us grow and change in sustainable ways in nurturing, building environments. This is not to say that your therapist will not sometimes have to say difficult words to you, but I am convinced it is both possible and preferable to say hard things in a soft way.

The greatest challenge to a person who is used to the direction and comfort of the Spirit is the apparent loss of that closeness to Heavenly Father. Many, many people, looking back on their depression from the other side of recovery, report the same experience: "I wasn't aware of it at the time, but I really did receive direction from Heavenly Father. I couldn't feel any burning or joy. I couldn't feel the Spirit the way I was used to. I doubted my own worthiness. But the Lord did direct me to where I could find help. He sent me other people to support me. He was watching over me, even though I felt that no one heard my prayers."

Depression can be one of the most searing of all trials, because we feel so alone and abandoned. But as we start to recognize the ways the Lord may be directing us, we can start to gain a sense of his continued blessings and presence.

Visiting with your bishop or stake president can provide you with healing words and healing lessons. These priesthood leaders will be able to reassure you of your goodness and worthiness. Or, if there is a transgression to resolve, they can assist you with your repentance so you no longer have to carry that burden. Priesthood leaders are an excellent resource in helping you apply the healing power of the Atonement. Though you may no longer feel the Lord's direction in response to your prayers, you can hear his voice through priesthood blessings. A loving husband, father, home teacher, bishop, or other worthy priesthood holder can give you a blessing and be the means through which the Lord can provide you with an awareness of his love and approval.

There is no simple spiritual formula to cure your physical depression. You will, however, find unexpected spiritual blessings as you seek to find meaning in your suffering and turn your burden over to Christ. The Savior taught that he was sent "to heal the broken-hearted" (Luke 4:18). Believe him, even though your current experience may not be telling you this. Some people discover that through their depression they have developed greater compassion; others understand more clearly the nature of mortality. Many people acquire a deeper, more profound appreciation for the Savior's atoning sacrifice. Through your increased wisdom, you will understand that suffering becomes payment for priceless blessings.

The world around us testifies of renewal and change. In chapter one you read this comparison:

> Looking out the window as we write this book, we see trees that have weathered a difficult winter beginning to put forth the first young leaves of spring. You will be like these trees. Though you may now, in the darkness and chill of your depression, feel that hope is gone, you will again feel warmth and light. As you leave your winter of depression behind you and begin to reach for hope, you will one day return to joy, richness, and light.

The oak trees behind my house, which in winter's darkness appear dead, respond to the prolonged light of spring by putting out the first tender leaves of a new season. The first hope a depressed woman feels will be tentative and tender, also. Her confidence will emerge slowly, though she will eventually return to her former abilities, with the addition of a new compassion borne of her suffering. That return will be gradual and careful. She may wish she could do more, faster. John Milton's Sonnet XIX, on his blindness,[1] reflects this frustration and the Lord's acceptance of the least we can do:

> When I consider how my light is spent,
> Ere half my days, in this dark world and wide,
> And that one Talent which is death to hide,
> Lodg'd with me useless, though my Soul more bent
> To serve therewith my Maker, and present
> My true account, lest he returning chide;*
> "Doth God exact day-labor, light denied,"
> I fondly** ask; But patience to prevent
> That murmur, soon replies, "God doth not need
> Either man's work or his own gifts; who best
> Bear his mild yoke, they serve him best; his State
> Is Kingly. Thousands at his bidding speed
> And post o'er Land and Ocean without rest:
> They also serve who only stand and wait."

* scold
** foolishly

Like Milton, we may feel we need to "earn our keep," or magnify our talents in mortality, but we are frustrated by our inability to do the things we used to do. This is where an understanding of the Atonement is vital. The Lord is not measuring our worth by our good works: there is no scale in eternity which counts our righteous deeds to see if we did enough to earn salvation. He asks us for our hearts. Our love for the Lord is enough, if it is all we can give. If we can also make dinner for a new mother, fine. If not, if it is beyond our capability at the moment, then remember, "they also serve who only stand and wait." And as we wait for the ability to do more, it is important to realize that what we are doing now is enough. The Lord judges the intents of our hearts.

I had a sacred experience in the temple that has engraved the truth of God's love into my heart. I was in a part of the temple where I was working one-on-one with the women who had come as patrons. A sister from my ward came to be proxy in an ordinance for her ancestors. I had never really felt that this sister liked me much. I was also aware of her feelings of inadequacy and her sorrow and guilt for the wayward paths her children had chosen. After we finished the ordinance, I realized with a sense of panic that I had left something out. We would have to start over at the beginning. I was embarrassed and was sure that my mistake would serve to confirm this sister's low opinion of me. I explained that I had made a mistake, apologized, and started over.

I was ashamed and determined that this time I would do everything exactly right. I concentrated carefully on what I was saying, thinking more of the mechanics of the ordinance than of the meaning. I *was not* going to make another mistake with this sister. Suddenly, as I came to a part that mentioned her faithfulness, I became so overwhelmed with emotion that I could not speak. It was revealed to my mind an awareness of how Heavenly Father looks upon this sister. I felt an immense love and tenderness, which acknowledged her faults and struggles, but didn't condemn her for them—instead loved her for her continuing desire to do right. It was the most tender, gentle, compassionate love I have ever imagined.

I blinked to clear my eyes of tears and saw that she was struggling for composure too. I hope that she felt what I felt. I continued, and finished, and she moved on. But the power of that sweet insight stays with me.

This is no statement of new doctrine. The Lord tells us of his infinite, unconditional love continuously. Then why do we limit it in our own minds? Why do we think it is dependent upon our actions? Why do we feel we must attain perfection to merit his approval?

He has been here, where we are. He has experienced all pain, all sorrow, all trauma, all regrets, and all remorse as a part of his atoning sacrifice. He understands us better than we understand ourselves, and he loves us with a love both infinite and tender. We don't have to earn it. We do need to believe it, accept it, and trust in it.

I think the love I have for young children helps me to understand the Lord's love for me. I don't expect them to be as competent as an adult. They're still young and growing and learning. But when they make a good effort, out of a desire to please me, I am filled with love and appreciation for them. If a four-year-old in sacrament meeting passes me a picture she has drawn, I don't judge it by rules of perspective or appropriate color. I am touched by the love for me that her effort reveals.

We are not perfect in our service to the Lord in this life. But the Lord doesn't judge us solely by our works: He looks upon our hearts. " . . . for the Lord seeth not as man seeth; for man looketh on the outward appearance, but the Lord looketh on the heart" (I Samuel 16:7).

Be patient with yourself, as the Lord is patient with all his children. He loves you and knows your difficulties as well as you do. He knows your desire to please him and return to his presence. He has said, "Greater love hath no man than this, that a man lay down his life for his friends" (John 15:13). You are his friend. If you can believe in little else for yourself right now, believe in his love for you. Trust his word: He knows you and loves you.

---

1. John Milton, seventeenth-century author of numerous works including *Paradise Lost*, wrote this poem after he became completely blind. He is expressing his grief at his inability to continue writing as he had before losing his sight.

# Suggested Reading

## LDS Perspectives on Depression and Hope

Broderick, Dr. Carlfred. *One Heart, One Flesh*. Salt Lake City: Deseret Book, 1986. Chapter eight of this book, "To Give unto Them Beauty for Ashes," was the beginning point of understanding depression from a spiritual perspective for both Meghan and Betsy. Dr. Broderick's ten pages addressing depression from a LDS framework was the impetus for our book.

Covey, Stephen R. *The Divine Center*. Salt Lake City: Bookcraft, 1982. Answers to why we need a life centered on God and Christ and how we can attain this goal.

Covey, Stephen R. *The Seven Habits of Highly Effective People*. New York: Simon & Schuster, 1989. How to restore our character ethic by embracing "powerful lessons in personal change."

Covey, Stephen R. *Spiritual Roots of Human Relations*. Salt Lake City: Deseret Book, 1970. Help in seeking spiritual solutions to everyday problems.

Hafen, Bruce C. *The Broken Heart: Applying the Atonement to Life's Experiences*. Salt Lake City: Deseret Book, 1989. An invitation to examine the Atonement as the healing power for sin, as well as for pain, discouragement, and inadequacy.

Horton, Anne L., et al. *Confronting Abuse*. Salt Lake City: Deseret Book,

1993. A compilation of essays and articles on abuse to help victims, family, and church leaders. Several perspectives on a multitude of abuse issues.

Maxwell, Neal A. *All These Things Shall Give Thee Experience*. Salt Lake City: Deseret Book, 1979. A wonderful book about finding meaning in our suffering.

Okazaki, Chieko. *Lighten Up!* Salt Lake City: Deseret Book, 1993. A book about optimism: how to enjoy living the gospel by increasing our charity to others and to ourselves.

Okazaki, Chieko. *Sanctuary*. Salt Lake City: Deseret Book, 1997. Finding peace amid the chaos of life by accepting sanctuary as an inner place of peace.

Robinson, Stephen E.. *Believing Christ*. Salt Lake City: Deseret Book, 1992. Accepting the good news of the gospel that says we need to "believe" Christ as well as "believe in" Christ. A wonderful book for understanding the Atonement in our lives.

## *Professional/Clinical Literature Related to Depression*

Benson, Dr. Herbert. *The Relaxation Response*. New York: Outlet, 1993. Offers meditation techniques to promote relaxation from "everyday" kinds of pressures that can or may have already escalated into depression.

Berger, K. S. *The Developing Person through the Life Span*. 2d ed. New York: Worth Publishers, 1988. Examines the "seasons of life" and emotional passages by reviewing some of the leading theorists and researchers in developmental psychology.

Bourne, Edmund J. *The Anxiety and Phobia Workbook*. Oakland, CA: New Harbinger, 1990. The most practical guide we've seen for assisting people who are suffering from anxiety and/or phobias. (We have included this guide because some of the women whose stories you have read in this book have co-existing disorders of depression and anxiety.)

Burns, David, M.D. *Feeling Good: The New Mood Therapy*. New York: Avon, 1992. Excellent guide book in self-help format for understanding cognitive treatment for depression. Presents therapy particularly effective in dealing with depression.

Burns, David, M.D. *The Feeling Good Handbook: Using the New Mood Therapy in Everyday Life*. New York: Plume Book, 1990. A handbook using the principles introduced in *Feeling Good*. Exercises and explanations included. (Though this won't substitute for therapy, it gives a good idea of what to expect.)

Fieve, Ronald R., M.D. *Moodswing*. Rev. ed. New York: Morrow, 1989. This has been a standard on bi-polar disorder since 1975.

Freeman, Dr. Arthur, and Rose DeWolf. *The 10 Dumbest Mistakes Smart People Make and How to Avoid Them*. New York: HarperPerennial, 1992. Not a great title, but a good book for recognizing and confronting negative thinking, while gaining greater control over your life. Based on Cognitive Therapy (see also David Burns, *Feeling Good*).

Jamison, Dr. Kay Redfield. *An Unquiet Mind*. New York: Alfred A. Knopf, 1997. A penetrating autobiographical account of the ravages of bi-polar disorder.

Kubler-Ross, Elizabeth. *On Death and Dying*. Reprint. New York: Simon & Schuster, 1997. Stages of the grief process. (Although this book is directed towards physical death, much can also be applied to accepting other losses.)

Lewis, C. S. *A Grief Observed*. San Francisco: Harper, 1994. A book which gives permission to admit our fears related to death and grief, but then turns us toward understanding the growth that may emerge from them.

O'Connor, Dr. Richard. *Undoing Depression: What Therapy Doesn't Teach You and Medication Can't Give You*. New York: Berkley Publ. Group, 1999. Offers specific techniques and exercises designed to assist the depressed person in creating healthy habits. Centers on medication and talk therapy; does not address the spiritual component.

Pipher, Mary. *Reviving Ophelia*. New York: Putnam Publishing Company, 1994. Penetrating glimpse into female adolescent depression with thoughtful prescriptions for change. Good insight into the changes and stresses that occur in a girl's life in early adolescence.

Richards, B. M. *Sudden Trauma! When Life Will Never Be the Same Again*. Salt Lake City: Gold Mind Publications, 2000. The single best resource book I have read for both accurate and practical information for those afflicted with Post Traumatic Stress Disorder (PTSD).

Sheffield, Anne. *How You Can Survive When They're Depressed*. New York: Harmony, 1998. A candid and informative guide to those who are the family or significant others of the depressed person.

Siegel, Dr. Bernie S. *Love, Medicine and Miracles: Lessons Learned about Self-Healing*. New York: HarperPerennial Library, 1990. Written from the premise that patients/clients who have the courage to love and be loved may influence their own recovery in miraculous ways.

Styron, William. *Darkness Visible: A Memoir of Madness*. New York: Random House, 1990. A most literary description of depression, written by a Pulitzer Prize–winning author stricken at the height of his fame.

Tavris, Carol. *Anger: The Misunderstood Emotion*. New York: Touchstone, 1989. A must read for anyone struggling with anger issues.

## Children's Literature

De Saint Exupery, Antoine, *The Little Prince*. New York: Harcourt, Brace & World, 1943. A child's story with the grown-up theme of "what is essential is invisible to the eye—it is only with the heart that one can see rightly."

Ellsworth, Barry, *The Little Stream*. Los Angeles: Bonneville Classic Books,

1995. A story of hope and renewal based on the children's song "Give, Said the Little Stream."

Estes, Eleanor, *The Hundred Dresses*. New York: Harcourt, Brace & World, 1944. A classic and poignant tale of catty little girls and the forgiveness that comes to them.

Seuss, Dr. *Oh, The Places You'll Go!* New York: Random House, 1990. Advice for "hoping" when confronted with fear, loneliness, and confusion; being in charge of yourself.

Silverstein, Shel. *The Giving Tree*. New York: HarperCollins Juvenile Books, 1986. Develops the theme of unconditional love: giving and giving without feeling a sense of sacrifice or expectation, and the hope that follows serene acceptance.

Williams, Margery. *The Velveteen Rabbit*. New York: Barnes and Noble, 1991. A children's classic which speaks of how we become "real"— ourbest self which grows and develops through challenges and hard things.

## *Forgiveness*

Burton, Theodore M. "The Meaning of Repentance." *Ensign* (August 1988), 7–9. A short but powerful admonition to view repentance as a "change" process. Finding hope as a result of truly understanding the Atonement as a personal gift.

Eldridge, Erin. *Born That Way?* A powerfully written book on seeking the change of heart which will leave us with no more desire to sin. Though the subject of this book is same-sex attraction, it is grounded in gospel doctrine and teaches a powerful lesson about seeing ourselves not as alcoholic, survivors of abuse, or homosexual, but as children of God and disciples of Christ.

Kimball, Spencer W. *The Miracle of Forgiveness*. Salt Lake City: Bookcraft, 1969. Hope is achieved through the healing powers of repentance and forgiveness.

Speare, Elizabeth George. *The Bronze Bow*. Boston: Houghton Mifflin, 1997. A novel which develops the theme of forgiveness as movement toward having hope.

Yorgason, Blaine M. *Into the Rainbow*. Orem, UT: Keepsake Books, 1990. A short and lyrical book about forgiveness. Easy to read and hopeful, this book will appeal to teenagers and adults.

Yorgason, Blaine M. and Sunny Oaks. *Secrets*. Salt Lake City: Deseret Book, 1992. A tender novel based on real stories of the ravages of sexual abuse. Stands as a powerful witness to those who are victims of sexual abuse that they are not alone, that forgiveness comes in stages, and that healing is "line upon line."

## *Inspirational Literature*

Cameron, Julia. *The Artist's Way*. New York: Jeremy P. Tarcher/Putnam, 1992. A workbook on the creative processes using inspirational thoughts and directed exercises to assist in finding and achieving harmony and hope in day-to-day living.

Colgrave, Melba, Harold H. Bloomfield, and Peter McWilliams. *How to Survive the Loss of a Love*. New York: Bantam, 1991. A pithy collection of essay, prose, poetry, and wry observations for the person who has suffered the loss of a relationship.

Cousins, N. *Anatomy of an Illness as Perceived by the Patient*. New York: W. W. Norton & Company, 1979. The author uses humor and positive reflections to help face a life-threatening disease.

Lindbergh, Anne Morrow. *Gift from the Sea*. New York: Pantheon Books, 1955. Sensitive and compelling meditations by a woman about finding balance and hope in life.

Frankl, Dr. Victor. *Man's Search for Meaning*. Boston: Beacon, 1992. A compelling and moving account of one man's search for meaning while interned in Auschwitz. Also includes an introduction to a type of therapy, logotherapy.

Kushner, Harold S. *When Bad Things Happen to Good People*. New York: Avon, 1983. A tender story of a rabbi and his family who are confronted with the tragic and fatal illness of their child. Using their faith, they find ways to break out of the anger and confusion of their initial response.

Lerner, Harriet Goldhor. *The Dance of Anger: A Woman's Guide to Changing the Patterns of Intimate Relationships*. New York: Harper-Collins, 1989. An insightful and challenging book to address anger management, particularly with women.

Ten Boom, Corrie. *The Hiding Place*. Grand Rapids, MI: Chosen Books, 1996. As a leader in the Dutch Underground during WW II, and later while imprisoned in a concentration camp, this author exemplifies hope and courage under extraordinary conditions.

Winawer, Dr. Sidney. *Healing Lessons*. Boston: Little, Brown, 1998. The moving account of a prominent cancer specialist who is faced with his own wife becoming afflicted with the cancer of his specialty. He and his wife must find hope between the worlds of medicine, alternative medicine, and spiritual choices.

# Bibliography

Barry, P. (1999, April). "It's No Joke: Humor Heals." *AARP Bulletin*, 14–17.

Berger, K. S. (1988). *The Developing Person through the Life Span*. 2d ed. New York: Worth Publishers.

Broderick, C. (1986). *One Heart, One Flesh*. Salt Lake City: Deseret Book.

Burns, D. D. (1980). *Feeling Good: The New Mood Therapy*. New York: Signet Book, New American Library.

Cousins, N. (1979). *Anatomy of an Illness as Perceived by the Patient*. New York: W. W. Norton & Company.

*Diagnostic and Statistical Manual of Mental Disorder—4th Edition*. (1994). Washington, D.C.: American Psychiatric Society.

Erikson, E. H. (1963). *Childhood and Society*. 2d. ed. New York: Norton.

———. (1968). *Identity, Youth and Crisis*. New York: Norton.

———. (1975). *Life History and the Historical Movement*. New York: Norton.

Fieve, R. R. (1981). *Moodswing*. 4th printing. Toronto, New York, London: Bantam Books.

Foote, D. and S. Seibert. (1999, Spring/Summer). "The Age of Anxiety." *Newsweek: Special Edition, Health for Life*, 68–72.

Goleman, D. (1992, January/February). "Wounds That Never Heal (How Trauma Changes Your Brain)." *Psychology Today*, 25.1, 62–66.

Healy, B. (1999, Spring/Summer). "A Medical Revolution." *Newsweek: Special Edition, Health for Life*, 64–65.

Lindbergh, A. M. (1955). *Gift from the Sea*. New York: Pantheon Books.

Mann, J. J. (1999, February/March). "Brain Biology Influences the Risk for Suicide."

Maxwell, N. A. (1986). *But for a Small Moment*. Salt Lake City: Bookcraft.

"Mood Disorders: An Overview—Part 1." (1997). *Harvard Mental Health Letter*. 1, 4, 7.

"Mood Disorders: An Overview—Part 2." (1998). *Harvard Mental Health Letter*. 1, 5–6.

"Mood Disorders: An Overview—Part 3." (1998). *Harvard Mental Health Letter*. 1, 1–5.

*NAMI Advocate*. (1995, September/October), 17.2, 13–14.

Packer, B. K. (1982). *That All May Be Edified*. Salt Lake City: Bookcraft.

Pipher, M. (1994). *Reviving Ophelia: Saving the Lives of Adolescent Girls*. New York: Putnam.

Schrof, J. M., and S. Schultz. (1999, 8 March). "Melancholy Nation." *U.S. News and World Report*, 56–63.

Seibert, S., and D. Foote. (1999, Spring/Summer). "The Age of Anxiety." *Newsweek: Special Edition, Health for Life*, 68–72.

Simon, R. (1997, January/February). "The Family Unplugged." *Family Therapy Networker*, 24–33.

Styron, W. (1989). *Darkness Visible*. New York: Random House.

Swerdlow, J. L. (1995, June). "Quiet Miracles of the Brain." *National Geographic*, 2–41.

vos Savant, M. (1993). "Ask Marilyn." *Parade Magazine*.

Watson, W. (1999, Spring). "Change: It's Always a Possibility!" *Brigham Young Magazine*, 66–67.

# Index

abandonment, 57–58;
family of origin issues,
57–58; adversity, 58;
situational, 58; physi-
cal, 58–60; develop-
mental crises, 60–66;
passing through life
stages, 60–66; disen-
chantment in mar-
riage, 62–63; pressures
of young motherhood,
63–66; "baby blues,"
66; losing your role as
caretaker, 66–67; posi-
tive life changes,
66–67; job changes,
67; moving to a new
neighborhood, 67

Unworthiness, feelings of,
88–89

vos Savant, Marilyn,
94–95

Watson, Wendy, 103–4
Whybrow, Peter, 32–33
Withdrawal, 3, 6

# About the Authors

Meghan Decker received her B.A. and master's degree in English from Brigham Young University. She is currently pursuing her interest in writing; she serves as the president of a local writer's group and is working on a novel. She and her husband, David, are the parents of five daughters and live in Portage, Michigan.

Betsy Chatlin received her B.S. from Brigham Young University in Teacher Education and her MSW degree from the University of Utah. She is currently licensed to practice as a clinical social worker in three states: Michigan, Utah, and Virginia. She has worked in private practice, family counseling, LDS Family Services, and mental health and social services. She is the mother of three daughters. She and her husband, Gene, live in Portage, Michigan.

Both Meghan and Betsy have served as Relief Society president in their ward, the Portage Ward in the Kalamazoo, Michigan Stake.